Breath of Life

Breath of Life

A Theology of the Creator Spirit

DENIS EDWARDS

ORBIS BOOKS

Maryknoll, New York 10545

Founded in 1970, Orbis Books endeavors to publish works that enlighten the mind, nourish the spirit, and challenge the conscience. The publishing arm of the Maryknoll Fathers and Brothers, Orbis seeks to explore the global dimensions of the Christian faith and mission, to invite dialogue with diverse cultures and religious traditions, and to serve the cause of reconciliation and peace. The books published reflect the opinions of their authors and are not meant to represent the official position of the Maryknoll Society. To obtain more information about Maryknoll and Orbis Books, please visit our website at www.maryknoll.org.

Cover art is from the "Ex Nihilo" Working Model, cast marble, copyright © 2002 F. Hart and P.E.C.F. Authorized by Washington National Cathedral. This work was created as part of *The Creation Sculptures* commissioned for Washington National Cathedral. Provided to Orbis through the courtesy of Chesley, L.L.C., Northbrook, Illinois. Visit www.frederickhart.com for information on Frederick Hart and his work.

Library of Congress Cataloging in Publication Data

Edwards, Denis, 1943-
 Breath of life : a theology of the Creator Spirit / Denis Edwards.
  p. cm.
 Includes bibliographical references and indexes.
 ISBN 1-57075-525-6
 1. Holy Spirit—History of doctrines. 2. Creation—History of doctrines. I. Title.
 BT119 .E39 2004
 231'.3—dc22
                                               2003021370

Contents

Part 3
Exploring the Theology of the Creator Spirit

Part 4
Two Particular Issues in Spirit Theology

Acknowledgments

Coming to the end of *Breath of Life* leads me to give thanks for all the ways the Spirit of God has brought life to the process of writing. I am grateful to those who have read my manuscript and offered invaluable critical suggestions and very welcome encouragement. They include Andrew Louth, Professor of Patristic and Byzantine Studies at the University of Durham; Robert John Russell, Founder and Director of the Center for Theology and the Natural Sciences at Berkeley; and Patricia Fox, trinitarian theologian and President of the Sisters of Mercy in Australia.

I had helpful discussions about the themes and structure of this work with John Haught, Elizabeth Johnson, Mary Catherine Hilkert, and William Stoeger. In Adelaide, my colleagues and friends at Catholic Theological College, the Flinders University School of Theology and Adelaide Theological Library have been generous and supportive. Alastair Blake and James McEvoy read the whole manuscript with a critical eye. Michael Trainor, Christine Burke, Jan Bate, and Trevor Bate read particular chapters. The friendly critics I mention here are not responsible for the positions I have taken. But this book owes a great deal to all of them.

An important part of the work for this book was done during a sabbatical time at the Catholic Institute of Sydney. I was made to feel welcome and at home by Fr. Neil Brown and the faculty members and much enjoyed our shared meals and collegial discussions. I was generously assisted by the staff of CIS and the librarians of the Veech Library. This sabbatical was financially supported by the Archdiocese of Adelaide through its Jordan-Kennedy Committee.

Versions of some chapters of this book have appeared in journals and in conference papers. Part of chapter 4 was given at a colloquium sponsored by the Australian Theological Forum in Adelaide in 2001 and appeared in the book *Sin and Salvation*, edited by Duncan Reid and Mark Worthing (Adelaide: ATF Press, 2003), 205-21. A first approach to chapter 6 appeared in the *Australasian Catholic Record* 76 (1999): 259-69. Versions of chapter 7 were published in *Pacifica* 13 (2000): 142-59 and in *Starting with the Spirit*, edited by Steven Pickard and Gordon Preece (Adelaide: ATF Press, 2001), 238-60. Chapter 9 was first given as the May 2001 Veech Lecture at the Catholic Institute of Sydney. In a revised form it was presented at the conference on panentheism at St. George's House, Windsor Castle, in December 2001. Further revised in the light of comments from participants, it will appear in a book forthcoming from Eerdmans, edited by the conference conveners, Arthur Peacocke and Philip Clayton. This project was generously supported by the John Templeton Foundation.

Finally, I am very grateful to Bill Burrows, my editor, and to all at Orbis who have worked on this book. I am delighted that *Breath of Life* is being published by Orbis Books.

Introduction

The stunning world opened up by Big Bang cosmology and evolutionary biology calls for a renewed theology of the Creator Spirit. The widely felt need for respectful dialogue with other religious traditions requires that Christians dig more deeply into their tradition of the uncontrollable Spirit as the wild wind that "blows where it wills" (John 3:8). Among the Christian churches, it seems that only the blazing fire of the Spirit will be able to energize the stalled ecumenical movement. My own church is confronted with diminishing numbers, loss of many of its young people, painful divisions over the ministry of women, excessive centralism, serious problems over authority, the scandal of sexual abuse, and a growing inability to provide the Eucharist. I am convinced that such issues can be addressed with fidelity and integrity only from a perspective that gives a proper place to the Spirit. Finally, I will argue that a renewed theology of the Creator Spirit can contribute not only to right relations between human beings but also to right relations with plants and insects, animals and birds, deserts and forests, and with the rivers, the seas, and the atmosphere that sustain our lives.

What is required is a holistic theology of the Spirit, one that begins not with Pentecost but with the origin of the universe 14 billion years ago. Christians tend to operate from an implied story of the Spirit that begins with Pentecost. Because the larger story of the Spirit is seldom told, I have chosen to tell a story of the Creator Spirit that begins with the first second of the observable universe.

Before telling this story, I begin with two foundational chapters. The first outlines a story of creation based on insights from the sciences, particularly cosmology and evolutionary biology. This scientific account will provide one of the building blocks for the theology of the Creator Spirit developed in the following pages. Then, in a second foundational chapter, I will turn to the Spirit theology of Basil of Caesarea (ca. 330-379). Basil was the most important contributor to the fourth-century development of the doctrine of the Spirit that culminated in the Council of Constantinople of 381. It is my wager that Basil's theology not only can offer a contribution to ecumenical healing on the theology of the Spirit but also can provide the elements for a contemporary ecological theology of the Spirit. In particular, I will seek to build on Basil's understanding of the Trinity as

1

Communion and of the Spirit as the *Breath of God that always accompanies the Word.*

The second section of this book tells a story of the Spirit in four chapters. It begins with the Spirit's work in creation from the first moment of the universe, moves to the Spirit's work among human beings in grace, culminates in the Christ event, and continues in a radically new way in the life of the church. It is a story of the Spirit told from below, from the side of creation. Because my view of the Spirit is determined by the Christ event, a central part of this story is the story of Jesus and the Spirit. In this section I will outline an approach to Spirit Christology in which Word and Spirit are closely interrelated. I will propose a theology of reciprocal relations between Word and Spirit that encompasses the theology of creation, grace, incarnation, and church.

The third part of this book is devoted to further exploration of the theology of the Creator Spirit. It begins by attempting to face what is an unavoidable issue for ecological theology—the pain, death, and extinction of so many creatures. In this section I envisage the Spirit as companion to all creatures in their travail and as the midwife to the birth of the new. The second chapter in this section argues for the idea that there is a role of the Spirit in creation that can be thought of as proper to the Spirit. Finally, I suggest that insights from science and theology lead to a panentheistic worldview, in which the Spirit can be thought of as "making space" for an interrelated universe of creatures to evolve within the life of the divine Communion.

The fourth section deals with two particular issues in the theology of the Spirit. The first is the procession of the Spirit, the issue that has divided East and West. I propose a theology of reciprocal relations between Word and Spirit, in which the Spirit is thought of as coming eternally from the Source of All *through* the Word, and the Word is thought of as generated eternally from the Source of All with the Spirit eternally *resting on* the Word. The second particular issue I address is that of discernment. I will discuss insights from the Christian tradition that offer help in the process of discerning what is truly of the Spirit of God in the chaos of diverse internal and external voices that impinge upon us. The book concludes with a chapter that attempts to bring together what has gone before in an overview of the theology of the Creator Spirit.

The theology of the Spirit has contributed to the thousand-year-old division between East and West and has been a significant symbol of the division. I attempt to make a small contribution to healing on this issue by going behind the divisions between East and West to the theology of Basil of Caesarea, which is common to both. While respecting and seeking to integrate the tradition of the Western church, I have chosen not to build directly on Augustine's theology of the procession of the Spirit from the Father *and the Son* (the *filioque*). I have not taken up his psychological model of the Trinity, nor his idea of the Spirit as the mutual love between the other two persons. Augustine's ideas were taken to a new depth in the theology of Thomas Aquinas, and this tradition has been creatively explored in contemporary theology.[1] But, because I believe that Basil's thought can contribute to an ecumenical theology and at the same time bring new life to a contemporary theology of the Spirit, I have chosen to stay with his concept of the Spirit as the Breath of God that always accompanies the Word.

I decided against attempting a summary of biblical approaches to the theology of the Spirit of God. There is little value in summarizing widely available material.[2] It seemed more useful in this kind of book to focus on particular biblical insights in specific sections of the work. So, for example, I deal with the Old Testament image of the Spirit as the Breath of Life in chapter 4, with the Spirit theologies of the four evangelists in chapter 6, and with aspects of Paul's theology of the Spirit in chapter 8.

Language about God is an important issue for a book like this. With feminist theologians, I believe that in order to speak rightly about the God who embraces and transcends both male and female, we need to make use of female as well as male images for God. Because of this I will speak of the Source of All Being not only as *Abba*-Father (Rom. 8:15) but also as the Mother comforting her child (Isa. 66:13). I will speak of Jesus not only as Son of God but also as *Sophia*, the Wisdom of God. Where speaking in my own voice, as opposed to reporting others, I will use a variety of terms for the divine persons. An ecological theology needs trinitarian language that embraces and includes the nonhuman. It needs more than parent-child images. The tradition of Wisdom and Word language is more helpful here than that of Father-Son. It makes it possible to think of *all* things as created in the Wisdom/Word of God and of every creature as a reflection of the eternal Wisdom/Word.[3]

Spirit language (breath, wind, oil, fire) is particularly useful in evoking the presence of God in ways that are beyond the human. While I want to maintain and build on this reference to nonhuman creatures, I will at times use feminine pronouns in speaking of the Spirit to bring out the personal nature of the Spirit's presence. I will use the feminine form not because I think that the Spirit is any more or less feminine than the other trinitarian persons, but simply as a balance to the overwhelming use of male images and words for God in the material I am using and in the Christian tradition in general. The Holy Spirit is sometimes spoken of as "the unknown" one, a phrase that suggests the radical otherness of the Spirit, the wind that blows where it wills (John 3:8). I will advocate an approach to the Spirit that understands this otherness in positive terms, as leading to an appreciation of the Spirit as present and at work in the otherness of the nonhuman as well as in the mysterious depths of the human.

PART 1

Two Building Blocks
for a Theology of the Spirit

ONE

The Story of the Universe

One of the joys of being in the Australian "outback" is gazing up into the sky on a moonless night. The Milky Way stretches right across the sky toward the Southern Cross. I find it astonishing to gaze into this stretch of sky and to know that I am looking toward the center of our galaxy, and that it contains something like 100 billion stars that are more or less like the Sun. It is hard to grasp the size of the Milky Way. Astronomers tell us that it is shaped like a disc that is about 100,000 light years across and 1,000 light years through the middle. The Sun is located about two-thirds of the way out on the radius of the disc and slowly orbits the galactic center.

It is easy to find the cloudy areas of sky known as the Large and Small Magellanic Clouds. In observing these "clouds" we are in fact looking out of our own galaxy. The Magellanic Clouds are our nearest neighboring galaxies, 170,000 and 190,000 light years from us. For some of the year the constellation Pegasus stands in the northwestern sky, and at the base of Pegasus there is a faint smudge of light, the Andromeda Galaxy. This is a spiral galaxy, very like the Milky Way in size and shape but about two million light years from us. I am always amazed to recall the simple astronomical fact that light from our close neighbor Andromeda has been traveling for two million years to reach my eyes, at the speed of 300,000 kilometers per second. We see Andromeda not as it is now, but as it was two million years ago.

Andromeda, the Magellanic Clouds, and the Milky Way belong to what is called the Local Group of galaxies. Galaxies are linked together in clusters and superclusters. Astronomers have begun to map the large-scale structure of the universe. In these maps, superclusters are grouped in enormous walls, surrounding vast voids where there are few galaxies and no large clusters. At the beginning of the twentieth century, it was not clear that the universe contained more than one galaxy, although some, like Immanuel Kant, had already speculated that the nebulae visible in the night sky might be "island universes." At the beginning of the twenty-first century astronomers estimate that there are about 100 billion galaxies in the observable universe.

Twentieth-century science radically changed our worldview. Not only do we now have a new understanding of the mind-numbing size of the universe, but we also understand the universe as expanding and evolving. The concept of an expanding universe has its theoretical base in Albert Einstein's General Theory of Relativity, even though Einstein initially resisted the idea. Theorists using Einstein's work to develop models of the universe found that in their models the universe was not static but expanding. And if the universe is expanding, and decreasing in temperature and density, as the models suggest, then this points back to a beginning of the universe of unthinkable smallness, density, and heat. In these theoretical models, not only matter but also space-time itself emerges and stretches in the process of cosmic expansion.

During the twentieth century, a number of lines of evidence gave empirical support to what came to be called Big Bang models of the universe. First, in the 1920s the astronomer Edwin Hubble showed conclusively that faint objects in the night sky are indeed other galaxies. He found that the absorption lines in the spectra of light coming from distant galaxies are shifted toward the red end of the spectrum. He saw these redshifts as indicating that these galaxies are moving away from us. Hubble found that the farther away they are, the faster they are receding. Second, theorists predicted that the high temperatures of the early universe would have produced a universe made up of about 75 percent hydrogen, about 25 percent helium, and tiny amounts of deuterium and lithium. Observation has confirmed this prediction. Third, theory also predicted that remnants of the original radiation should still be present in the universe. This background microwave radiation was discovered in 1965 by Arno Penzias and Robert Wilson. The discovery of this "afterglow" of the Big Bang finally overcame most of the resistance to the Big Bang scenario. It confirmed the theory of an expanding universe.[1] Even though there is still much controversy about the origin of the universe and about what happened within the first second of its existence, the general picture of the expanding universe is widely accepted. As Stephen Hawking has written, "the discovery that the universe is expanding is one of the great intellectual revolutions of the twentieth century."[2]

This truly revolutionary idea in cosmology needs to be understood in conjunction with the great revolutionary idea in biology from the nineteenth century. In *The Origin of Species,* published in 1859, Charles Darwin proposed that evolutionary change occurs through natural selection, based on inherited variations that give some creatures an edge in successful adaptation to new environments. Twentieth-century work in genetics, molecular biology, and many other fields has developed and confirmed Darwin's fundamental insights. The story of life can now be traced back to

3.8 billion years ago. Scientists have discovered the remains of communities of microbes in rock formations that suggest that there were well-developed communities of bacteria on Earth by three and a half billion years ago. The evidence from a number of disciplines leads to the conclusion that all the wonderfully diverse creatures that inhabit our planet have evolved from these communities of simple cells.

The combination of the story of the universe and the story of life on Earth constitutes a new worldview—and, of course, a new view of the human being in relation to it. It is a worldview that will be taken for granted by many young people growing up in the twenty-first century. When a new worldview emerges that springs from a broadly held scientific consensus, theology must engage with it in order to be faithful to its own task. It may be, of course, that some dimensions of a broadly held scientific consensus will change over time. But I am convinced that theology must take the risk of engaging with the best available information at the time. This means, of course, that such theology, including the theology represented by this book, will always have a tentative and provisional character.

In what follows I will attempt to sketch an account of the worldview that emerges from scientific work in cosmology and evolutionary biology. This will form an important part of the context for the theology of the Holy Spirit that follows. This account is in narrative form.[3] It tells a story, the story of the unfolding universe and the story of life on Earth. It describes what I take to be the broadly accepted story of the visible universe. I will not deal in any detail with speculative theories about what occurred within the first second.[4]

It is important to note, however, that in some theoretical models of the universe, particularly those based on a period of rapid inflation, the observable universe may be a small part of a much bigger universe, even an infinite one.[5] Astronomer Martin Rees uses the word "multiverse" to describe the idea that our universe may be just one member of an ensemble of universes.[6] But there are cosmologists who, on the contrary, argue that there is a boundary or edge to the space-time of our universe, and that therefore it has a beginning.[7] While cosmologists agree on much of the history of the observable universe back to the first second, there is a great deal that is necessarily theoretical and also highly controversial beyond that. To my mind, these ongoing controversies serve as a healthy caution to theology. They caution against simply identifying the first moment of the Big Bang with the beginning of God's act of creation.

As a theologian, I am not concerned primarily with these controversies but with what is common ground in cosmology, the worldview of the expanding universe. I believe that theology is called to respond to what we can know with reasonable confidence about the universe we inhabit. The information to which we have access is limited by the speed of light and by the amount of time that light has had to travel toward us (roughly 14 bil-

lion years). The observable universe, then, stretches out from us in all directions for about 14 billion light years. It is this observable universe that is
the focus of the following account.

THE STORY OF THE UNIVERSE

The First Second

The observable universe began from an unthinkably small, hot, and
dense state about 14 billion years ago. Cosmologists believe that an enormous amount of cosmic history happened within the tiniest fraction of the
first second. Many think that in this period the universe went through a
time of extremely rapid expansion—the inflation era. Within the first second, particles existed only for the briefest interval before interacting with
other particles and going out of existence. Particles and antiparticles met
and disappeared for ever. By the end of the first second, a billionth of the
original matter had survived and was stabilized. The fundamental forces of
the universe had emerged (gravity, electromagnetism, and the strong and
weak nuclear forces), and the universe existed as an expanding and cooling
"soup" of elementary particles such as electrons, neutrinos, and photons.

The Emergence of Nuclei of Hydrogen and Helium

From about the first second, protons and neutrons were able to bond
together in the cooling universe to form the nuclei of hydrogen and helium.
It was still too hot for them to form into atoms. The nuclei of hydrogen
accounted for about three-quarters of the matter of the early universe, with
the nuclei of helium making up the other quarter, alongside small amounts
of other elements. Matter and radiation were still coupled together in an
opaque world. Nuclei of hydrogen and helium still interacted with photons, the particles that constitute light. By the end of the first three minutes,
the universe existed as an expanding and cooling plasma of nuclei of
hydrogen and helium.

The Formation of Atoms

The universe continued to expand and to cool down. When it was about
300,000 years old, it was cool enough for the first atoms of hydrogen and
helium to form and for matter to be separated out from radiation. These
primordial atoms gave a radically new structure to the universe. They
allowed light to go through them. Photons were set free and from then on
seldom interacted with matter or with each other. As the early universe
thinned out and became transparent to light, it was filled with a universal
sea of radiation. This is the origin of the cosmic microwave background,

which was detected by Arno Penzias and Martin Wilson in 1965. This radiation comes from all directions of the sky and it has a temperature of about three degrees Kelvin.

The Emergence of Galaxies and Stars

After about a billion years, small fluctuations in the expanding and cooling universe produced sites where clouds of gas formed. These would evolve into the first galaxies. Stars were born as the matter within regions of these proto-galaxies contracted because of gravity, began to heat up, and eventually ignited in nuclear reactions, in which hydrogen was converted into helium. The universe lit up with starlight. There is much that is still unknown about galaxy formation. But astronomers using radio telescopes can observe massive clouds of gas about 12 billion light years away from us, proto-galaxies with enough gas to form something like 100 billion stars. They have discovered intense star formation in galaxies 11 billion light years away. As they observe these distant galaxies, astronomers are looking back into the early universe.

The Birth of the Solar System and Earth

About 4.6 billion years ago our Sun emerged as one of a new generation of stars in the Milky Way galaxy. Planets began to build from the disk of dust and gas that circled the young Sun. Earth probably began from grains of dust in this disk, developing into a ball that was constructed through collisions and held together by gravity. The young Earth continued to develop by means of the ongoing bombardment of comets. It began to heat up because of this bombardment and because of internal radioactive heat. Iron sank to the core and lighter minerals came to the surface. Comets ferried large amounts of ice to Earth, contributing to the formation of the oceans. They also brought organic material that would contribute to the emergence of life. By four billion years ago, the bombardment had slowed, a crust had developed, the surface had cooled, seas had formed, and a first atmosphere had emerged.

The Beginning of Life on Earth

About 3.8 billion years ago, life appeared on Earth in the form of bacteria, simple cells without a nucleus (prokaryotes).[8] It is not known where or how life began. The recent discovery of the importance of thermophiles (heat-loving bacteria) has led to the hypothesis of an origin near deep-sea volcanic vents. In recent years more attention has been given to the extraterrestrial origins of some of the building blocks of life.[9] The earliest fossils we have of living things are stromatolites, structures that formed when bacteria deposited mats formed from mineral grains. Some of these, found near Marble Bar in Western Australia, are dated at 3.5 billion years old. There is evidence of life's signature found in the carbon of rocks from Greenland dated at 3.85 billion years old.

The Eukaryotes

For about a billion years the only life on Earth was bacterial. But then something dramatically new happened. The *eukaryotes* appear. These cells differ markedly from *prokaryotes*. Although they are still single-celled creatures, they possess a nucleus surrounded by a membrane that contains individual chromosomes. These nucleated cells apparently had their origin about 2.7 billion years ago, from a symbiotic merger between two kinds of bacteria.[10] In a further symbiosis, some eukaryotes would incorporate other cells within themselves as cellular organelles. This is the origin of the mitochondria that play a fundamental role in our bodies today. The emergence of the first nucleated cells was an enormous step in evolutionary history. It provides the necessary foundation for all the multicellular forms of life that have emerged over the last 600 million years.

The Flourishing of Plants and Animals

Over several billion years, the atmosphere of the Earth, originally composed of methane, hydrogen, ammonia, and carbon dioxide, was converted into one that was oxygen-rich. This occurred because of photosynthesis by blue-green bacteria. Gradually eukaryotes evolved into multicellular organisms that could use oxygen to produce energy. The first multicellular animals that appear in the fossil record are the Ediacara fauna of around 580 million years ago. The fossils tell of a wonderful explosion of diverse life forms in the seas during the Cambrian period (545-495 million years ago), as animals became bigger and developed shells and skeletons. About 375 million years ago the first vertebrates moved onto land. There was a terrible extinction of life 248 million years ago, in which 90 percent of marine species were lost. This was to be followed by a period in which life bloomed with dinosaurs, flying reptiles, marine reptiles, and mammals during the Triassic (248-206 million years ago) and Jurassic (206-144 million years ago) periods. Birds and flowering plants appeared at the beginning of the Cretaceous period (144-65 million years ago). At the end of this period, 65 million years ago, probably because of the impact of a large comet hitting Earth, the dinosaurs, along with more than half of Earth's living species, were wiped out. The extinction of the dinosaurs left habitats for mammals to fill. They diversified and flourished. Primates, horses, and marine mammals made their appearance.

Human Life

About five to eight million years ago, some species of chimpanzee-like apes succeeded in establishing themselves in the tree savanna that surrounded the African rain forest. They developed a more upright (bipedal) style of walking. Various bipedal species evolved between four million and two million years ago (the australopithecines). About two million years ago, *Homo rudolfensis* appeared with a significantly larger brain, shorter arms, and longer legs. *Homo erectus* seems to have emerged about the same time and quickly spread from Africa to Europe and Asia. *Homo erectus* used fire, could run like modern humans, and made stone tools according to plan.[11] They evolved into various groups including the Neanderthals, who flourished between 250,000 and 30,000 years ago. *Homo sapiens* evolved from *Homo erectus* in Africa about 150,000 years ago. They were lighter in body weight than *Homo erectus*, but their brain size had increased from about 826 to 1250 grams. They spread from Africa to the world, reaching Australia about 60,000 years ago, western Europe about 35,000 years ago, eastern Asia about 30,000 years ago and North America about 12,000 years ago (although there is some evidence of an earlier colonization of North America).

MADE FROM STARDUST

In tracing the story of the universe and of life on Earth, it becomes startlingly clear that everything in our universe is interconnected. There is an inner relationship between what happens in the stars and what happens in the evolution of life on Earth. In this final section of this chapter I will reflect a little further on this interconnection. It reveals something about the nature of the universe that I will argue is fundamental to a contemporary articulation of the theology of the Creator Spirit.

Trees, birds, and human beings are made from the stars. The universe is dominated by just two elements, hydrogen and helium. As is clear from the story told above, these elements have their origin in the Big Bang itself. While all hydrogen is produced primordially, helium is produced in two ways, primordially in the first three minutes and then again in stars by means of the nuclear fusion of hydrogen. There are about ninety-two elements that occur naturally on Earth. All these elements, apart from the primordial hydrogen and helium, have been made in stars. The living creatures of Earth are made up of molecules composed of atoms of carbon, hydrogen, oxygen, nitrogen, and phosphorus. Every atom of each of these elements, apart from hydrogen, has been made by nuclear fusion in stars. Every atom of every body found on Earth originates in a star. Life is intimately related to the stars. If there were no stars there could be no trees, flowers, kangaroos, or human beings. We are all made from stardust.

As living creatures, we are directly connected to the very origin of the universe through the atoms of hydrogen in the cells of our bodies. Hydrogen is a fundamental element in the structure of the cells of all living things. And when combined with oxygen, it also forms the water that provides the context for the emergence of life. The hydrogen atoms that constitute each cell of my body and the hydrogen atoms I drink in a glass of water were all formed in the Big Bang. None of this is true of the primeval helium. Helium is chemically inert and very light, so that most of the helium in our part of the solar system was lost into space. But the hydrogen from which we are made links us directly to the cosmic processes of the early universe. In this very concrete sense, we are children of the universe.

Stars form when clouds of gas condense because of gravity and heat up until the internal temperature is high enough to start a thermonuclear furnace in which hydrogen is converted into helium. When a star exhausts its supply of hydrogen, a chain of nuclear reactions occurs that can convert helium into heavier elements, including carbon, which is fundamental for terrestrial life like ours, along with nitrogen and oxygen and finally iron. Some stars finish their lives in supernova explosions, producing even heavier elements. These supernovas, along with other dispersion processes, seed the nearby universe with elements for the formation of further stars and their planets.

With each generation of stars, the chemical elements of the galaxy are being transformed from lighter to heavier elements. Astronomers estimate that it takes about three generations of stars to provide the chemicals that are necessary to form whales and parrots and human beings. John Barrow states that it takes at least ten billion years of stellar burning to produce the carbon and the other elements from which we are made.[12]

Our galaxy, the Milky Way, is filled with the raw materials for life produced by generations of stars. Scientists have been able to identify complex organic molecules and amino acids in interstellar clouds. While there is still no adequate explanation for the origin of life on Earth, the resources for life are abundantly available in these interstellar clouds of the Milky Way. This material arrived on Earth via comets. John Gribbin writes: "The raw material from which the first living molecules were assembled on Earth was brought down to the surface of the Earth in tiny grains of interplanetary material, preserved in the frozen hearts of comets from the interstellar debris of the giant molecular cloud from which the Solar System formed." He insists that these grains of matter are not metaphorically but quite literally formed from material that comes from the stars.[13]

The relationship between the stars and the biosphere on Earth is such that NASA scientists and university departments now describe themselves as working in the field of astrobiology. The astronomer Martin Rees speaks of a "galactic ecology" of the Milky Way. He says that a galaxy resembles a large ecological system in which pristine hydrogen is transformed into the basic building blocks of life such as carbon and oxygen, and then some of this is returned to interstellar space to be recycled in new generations of stars.

Rees tells a story of a single carbon atom, which I have adapted in this paragraph. Imagine a carbon atom born from a dying star that ends its life in a supernova explosion. The atom is propelled out into space, where it wanders for hundreds of millions of years. Eventually it finds itself in an interstellar cloud of gas. This cloud collapses under its own gravity and new stars begin to form. The atom we are following becomes part of a spinning gaseous disk surrounding one of these new stars, the Sun. It coalesces with other material to constitute part of a newly forming planet, Earth. Over a billion years it plays out its own role, first in the geological processes that mold the Earth's surface and then in the chemistry that allows living creatures to emerge and to evolve. Today it has ended up in a brain cell of the reader of these words.[14]

Carbon atoms, like those in every cell of my brain and my blood, have a pedigree that extends back before the birth of the solar system 4.5 billion years ago. Rees points out that if we traced the history of atoms that make us up back to about seven billion years ago, we would find them spread throughout the whole Milky Way galaxy—"Atoms now linked together in a single strand of DNA were then inside different stars spread around the Galaxy or dispersed in the medium between stars."[15]

Human beings, along with all other life forms of Earth, are intimately related to and dependent on the long history of the universe. We are all made of stardust. Because of these connections, the astronomers George Coyne and Alessandro Omizzolo speak of a "social" character to the universe. They point out that all things are interconnected in the "families" of galaxies, stars, planets, nations, and people. The common bond among these families is shown by the fact that "the more abundant chemical elements in our own bodies came from three generations of stars" and that "some of the less abundant elements may have required nucleosynthesis in millions of distant galaxies." They conclude that "no element in the universe, including ourselves, can be ultimately understood, except in relation to the whole."[16]

The story of the universe that science tells with all its implications for the interconnectedness of all things in our universe will be one of the building blocks on which I will attempt to construct a theology of the Spirit. The second, which I will outline in the next chapter, has a very different nature. It will take the form of an exploration of the theology of Basil of Caesarea on the Holy Spirit, a theology that comes from the fourth century of the Christian era. I will be suggesting that some of the key ideas of Basil's theology can be brought into a creative dialogue with the story of the universe that science puts before us. With these two building blocks in place, I will attempt to articulate a theology, that is also a story, of the Spirit.

TWO

Basil on the Holy Spirit

Basil of Caesarea will be foundational for the theology of the Spirit developed in the rest of this book. I will build on his understanding of God as Communion and on his vision of the Spirit as the Breath of God who always accompanies the Word. The argument will be that these insights can develop in new ways today, particularly in dialogue with the scientific worldview presented in the previous chapter, and thus can contribute to a renewed theology of the Spirit. My hope is that such a theology may have practical effects in the life of the church, in ecumenical relations between East and West, in a communitarian politics, and in an ecological vision and praxis.

The Pentecostal experiences of the Spirit constituted those who assembled after the death of Jesus as the church of Jesus Christ. These experiences, interpreted in the light of the Christ event and by means of the ancient Hebrew theology of the Spirit of God, provided the basis for the various theologies of the Spirit that can be found in the New Testament. These biblical articulations of the experience of the Spirit are the primary resource for all later Christian theologies of the Spirit, including the one developed here.

If the first experience of intense creativity in the Christian theology of the Spirit occurs in the New Testament communities, I would propose that the second occurs between the councils of Nicaea (325) and Constantinople (381). This fourth-century development is built upon the Scriptures, the liturgical life and living traditions of the church, and the work of theologians like Athanasius (ca. 296-373), bishop of the great Christian center of Alexandria. It takes place in a community not known for its learning or culture in the district of Cappadocia, near the center of modern Turkey. It is largely the work of Basil of Caesarea (ca. 330-379), in collaboration with his friend Gregory of Nazianzus (ca. 329-389) and his brother, Gregory of Nyssa (ca. 335-394). They are part of a wider group of fourth-century contributors to the deepening of the theology of the Spirit that includes

16

Athanasius and Didymus the Blind (ca. 313-398) in the East, and Hilary (ca. 315-367), Ambrose (ca. 339-397), and Augustine (354-430) in the West.

Basil's theology is the common heritage of East and West, predating the controversies over the procession of the Spirit. It provides the theological underpinning for the doctrine of the Spirit that would emerge at the Council of Constantinople (381) and be enshrined in the Nicene-Constantinopolitan Creed.[1] Because Basil's theology of the Spirit is the common tradition of East and West, I believe that it can offer the basis for an authentic ecumenical theology that seeks to bridge the millennium-long divide over the doctrine of the Spirit. I will begin this chapter by exploring Basil's lived theology of the Spirit, and then focus on his understanding of God as Communion. Finally, I will outline his view of the Holy Spirit as the Breath of God who enables creatures to participate in divine Communion.

BASIL'S LIVED THEOLOGY OF THE SPIRIT

Theology is always shaped by the context, experience, assumptions, biases, and priorities of the theologian. In Basil's case, I suggest that his theology of the Spirit is particularly related to his experience of the *social* nature of Christian life. Basil's theological reflection on the Spirit developed in the context of his commitment to the communion of the church and to the good of the wider society. His theology is a practical theology, directed toward the building up of the Christian community and toward participation in public life.[2] In a recent biography of Basil, Philip Rousseau shows that Basil valued the kind of truth that can be tested in action. He was interested in the truth that finds expression in generous and practical love of others and in the worship of God.[3] For Basil, theology involves the *praxis* of a life lived for God. Rousseau makes the point that, while Basil valued prayer and seclusion, he saw these not as opposed to public life but as leading naturally toward it.

In exploring Basil's theology of the Spirit, then, it is helpful to begin from his attempt to live a God-centered life in the Christian community of fourth-century Cappadocia. Basil came from a large and moderately wealthy Christian family who lived at Pontus, near the coast of the Black Sea. He received a classical education in Caesarea, Constantinople, and finally in Athens in the company of his friend Gregory of Nazianzus.[4] Soon after returning to Cappadocia, Basil abandoned the life of rhetoric for one of prayer and seclusion. After the death of their father, Basil's elder sister Macrina had persuaded her mother to abandon their accustomed way of life and to transform the family home into a Christian community based on equality. In Gregory of Nyssa's words, she had "put herself on a level with the many by entering into a common life with her maids, making them her sisters and equals rather than her slaves and underlings."[5] Later, Macrina set up a monastic-style community on the family property at Annisa on the Iris River. Basil took up a life of prayer and asceticism on the opposite bank of the Iris, inspired by Macrina and particularly by his friend and mentor Eustathius of Sebaste.

In 356 Basil followed Eustathius on a tour of the monastic settlements of Syria, Mesopotamia, Palestine, and Egypt. On his return, probably in 357, Basil was baptized by Bishop Dianus of Caesarea. He began to live in his retreat at Annisa, where he was joined for a time by Gregory of Nazianzus in 358. Basil was soon drawn into the life of the church at Caesarea, although he several times retreated back to Annisa. He was ordained a priest around 362. Well before his ordination, he was involved in theological controversies over the divinity of the Word and of the Holy Spirit.

There had been widespread difficulty in the East in accepting Nicaea's teaching that the Word is of the same substance (*homoousios*) as the Father. On top of this, Aetius and his disciple Eunomius had revived a sophisticated form of Arian theology at Antioch, teaching that the Word and Spirit were "unlike" the Father. Many ordinary Christians, bewildered by the range of competing theological options on offer, held views that tended toward Arianism.[6] The emperors Constantius and Valens supported Arian tendencies. It was in this context that Jerome remarked that the whole world groaned in amazement to find itself Arian. Basil was ordained bishop of Caearea in 370 and, in the last decade of his life, did all he could for the truth of the faith and the peace of the church. As he saw it, this meant opposing those who denied the divinity of Christ or the Spirit. But, importantly, it also meant attempting to hold together in the communion of the one church both those who adhered to Nicaea strictly and those who shared the faith of the church but had difficulties with the unbiblical language used at Nicaea.

Nicaea (325) had taught the eternal divinity of the Word and, fifty-six years later, the Council of Constantinople (381) would teach the eternal divinity of the Holy Spirit. In between was a time of turmoil and strife. For the first time in Christian history, the divinity of the Spirit had become a matter of intense and sustained controversy. Eunomius, of course, had denied the full divinity of the Spirit; and in Egypt, Serapion, bishop of Thmuis, drew to the attention of Athanasius the claim made by a group of Egyptian Christians that the Spirit was a creature, a superior angelic being. Athanasius's response in his *Letter to Serapion*, defending the divinity of the Spirit against those he called "Tropici," was a pioneering work in the development of the doctrine of the Spirit.[7] Basil now found himself confronted with others opposed to the divinity and equality of the Spirit. He called them the Spirit-fighters (*pneumatomachi*) and, sadly, would find his former friend Eustathius associated with them.[8]

In addition to theological issues over the divinity of the Word and the Spirit, Basil faced grave problems of ecclesiastical politics. A central instance is the fact there were rival bishops in the great Christian center of

Antioch. Basil was in communion with one contender, Meletius, while Athanasius and Rome acknowledged another, Paulinus. It was a complex and disturbing period of church life. At the end of his *On the Holy Spirit*, Basil describes the situation he faced as like being caught up in a violent sea battle that takes place in the midst of a wild storm. He presents a detailed picture of a battle fought in darkness, with huge winds, torrential rain, and enormous waves. While some combatants change sides, others massacre each other in rebellion against authority. Everywhere there is confusion, betrayal and hatred.[9] With these images, Basil communicates something of the circumstances in which he wrote his important work on the Holy Spirit and attempted to live a life of generosity and fidelity in response to the same Spirit.

It is clear that Basil had flaws and failures, but, in spite of these, his pastoral and theological work finally helped to bring a measure of unity to the church. Anthony Meredith suggests that Basil can be summed up as a leader, a founder, an organizer, an ecclesiastical politician, and someone to whom subsequent generations could look back with gratitude. He writes of Basil: "He tamed and organized the wild wandering ascetics and brought them under a stable rule; he brought together a faction-ridden Church and was in large measure responsible for the adoption of the Creed of Nicaea."[10] By the end of Basil's life, the greater part of the church had finally received the teaching of Nicaea on the divinity of Christ, and the ground had been thoroughly prepared for Constantinople's teaching of the divinity of the Holy Spirit.

Basil's theology of the Spirit has its foundation in his experience of baptismal and eucharistic communion. John Zizioulas has pointed out that a significant number of the key theologians who contributed to the development of the doctrine of the Trinity were pastoral bishops like Basil. The theology of God they articulated was not an abstract theoretical truth but a truth of lived communion (*koinōnia*).[11] Their pastoral responsibility involved building up the communion of the local church and working to maintain communion with other local churches. All was centered on the Eucharist as the event of communion. In the Eucharist, God was experienced and tasted as eschatological trinitarian communion. It was not at all surprising, then, that a bishop like Basil would see the work of the Spirit in terms of communion.

Communal life had always run deep in Basil. He was the third of ten children in a family that counted heroes of persecution among its ancestors. He formed close, intense, and often troubled friendships throughout his life. Rousseau says that Basil "could not have achieved even his own limited success without the intellectual stimulus and moral counsel of some half a dozen close colleagues." Basil's letters reveal just how much his friends mattered to him. But his relational approach to life went far beyond his family and close friends. His whole vision was relational and communal. It involved the well-being of both the church and civil society.

Rousseau tells us that Basil "thought relentlessly in social terms."[12] He constantly encouraged a sense of responsibility for others, and consistently gave priority to those who were poor or ill.

In his work as a priest and bishop, Basil gave expression to his commitment to the good of society. He preached vigorous sermons on the need to share wealth. He taught that hoarding to oneself property that one does not need is a theft from the poor:

> If we call someone who strips clothes from others a thief, what else would we call those who do not clothe the naked, even though they can? The excess bread you have does not belong to you but to the hungry. The clothes you keep in your cupboard belong to the naked. The shoes that go to rot belong to those with bare feet. The treasure stored in your cellar belongs to those in need. When you do not help those whom you can help, you injure them.[13]

In his *Sermon 8*, he gives a vivid picture of the human consequences of the drought that afflicted Cappadocia in 369. He vigorously challenges the wealthy, urging his hearers to respond to those who suffer hunger.[14] Gregory of Nazianzus tells us that, by his exhortations, Basil opened the "storehouses of the rich." Then Basil himself oversaw the subsequent redistribution of food, serving "cauldrons of soup and salted meats" to the hungry.[15]

Basil's commitment to social welfare went beyond preaching and personal charity. He built an enormous community center on the outskirts of Caesarea. It involved a large complex of buildings, with housing for the bishop and clergy and shelter for travelers, strangers, and those who were ill. There were nurses, doctors, and workers in a number of trades, as well as pack animals.[16] Basil himself cared for lepers and dressed the wounds of the sick.[17] This area became known as Newtown, and the population of Caesarea came to be recentered around it. Later it would be known as the Basilead. Basil encouraged assistant bishops to set up similar systems with their monks in nearby villages.[18]

Basil's teaching on the ascetical life also gave significant expression to his commitment to community. Augustine Holmes makes the important point that Basil's teaching on asceticism was addressed not just to monastic communities but to all Christians.[19] Basil saw continuity rather than a boundary between those who lived the faith in ordinary families and those who lived a more monastic Christian life. All are part of the local church. All are called to a life that is pleasing to God. Right at the beginning of his *Longer Rule*, Basil centers the whole ascetical life on the dual command from Matthew 22:37-39 to love God and neighbor.[20] In his third rule, he explains that communal love is based on the very *nature* of human beings as well as on the Gospel. Human beings are by nature relational. Basil writes: "nothing is so characteristic of our nature as to associate with one another, to need one another and to love our kind."[21] When the Gospels command us to mutual love—Basil points to John 13:34: "I give you a new commandment, that you love one another"—what they command is true to the nature that God has given to us.

Basil teaches that love of neighbor is already a fulfillment of the command to love God. Pointing to Matthew 25:35, where Christ identifies himself with the hungry, the thirsty, the stranger, the naked, and the prisoner, Basil insists that this love must involve the poor and the needy. It is Christ we meet in all those in need. Basil opposes the kind of solitary withdrawal common in Egypt. He consistently stresses the communal ideal of the life of faith. In his rule 7, Basil presents a controversial series of arguments opposing the solitary life (*monōsis*) and supporting a communion (*koinōnia*) of life. He sees the diverse gifts of the Spirit as given to individuals for the good of the community. He claims that these gifts cannot find expression in the solitary life; the charisms of the Spirit can be lived out only in community. Among a number of biblical arguments in support of the common life, Basil puts the question to those who would choose the solitary life: "Whose feet will you wash?" For Basil, the key model for Christian life is found in the texts from Acts that describe the common life of the apostolic community: "All who believed were together and had all things in common" (Acts 2:44 and 4:32).[22]

All of this, I believe, is the practical foundation for Basil's theology of the Holy Spirit. The Spirit is found in the living of communion — in nursing the sick, in sharing food with the hungry, in hospitality, and in friendship. This is already a kind of lived theology. Basil saw the whole of Christian life as built up through the gifts or charisms of the Holy Spirit. He understood these charisms to include not only spiritual gifts such as prophecy and healing, but also earthly goods and services. He tells us that the Spirit, who is "one whole," gives diverse gifts for the good of the one whole community. Christian unity consists in the harmonious relationships between the members of the Body of Christ, as they share with one another the diverse gifts of the one Spirit. Basil tells us that "all the members complete the Body of Christ in the unity of the Spirit, each member assisting the others with aid provided by the unique gifts it has received."[23]

Basil's lived theology is a theology of communion. He lived it sometimes successfully and sometimes unsuccessfully in his intimate friendships, in his wide circle of acquaintances, in his commitment to the poor and needy through word and action, and in his pastoral ministry. He lived communion in his efforts to build up the church, in his pastoral inclusivity, and in his tolerance of a level of diversity within the one faith.

GOD AS COMMUNION

Basil's great work *On the Holy Spirit* was completed in 375, the only large-scale work written while he was a bishop. Much earlier, probably around 364, Basil had already defended the divinity of the Spirit in the third book of his *Against Eunomius*. However, as controversy about the Spirit raged around him in the 370s, Basil at first had remained silent. He tells us that he had been reluctant to enter again into the public dispute over the divinity of the Spirit. But finally he responded to the entreaty of his trusted friend and disciple Amphilochius of Iconium with his *On the Holy Spirit*. The whole book is a sustained argument for the full and equal divinity of the Holy Spirit, but nowhere do we find Basil calling the Spirit God, or stating that the Spirit is of the same substance (*homoousios*) as the Father.

Why this reluctance and caution? Gregory of Nazianzus, who was far more forthright than Basil, tells us that it was because of Basil's "economy" (*oikonomia*), or pastoral prudence. He points to the fact that Basil lived with the threat of banishment from his pastoral work at Casearea.[24] The emperor Valens was always a danger to Basil, but Jean Gribomont insists that Basil's economy went far deeper than this.[25] He argues that Basil consistently refused to take a hard line because of his concern for communion with the weak and scattered sheep of the church. He had no wish to alienate those who found it difficult to cope with new forms of language about the Spirit. So we find that Basil's strategy was to make only two requirements for communion. First, there was the positive requirement of accepting the faith of Nicaea, and, second, the negative requirement of *not* saying that the Spirit is a creature.[26] If someone honored Nicaea and agreed not to call the Spirit a creature, then he or she could be accepted in communion. Basil was concerned for the truth of faith, but he also was committed to the living communion of believers.

At a deeper level still, Basil believed that it was the Spirit who would lead the whole church forward in the doctrine of the Spirit. This living faith mattered far more than any one theological expression. What was essential was to share in the living faith of the church, in its tradition and in its liturgy. Basil was convinced of the radical incomprehensibility of God, which transcends all human formulations. Thus, as Gribomont puts it, he was not inclined to identify "the verbal formulations received at a given moment with the essence of the spiritual faith."[27] He trusted that the Spirit would lead the church forward into truth. Basil's flexibility, then, springs not only from prudence, and not only from pastoral care for the straying sheep, but also from openness to the leading of the Spirit in the life of the church. He was to be vindicated after his death, when, in the creed associated with the Council of Constantinople, faith in the full divinity of the Spirit was expressed in the same open kind of biblical language that he himself had used.[28]

Basil develops his theology of the Spirit in a very particular way. He begins by reflecting on the prayer of praise to the Blessed Trinity, the doxology. In his opening chapter, he tells of an incident that occurred on the feast of St. Eupsychus, September 7, 374. While in prayer with the gathered community, Basil had sometimes used the prayer: "Glory to the Father *with* (*meta*) the Son and *together with* (*syn*) the Holy Spirit." At other times he had prayed: "Glory to the Father *through* the Son and *in* the Holy Spirit." The first form of prayer provoked a reaction. Basil says: "Some of those present accused us of using strange and mutually contradictory terms."[29] They angrily rejected the first doxology. Later in the book, Basil tells us that what upset his opponents was his use of the word *with* in relation to the Holy Spirit: "Because of this they call us innovators, revolutionaries, phrase-coiners, and who knows how many other insults."[30]

This apparently trivial incident becomes the occasion for a powerful theological development. Basil is fully convinced that the Spirit is "divine by nature."[31] But he chooses to witness to the full equality of the Holy Spirit in terms of worship rather than in the language of philosophy. He insists on the equality of honor (*isotimia*) of the Three. The Three are equally to be praised and worshiped. He constantly refers to the liturgical experience of baptism, where all are baptized and saved in the name of the Father *and* the Son *and* the Holy Spirit. Salvation is given to us in the name of the Three and the Three are to be worshiped equally.

Basil argued so strongly for using the word "with" of the Spirit because it implies equality of worship. He would have been delighted with the words from the Nicene-Constantinopolitan Creed that can be literally translated from the Greek as: "I believe in the Holy Spirit . . . *who with the Father and the Son is co-worshiped and co-glorified.*" He was convinced that this kind of language expresses the ancient tradition of the church. He goes into detail to show how he had received this form of the doxology from ancient and respected sources.[32] Of course he was also perfectly happy with the traditional language that prayed "*through* the Son and *in* the Spirit." But he knew that his opponents could make use of this language while still maintaining that the Spirit was subordinate and less than fully divine. He knew, too, that prayer to the Spirit *with* the other divine persons unambiguously placed the Three together in unity and equality of worship.

In his discussion of this issue, Basil not only insists on the equality of the Spirit, but gives expression to his own distinctive theology of the Trinity. This is, above all, a theology of communion. God is always, for Basil, Persons-in-Communion. As Orthodox theologian Boris Bobrinskoy states: "The key term in *On the Holy Spirit* is *koinōnia* (communion)."[33] It is the key to two interrelated dimensions of Basil's thought. First, it describes the unity of the Three with each other. Second, it describes the Spirit's work in the sanctification of creatures.[34]

Taking up the first of these points, then, it is clear that Basil understands the unity of the Three as a unity in communion. He tells us that the unity of the divine nature is found in the "communion (*koinōnia*) of the Godhead."[35] He speaks of the Spirit as being united with God through "communion in the divine nature."[36] Basil consistently sees the divine persons as *with* each other in profound communion. The Father exists *with* the Word and *with* the Spirit in radical equality and unity. While Basil is happy with the use of the word *and* to link the persons, he believes that the word *with* adds another dimension:

> But *with* is an especially useful word because it testifies to eternal communion (*koinōnia*) and unceasing cooperation. If we say that the Son is *with* the Father, we mean two things: first that their persons are distinct, and second that they are inseparably united in fellowship (*koinōnia*).[37]

Basil's unity in communion is a unity entirely without subordination. As John Zizioulas says, Basil's use of *with* makes the inner-trinitarian relations look entirely different: "The three persons of the Trinity appear to be equal in honor and placed one next to the other without hierarchical distinction, almost as if the monarchy of the Father itself were an irrelevant matter."[38] Of course, Basil never forgets the monarchy, but he makes it abundantly clear that there is no hierarchy of power or honor in the Trinity. Nor is there any kind of priority in time. All are equally beyond time, equally eternal.

The Three share life with each other in complete mutuality. The Trinity is eternally Persons-in-Communion. The persons are distinct from each other but mutually abide in each other. This mutual abiding, central to the Cappadocian view of God, will later be called *perichōrēsis*—a word that brings to mind the mutual indwelling of the supper discourse in the Gospel of John. It points to a communion of radical unity. In this perichoretic communion, the distinctiveness of persons is not lost but immeasurably enhanced. Otherness is not obscured or denied but celebrated in love.

Basil, along with the two Gregorys, had long stressed the distinct and integral existence of each of the persons of the Trinity. While Nicaea, and Athanasius, had successfully brought out the unity in God, it was left to the Cappadocians to clarify the distinction of persons. Basil knew that simply teaching the divine unity was not enough. In both the East and the West there were those who were opposed to Arius, who were strong advocates of the divine unity, and therefore could certainly say yes to Nicaea, but who were not clear about the distinctions of persons.[39] Basil was particularly concerned with those like Marcellus of Ancyra, who seemed to oppose the diversity of persons. They were called Sabellians—after the third century Sabellius, who was thought of as holding that there is one God who simply appears to us in different modes. Basil belonged to a group of Eastern Christians who saw the need to defend not only the unity of God but also the distinction and diversity of the Three against forms of Sabellian modalism.

Until Basil's time, there had been no word in Greek that could bring out the full significance of the distinct individual person. The only word available was *prosōpon*, a word that originally referred to the mask an actor wore and came to refer to the role an individual played. There was no simple way of pointing to the ontological importance and dignity of the individual human, let alone of the divine Three. Basil, followed by the others, began to use the word *hypostasis* (meaning a *substantial* reality, much like *ousia*) of the Three. This meant that, while there were still some who spoke of one *hypostasis* in the Trinity, referring to the one divine nature, Basil and others were speaking of three *hypostases*, referring to the three persons. Athanasius wisely allowed both usages, as long as each was understood in conformity with the teaching of Nicaea.[40] Eventually Basil's usage would win the support of the wider church.

By using this word of persons, Basil gave ontological weight to the dignity and integrity of the person. Orthodox scholars have pointed out that this move was important not only for trinitarian theology but also for the development of the concept of the human person. It allowed the mystery of "the other" to be affirmed.[41] For the first time in Greek thought, an ontological category (*hypostasis*) is applied to divine and human persons. This was a step in the understanding of the dignity of the human person that evolved eventually toward the contemporary notion of human rights. In terms of a theology of God, it was one of the ways by which Basil and the other Cappadocians brought out the reality, integrity and significance of each person of the Trinity, while also maintaining their radical equality and unity in the communion of the one divine being (*ousia*).

For Basil, then, God is to be understood as radically relational. God exists only as Persons-in-Relationship. God's being is communion. Zizioulas writes:

> It would be unthinkable to speak of the "one God" before speaking of the God who is "communion," that is to say of the Holy Trinity. The Holy Trinity is a primordial ontological concept and not a notion which is added to the divine substance or rather which follows it, as is the case in the dogmatic manuals of the West, and alas, in those of the East in modern times. The substance of God, "God," has no ontological content, no true being, apart from communion.[42]

Being is understood as communion. The being of God is understood as a relational being. Zizioulas goes on to state that it is "communion which makes things be. Nothing exists without it, not even God." It is the divine Communion of the Three that brings forth a universe that is radically other than God, yet exists only in communion with the divine Three. It is the Spirit who mediates this communion to all creatures and thus enables them to be and to become what is new.

Zizioulas has been criticized for overstating the place of communion in Basil's view of the Trinity.[43] Certainly Basil does not think of the Trinity exclusively in terms of communion. Perhaps the point to be made is that for Basil the Trinity is understood as *both* a communion and as one divine

being or substance (*ousia*). But there is no doubt that Basil has a rich theology of trinitarian communion, and it is this theology that I will take up
in the rest of this book. If divine being is communion, then created being
too exists only in and from communion. This suggests that being-in-relationship is of the essence of things. This has consequences for the understanding of the human person. It also has consequences for understanding
every dimension of the universe.

It will be the argument of this book that it is *Communion that makes
things be and become in an evolutionary universe.* An emergent and interrelational universe springs from within the divine Communion. This same
divine Communion is creation's eschatological destiny.

THE BREATH OF GOD
AS THE COMMUNION-BRINGER

Basil has a favorite image for the Spirit. He sees the Spirit as the *Breath
of God who always accompanies the Word.*[44] It is the Breath of God that
gives life—both in the sense of biological life and in the sense of resurrection life. Basil refers constantly to Psalm 33:6: "By the word of the Lord
the heavens were made, and all their host by the breath of his mouth."
Much of the West would draw upon an analogy taken from psychological
experience, describing the Trinity in terms of the two interior activities of
knowing (the Word) and loving (the Spirit). Basil, along with Eastern theology, would stay with the biblical images of the Breath that comes from
God's mouth and the Word that God speaks. Breath is an obvious sign of
life, and the divine act of bringing life to creatures is naturally imaged as
breathing life into them (Gen. 2:7).

In Basil's thought, it is the Breath of God who mediates the divine Communion to a world of creatures. The Holy Spirit *is* communion, in the sense
that it is only in the Spirit that we are brought into communion with the
Blessed Trinity. For Basil, the Spirit is above all the gift of divine Communion given to angelic and human creatures by which they are sanctified.
They are made spiritual "through communion (*koinōnia*)" with the Spirit.[45]

As I have already indicated, Basil thought a great deal about the language used for the Holy Spirit. He was convinced that we should not be
restricted to any one set of terms. Basil's adversaries, such as Eunomius and
his teacher, Aetius, had claimed that the language about the Trinity was
fixed. They asserted that the prepositions *from* the Father, *through* the Son
and *in* the Spirit could not be changed. They held that the three prepositions say all that can be known about the Trinity. They taught that this
fixed order showed that the Spirit has a different and *inferior* nature to the
Father.[46]

Basil rejects all this completely. He has three lines of argument in
response. First, he opposes a rationalism that reduces the incomprehensible

God to any kind of human system. The Spirit cannot be contained by our concepts or images but remains utterly mysterious to us and transcends all our language. Second, Basil undertakes a learned and thorough study of the Scriptures and shows that *from, through,* and *in* are not restricted in biblical usage to any one of the divine Persons, but are used of the Three in various ways. Third, Basil appeals to the liturgical tradition and locates his own doxology (*with* the Spirit) in the ancient tradition of the church. Above all, of course, he situates it in close relationship to the baptism formula "in the name of the Father *and* of the Son *and* of the Holy Spirit" (Matt. 28:19).

Basil demonstrates that there are many legitimate ways of speaking about the Spirit. The trinitarian God cannot be encapsulated by or limited to any one expression. We cannot even be limited to any one order between the Three. He points out that when reflecting on the work of the Trinity from the point of view of our experience, it is natural and appropriate to start from the Spirit. But if we consider this same work from the perspective of its ultimate origin, it is natural to start from the Source of All:

> The way to divine knowledge ascends from the one Spirit through the one Son to the one Father. Likewise, natural goodness, inherent holiness and royal dignity reach from the Father through the Only-Begotten to the Spirit.[47]

We begin from the Spirit because our whole life in God comes to us through communion in the Spirit. Basil insists that it is only in the Spirit that we can come to Christ. He does not tend to think of the Spirit as simply following the Word. In his theology there is a mutual and reciprocal relation between Word and Spirit. We should not think of the Spirit as coming only after the death and resurrection of Jesus. The Spirit is active in every stage of the history of salvation. The Breath of God and the Word of God go together. They can never be separated. Basil describes the presence and action of the Spirit in the ministry of Jesus:

> Christ comes, and the Spirit prepares his way. He comes in the flesh, but the Spirit is never separated from him. Working of miracles and gifts of healing come from the Holy Spirit. Demons are driven out by the Spirit of God. The presence of the Spirit despoils the devil. Remission of sins is given through the gift of the Spirit.[48]

This view was shared by the other Cappadocians. Gregory of Nazianzus says something very similar:

> Christ is born; the Spirit is his forerunner. He is baptized; the Spirit bears witness. He is tempted; the Spirit leads him up. He works miracles; the Spirit accompanies him. He ascends; the Spirit takes his place.[49]

Basil describes the sweep of the Spirit's action as encompassing not only creation but also the whole drama of God's saving action. The Spirit is present and active in the blessings on the patriarchs, in the law given to Israel, in prophecies and miracles, in the event of the incarnation, in the anointing of Jesus by the Spirit, in the deeds of Jesus, in the appearances of the risen Christ, in the church with its various ministries, in the conversion of sinners and the renewal of lives, in the new creation, and in the final judgment.[50]

In all of this, Basil thinks of the Spirit as the Sanctifier, as Life-Giver and as Completer. The Spirit is the refreshing Breath, who, "lacking nothing, *brings all things to perfection.*" He tells us that the Spirit who is "never depleted, *gives life to all things.*"[51] He sees the Spirit as the indwelling Sanctifier, bringing creatures into communion with the Trinity. He says that human lives can be transformed in God only if the Spirit creates an event of communion with human beings. Then, in the Spirit, "hearts are lifted up, the infirm are held by the hand, and those who progress are brought to perfection." Basil describes the illumination and transformation that this communion of the Spirit brings:

> When a sunbeam falls on a transparent substance, the substance itself becomes brilliant, and radiates life from itself. So too, Spirit-bearing souls, illumined by him, finally become spiritual themselves, and their grace is sent forth to others. From this comes knowledge of the future, understanding of mysteries, apprehension of hidden things, distribution of wonderful gifts, heavenly citizenship, a place in the choir of angels, endless joy in the presence of God, becoming like God, and, the highest of all desires, becoming God.[52]

Because Basil sees the Spirit as the one who brings creatures into communion with God, he embraces the expression "*in* the Spirit." While denying that it is the only way of speaking about the Spirit, he holds that the use of the preposition *in* is a helpful way of speaking about the Spirit's presence to creatures. When properly understood, it does not diminish the Spirit, but says a great deal about the Spirit's creative and life-giving work *in* creatures.

He develops the idea that we dwell in the Spirit as in a place (*chōra*). He writes: "Although paradoxical, it is nevertheless true that Scripture frequently speaks of the Spirit in terms of *place*—a place *in* which people are made holy."[53] Among his examples he points to the Psalms, where God is spoken of as "a place of strength" (Ps. 71:3). He mentions Exodus, where God says to Moses: "See there is a place by me where you shall stand upon the rock" (Exod. 33:21). Basil comments that this place is "contemplation in the Spirit." When Moses entered this place, God was revealed to him. Basil asks: "What is the place of the sacrifice of praise?" He answers: "Only in the Holy Spirit." He reminds us that Jesus has said that true sacrifice is offered in spirit and in truth (John 4:23). He recalls that Jacob saw this place and said "The Lord is in this place" (Gen. 28:16). All of this leads Basil to conclude that the Spirit is the *dwelling place* of the saints.

Basil sees it as entirely possible and appropriate to speak not only of creatures like us as dwelling in the Spirit but also of the Spirit dwelling in creatures. Both are proper ways of speaking about the Holy Spirit. Basil tells us that the Spirit is present everywhere in the universe, and dwells in creatures in many diverse ways.[54] In a particular way the Spirit dwells in human beings, enabling them to cry out "Abba! Father!" But Basil never sees the indwelling Spirit in individualistic terms. Again his theology presses toward the social. God gives the gift of the one Spirit to the one Body of Christ, that all the members may have the same care for one another since they are united in "the communion (*koinōnia*) of mutual sympathy."[55] Basil often uses the word *sympathy,* with the meaning of "feeling with others." Implicit here is the idea that it is the Spirit who makes us genuinely empathetic to others. This kind of feeling *with* others is at the heart of his idea of communion.

Basil understands the life of being in the Spirit is a process of illumination. The Spirit is the light by which we see Christ, the Image of God. The Spirit of God is the place where this Image is communicated:

> The Holy Spirit cannot be divided from the Father and the Son in worship. If you remain outside the Spirit, you cannot worship at all, and if you are *in* him you cannot separate him from God. Light cannot be separated from what it makes visible, and it is impossible for you to recognize Christ, the Image of the invisible God, unless the Spirit enlightens you. Once you see the Image, you cannot ignore the Light; you see the Light and the Image simultaneously. It is fitting that when we see Christ, the Brightness of God's glory, it is always through the illumination of the Spirit.[56]

Several times Basil makes the point that if we consider the work of the Spirit in the economy of creation and redemption, then we say that the Spirit dwells *in* creatures bringing them into communion with God. But if we consider the Spirit in the communion of the Trinity then we use the word *with* to bring out the radical equality and mutuality of the trinitarian relations.[57] At one point Basil puts it succinctly: "The preposition *in* expresses the relationship between ourselves and the Spirit, while *with* proclaims the communion (*koinōnia*) of the Spirit with God."[58]

All of this suggests that the Spirit is the presence of God to creation, the immanence of God. The immanent Breath of God is always in communion with the Word and the Source of All. But it is the Spirit's role to dwell in creatures, creating the bond of communion between the creature and the life of God. The Spirit is the Communion-Bringer and, as such, is the Life-Giver and Sanctifier.

CONCLUSION

For Basil, then, the Spirit of God is experienced in a God-centered life lived in communion with others. He sees the Spirit as the Breath of God, who exists eternally *with* the Word of God and *with* the Source of All, in the unity of the one divine nature that is a *unity in communion*. This is a dynamic union of mutual love, of mutual giving and receiving, of being with one another in ecstatic shared life. In such love, the distinctiveness and otherness of persons are not lost but flourish in all their exuberance and vitality. This is the kind of divine love that embraces the universe. It is this kind of Communion that makes things be. Creation springs forth freely from the exuberance of trinitarian life.

Communion is not only the mode of the Spirit's mutual relationship with the other persons of the Trinity. It is also the mode of the Spirit's communication with creatures. In the economy of creation and salvation, the Spirit is the *ek-stasis* of God toward creatures. The Breath of God dwells *in* each creature, enabling each to share in the existence and life that comes from the divine Communion. The Spirit is the one who brings all things to their completion in God. The Spirit *is* communion. This suggests a theology of the Creator Spirit that will be explored in the next chapter: the Holy Spirit is the creative presence of God to each creature, enabling each to be and to become in an interrelated universe of creatures.

While the Spirit of God is fully personal, this is not understood in an anthropomorphic sense. The Spirit is not personal in a humanlike way, but in a way that transcends the human, like the wind that blows where it wills. The Breath of God escapes the limits of the human and embraces the universe and infinitely more. The Spirit is the presence of God at the heart of the universe, a mysterious presence that fills the whole universe yet is intimately interior to each creature.

Basil's theology of the Spirit as life-giving Communion-Bringer has practical effects. It points beyond individualism to a social view of reality that is authentically communitarian, in which the poor have priority and diversity is valued. And, as I will attempt to make clear, it can be further developed toward an ecological view of creation as a diffentiated community of interrelated creatures. If it is Communion that makes things be, then interrelatedness is not an accidental or trivial characteristic of things. It is of the essence of things.

In the light of the scientific story of the universe sketched in chapter 1, and Basil's theology of the Holy Spirit as the communion-bringing Breath of God developed in this chapter, I will begin in the next section to tell the story of the Spirit. I will propose that this one story can be thought of as including four episodes, the Spirit's life-giving and renewing work in *creation, grace, incarnation,* and *church*.

PART 2

The Story of the Spirit

THREE

Breathing Life
into a Universe of Creatures

The story of the Spirit begins a long time before Pentecost. If the fourteen-billion-year story of the universe were condensed into one year, the event that Christians call Pentecost would come only in the last seconds of the final minute of the year. The history of the Spirit embraces the whole year. It is coextensive with the *total* life of the universe. God's Spirit has been breathing life into the processes of the evolving universe from the very first. The laws of nature and the initial conditions of the early universe exist only because of the empowering presence and action of the Creator Spirit.

The story of the Spirit involves all the mysterious processes of the first second, the formation of the nuclei of the primordial hydrogen and helium, the first atoms, the birth of galaxies and stars, the synthesis of elements in the stars, the development of our solar system around the young Sun, the origin of life with the marvelous DNA molecule, the evolution of multicellular creatures, the flowering of life and the emergence of humans with their highly developed brains.

At the end of his *Brief History of Time*, Stephen Hawking asks a famous question: "What is it that *breathes fire* into the equations and makes a universe for them to describe?"[1] In this chapter, I will begin to develop a theology of the Spirit as the Breath of God. I will propose that it is this Breath of God who breathes fire into the equations and continues to breathe life into the exuberant, diverse, interrelated community of living things.

The size and scale of the universe that we know today dwarf the world-views available to Moses, the Hebrew prophets, and Jesus himself. Yet I am convinced that the revelatory word they speak, a word of promise, a word of grace, a word about a world always open to God's future, a word about the creative Breath of God breathing life into the process of the world's unfolding, can offer enlightenment and hope to those with a twenty-first-century worldview. Both the prophetic promises and Jesus' preaching and praxis of the reign of God direct our gaze toward a God who comes to us

33

as our future. This future is anticipated in the experiences we already have of genuine community—with human beings, with other creatures, and with God. It is the Holy Breath of God that we encounter in all our experiences of authentic communion. It is the Breath of God who leads creation into an open future, who makes all things new.

In the kind of approach taken here, the Spirit is understood as creatively empowering a world in process, a world that has its own integrity and proper autonomy. It is a world of contingencies and chances, a world that evolves in its own way. It is a world that comes to what is new through exploring the possibilities offered in unpredictable events and random mutations. As Arthur Peacocke points out, the randomness and lawfulness that are built into creation are what one would expect if the evolving universe is to be able to explore options and to experiment with the fullest range of possibilities.[2] The Spirit is to be thought of as working with creation not according to a predetermined path or "design" but in dynamic open ways. These include Charles Darwin's evolution through natural selection and Ilya Prigogine's concept of new forms of order emerging at the edge of chaos in open "dissipative" systems. The zone of the Spirit embraces the chanciness of random mutations and the chaotic conditions of open systems.

The biblical Spirit is not constrained by human comfort zones. The Spirit of God blows where she wills (John 3:8). This wild and unpredictable Spirit can be envisaged in the image of the blazing flame of fire that confronts Moses in the burning bush (Exod. 3:2) and in the whirlwind that is the place of God for Job (38:1), but it can also be experienced in "the sound of sheer silence" that is the sign of the divine presence for Elijah (1 Kgs. 19:12). David Toolan beautifully describes the creative Spirit as:

> the wind-breath-sound that the Creator breathes forth into primordial big bang chaos, the "gentle breeze" that walks with Adam and Eve in the garden, Elijah's "small still voice," the Shekinah/Glory of the rabbis, the Advocate-Spirit that "blows where it wills" through the Gospel of John, and of course, Gerard Manley Hopkins's Holy Ghost that "over the bent / World broods with warm breast and with ah! bright wings."[3]

This whirlwind wild Spirit *is* the boundless love at work in the processes of the universe. How can this wind that blows where it wills be thought of more explicitly in terms of the Christian tradition? I will propose that the Spirit, always in the communion of the Trinity, is the immanent divine principle that enables an emergent universe to be and to evolve. In this chapter, I hope to begin the construction of a theology of the Creator Spirit that will offer a way of thinking about the unfolding of the universe that is both fully congruent with the Christian tradition and plausible and productive in the light of contemporary science. This will involve sketching the biblical notion of the Spirit as the Breath of Life and the development of the concept of the Creator Spirit in the patristic era, before offering some suggestions for a contemporary theology of the Spirit as the immanent source of the new in an emergent universe.

BIBLICAL TRADITION OF THE BREATH OF LIFE

The Bible puts before us the image of the Spirit as the Breath of God that breathes life into the dust of the Earth so that it becomes a living being (Gen. 2:7). All the wonderfully diverse things of the planet, all the things that creep, crawl, run, hop, swim and fly are brought to life by this Breath of God. Everything comes from the animating Breath. Before outlining this tradition, two preliminary comments are appropriate. First, the Spirit of God in the ancient Hebrew Scriptures is a way of talking about the presence and action of the one God of Jewish monotheism. This Spirit was not understood in personal or trinitarian terms. The second comment is that the concept of the Spirit of God has a complex history in the ancient biblical texts. In some of its early usages it refers simply to the morally neutral power to do mighty deeds. In the developing tradition, the Spirit becomes a way of talking about the powerful presence of the God of Israel. In this sense the Spirit is understood as the "vivifying, energizing power of God."[4] The Spirit is associated with early ecstatic prophecy, with kingship, and with messianic expectation. The word *Spirit* expresses God's creative, prophetic, or renewing presence to the people of Israel or to the world at large.[5] The texts that I take up here are one part of this wider tradition. They form one stream within it—that of the Spirit as the creative Breath of Life.

The Hebrew word *ruach* can mean "wind," "breath," or "spirit." In the book of Genesis, it is used a number of times of the Breath of God that enables things to live. Creatures exist because God gives them the *ruach*. First we find God forming an earthling from the dust of the ground and then breathing "the breath of life" (Gen. 2:7) into this first human's nostrils. Through the breath of life, the earthling "became a living being." We are told that human beings remain alive only so long as they have the divine breath abiding in them (Gen. 6:3). God threatens that the flood will "destroy from under heaven all flesh in which is the breath of life" (Gen. 6:17; 7:22). Those that are to be saved go into the ark with Noah "two of all flesh in which there is the breath of life" (Gen. 7:15).

In Job, Elihu says: "The spirit of God has made me, and the breath of the Almighty gives me life" (Job 33:4). A little later he declares of all living things: "If he should take back his spirit to himself, and gather to himself his breath, all flesh would perish together, and all mortals return to dust" (Job 34:14-15). In Isaiah, God is described as the one who "spreads out the earth and what comes from it, who gives breath to the people upon it and spirit to those who walk in it" (42:5). In Ecclesiastes, death is described in words that echo Genesis 2:7: "the dust returns to the earth as it was, and the breath returns to God who gave it" (12:7).

In the Psalms, the interconnected images of God's Breath and God's Word are linked together explicitly in the creation of the universe: "By the word of the Lord the heavens were made, and all their host by the breath of his mouth" (Ps. 33:6). Word and Breath acting together create not just living creatures but the whole cosmos. As I have pointed out, this text would be taken up in patristic theology and used thematically to insist that God's Word and the Breath of God's mouth always go together. Psalm 104, the great celebration of God's creation, sings of the heavens, the earth, the living creatures of the land and sky, and the sea with all its life forms small and great:

> These all look to you to give them their food in due season;
> when you give it to them, they gather it up;
> when you open your hand, they are filled with good things.
> When you hide your face, they are dismayed;
> when you take away their breath, they die and return to their dust.
> When you send forth your spirit, they are created;
> and you renew the face of the ground. (Ps. 104:27-30)

The Breath of God is understood here as the creative and life-giving presence of God. It is unlimited in scope and can be found wherever human beings journey. Psalm 139 points to the universal reach of this sustaining and providential presence of God:

> Where can I go from your spirit?
> Or where can I flee from your presence?
> If I ascend to heaven you are there;
> if I make my bed in Sheol you are there.
> If I take the wings of the morning
> and settle at the farthest limits of the sea,
> even there your hand shall lead me,
> and your right hand shall hold me fast. (Ps. 139:7-10)

With the prophet Ezekiel, we enter another imaginative world. He offers a spectacular image for the life-renewing Breath. The Spirit takes Ezekiel to the valley of dry bones. In this place of death, God commands Ezekiel to prophesy to the bones: "Thus says the Lord God to these bones: I will cause breath to enter you and you shall live." Ezekiel speaks the word of prophecy as he has been instructed. With a great rattling noise, the bones come together, but still there is no breath in them. God again instructs Ezekiel: "Prophesy to the breath, prophesy, mortal, and say to the breath: Thus says the Lord God: Come from the four winds, O breath, and breathe on these slain that they live." Ezekiel does what he is told and as a result "the breath came into them, and they lived, and stood on their feet, a vast multitude" (Ezek. 37:3-10).

The Wisdom of Solomon, written in Greek, presents the Breath of God (*pneuma*) as closely related to divine Wisdom (*sophia*). This text, which is apocryphal for some Christians but considered part of the canon by Greek Orthodox and Roman Catholics, proclaims the universal creative role of the Breath of God: "the spirit of the Lord has filled the world and that which holds all things together knows what is said" (Wis. 1:7). Later we read:

> For you love all things that exist,
> and detest none of the things you have made,
> for you would not have made anything if you had hated it.
> How would anything have endured if you had not willed it?
> Or how would anything not called forth by you have been
>   preserved?
> You spare all things, for they are yours, O Lord, you who love
>   the living.
> For your immortal spirit is in all things. (Wis. 11:24-12:1)

In these texts we find a basis for a developed theology of creation. The world of creatures is understood as contingent. Things exist only because God's Breath dwells in all things and holds them in being. Moreover, God's Spirit dwells in them because God loves them. In the book of Judith (also an apocryphal/deuterocanonical book), the ancient tradition of the creative Word and Breath of God is beautifully encapsulated in the prayer: "Let all creatures serve you, because you spoke, and they were made. You sent forth your spirit and it formed them" (Jdt. 16:14).

The New Testament communities understood this Spirit that breathed life into creatures in Genesis and was promised by the prophets to be the same Spirit who overshadowed Mary at the conception of Jesus (Matt. 1:18; Luke 1:35), who anointed Jesus at his baptism (Mark 1:10), and who was poured out on the Christian community at Pentecost (Acts 2:4). Even as they interpreted the Spirit in specifically Christian terms as the Spirit of the risen Christ, the early Christian community saw continuity between the Spirit they experienced in Christ and the Breath of God active in creation and in the history of Israel. Paul sees this same Breath of Life as now dwelling in Christians, adopting them into the divine life and enabling them to pray "Abba! Father!" (Rom. 8:15). The author of John's Gospel sees this same Spirit as given to Christians as their personal Advocate who will remain with them forever (John 14:16).

In the light of their postresurrection experiences, the early Christians identified the Spirit as the Life-Giver (*Zōopoion*) in the sense of the one who brings us a participation in resurrection life. This word "Life-Giver" would become a central affirmation of the Nicene-Constantinopolitan Creed. The word is found in John 6:63, but the idea of the Spirit as life-giving is found in various ways in both John and Paul. In the Gospel of John, Jesus, in dialogue with Nicodemus, explains the need to be born again of the Spirit. Only those who have been given a new birth and have come to a new life of water and the Holy Spirit can enter the reign of God (John 3:5). In his dialogue with the Samaritan woman, Jesus offers her living water that will become a spring gushing up to eternal life (4:14). At the feast of Tabernacles, Jesus invites all those who thirst to come to him to drink and promises that from them will flow rivers of living water. The Gospel says explicitly that this living water refers to the Spirit (7:39). We are told that as yet there was no Spirit, because Jesus was not yet glorified. With Jesus' death and resurrection the life-giving Spirit is freely poured out on all believers (19:34; 20:22).

Paul also sees the Spirit as the Life-Giver: "If the Spirit of him who raised Jesus from the dead dwells in you, he who raised Christ from the dead *will give life* to your mortal bodies also through his Spirit that dwells in you" (Rom. 8:11). He associates the risen Christ closely with the Spirit and speaks of Christ as the new Adam who "became a life-giving spirit" (1 Cor. 15:45). He sees the Spirit we have received as a spirit of adoption (Rom. 8:15, 23) into the life of God. All of creation waits and groans in labor pains along with those who have received the firstfruits of the Spirit (Rom. 8:23). The experience we already have of the Spirit is the down payment or guarantee of the life to come (2 Cor. 5:5). In the new life we have in Christ, we have already found freedom from the law and from sin. Paul contrasts the letter of the law with "the Spirit that gives life" (2 Cor. 3:6). He tells his readers: "The law of the Spirit of life in Christ Jesus has set you free from the law of sin and death" (Rom. 8:2). For Paul, the promise made in Joel 2:28 has been fulfilled—"I will pour out my spirit on all flesh." God's love has been poured into our hearts through the Holy Spirit that has been given to us (Rom. 5:5).

For the Christian, the theology of the Spirit is deepened and transformed in the Christ event. God is encountered in Jesus and in the outpouring of the Spirit in such a powerful way that the Christian community is convinced that God communicates God's very self to us both in the Word and in the Spirit. This is the experiential basis for the later development of a fully trinitarian doctrine of God. While this obviously represents an important development of their understanding of God, the Christian community maintains that it is a development in understanding of the same God who is the God of Israel. And, as the Nicene-Constantinopolitan Creed makes explicit, they believe that the Holy Spirit of trinitarian faith is the same Spirit "who has spoken through the prophets" of Israel.

Because of this conviction, the early theologians of the Holy Spirit could see the Spirit as the Breath of God who accompanies the Word of God in both creation and in the work of salvation. In both senses the Spirit is the Giver of Life.

PATRISTIC THEOLOGY OF THE CREATOR SPIRIT

The theology of the Spirit got off to a slow start. In the second and third centuries there was little attempt to develop an explicit theology of the Spirit and even less emphasis on the Spirit's work in creation. Theologians focused their attention on the Word of God as the *Logos*. The language of *logos* was the common currency of both Neoplatonists and Stoics, and early Christian theologians naturally developed their theology around the theme of Christ as the Logos of God. It was understood that God creates through the Logos (John 1:3). The issue that would come into dispute in the Arian debates at the beginning of the fourth century was the eternity and full divinity of the Logos.

There was no parallel development in the theology of the Spirit in the second and third centuries. Yves Congar comments that Justin Martyr, for example, "made no distinction between the Logos and the Spirit, yet he gave his life for the Christian faith."[6] There was a lack of clarity about the distinctiveness of the person and work of the Holy Spirit. Often there was overlap in the language of the Word and the Spirit, and in some cases what was said of Christ could be said of the Spirit. Louis Bouyer notes that the ambiguity of the word *spirit* is part of the problem. The word could be used in a number of senses, not all of them identical with the Holy Spirit.[7] Once the Council of Nicaea (325) had clarified the divinity of the Word, the theology of the Holy Spirit moved toward center stage. Only then would the Spirit's work in creation be addressed more explicitly. As Boris Bobrinskoy notes, "before Nicaea, in Rome and in Alexandria, there is an almost total lack of any mention of the work of the Holy Spirit in creation."[8]

Irenaeus (ca. 115-190) stands out in this context as a theologian who kept the Word and the Spirit together in a theology of creation and salvation. Like many who came after him in the Greek tradition, Irenaeus was inspired by Psalm 33:6: "By the word of the Lord the heavens were made, and all their host by the breath of his mouth."[9] For Irenaeus, God creates through the Word and the Spirit:

> For God needs none of these things, but is he who, by his Word and Spirit, makes and disposes, and governs all things, and commands all things into existence.[10]

> He is the creator, who made all things by himself, that is through his Word and his Wisdom—heaven and earth and the seas and all things that are in them.[11]

While most of the Christian tradition identified Wisdom with the Word of God, Irenaeus equates Wisdom with the Holy Spirit. He liked to speak of God creating *with two hands*, that of the Word and that of the Spirit. He says, for example, that humanity, "having been molded at the beginning *by the hands of God*, that is, of the Son and the Spirit, is made after the image and likeness of God."[12] While Irenaeus holds Word and Spirit together in creation and redemption, he can also differentiate the work of the Three in creation, telling us that the Father "plans and gives commands," the Son "performs and creates," and the Spirit "nourishes and increases."[13]

Irenaeus sets the stage for a balanced and reciprocal theology of Word and Spirit in creation. Unfortunately, the great Alexandrian theologian Origen (ca. 185-254) is less helpful. He spells out the work of the Spirit in human sanctification. But he explicitly excludes the Holy Spirit from the creation of nonhuman entities. He tells us that the Spirit is reserved for those human beings who are on the path of conversion and renewal. The Father and the Word of God are involved with ongoing creation, enabling the existence of all human and nonhuman creatures, but not the Spirit. The work of the Holy Spirit is reserved for faithful believers:

> The operation of the Holy Spirit does not take place at all in those things that are without life, or in those things, which although living are yet dumb; nay, is not found even in those who are endowed indeed with reason, but are engaged in an evil course, and not converted to a better life.[14]

Origen seems to hold that the Spirit is powerfully at work in grace, but not at all involved in the creation of a physical universe. He thus brings to the fore an issue that is crucial for this book: Is the Spirit actively involved in the process of the becoming of our universe over the last fifteen billion years or is the Spirit involved only with human beings? I am convinced that we need to go beyond the mistaken view of Origen to articulate a theology of the Spirit that involves the creation of all creatures, including nonhuman animals and inanimate creatures. This means understanding the Spirit as actively involved not only with sanctification but also with the creation of the physical universe.

Athanasius (ca. 296-377) is an important witness to a strong theology of the Spirit. About 360, while hiding in the desert after being exiled from Alexandria, he wrote on the Spirit in the *Letter to Serapion* mentioned in the last chapter. This was a defense of the doctrine of the Spirit against the Tropici—an Egyptian group who held that the Spirit was a creature. Athanasius vigorously affirms the divinity of the Spirit. The Spirit is one in substance (*homoousious*) with God.[15] He links the Spirit closely to the Word. The Spirit is "not outside the Word, but in the Word," and, being in the Word, the Spirit is in God.[16] Because of his conviction of the unity between the Word and the Spirit, Athanasius is able to extend the existing doctrine of the creative Word in the direction of a more clearly articulated theology of the Creator Spirit. The Spirit creates, participating in the one divine act of creation:

> It is clear that the Spirit is not a creature, but takes part in the act of creation. The Father creates all things through the Word in the Spirit; for where the Word is, there is the Spirit also, and the things which are created through the Word have their vital strength out of the Spirit from the Word. Thus it is written in the thirty-second Psalm: "By the Word of the Lord the heavens were established, and by the Spirit of his mouth is all their power."[17]

> There is, then, a Triad, holy and complete, confessed to be God in Father, Son and Holy Spirit, having nothing foreign or external mixed with it, not composed of one that creates and one that is originated, but all creative; and it is consistent and in nature indivisible, and its activity one. The Father does all things through the Word and in the Spirit. Thus the unity of the Holy Triad is preserved.[18]

Athanasius insists that God's action toward creation is *one*. The Three act in one undivided act. But this does not exclude that idea that there is something distinctive about the roles of the Three in this one act. For Athanasius, creation is from the Source of All, through the Word and in the Spirit. And he tells us that God's grace is given to us from the same Source and through the same Word, and that we can have communion (*koinōnia*) in this grace only *in* the same Holy Spirit.[19]

Basil builds on Athanasius. In his *Against Eunomius* of 364, he associates the Spirit's work with life-giving, completing, and sanctifying.[20] These same themes are found throughout his work. In chapter 16 of his *On the Holy Spirit,* Basil considers creation directly. He tells us that "in every operation the Holy Spirit is indivisibly united with the Father and the Son." He says that the divine persons act in communion (*koinōnia*) in creating.[21] Basil speaks of "the original cause of all things, the Father, the creative cause, the Son, and the completing cause, the Spirit." He tells us that "the Source of all being is one, creating *through* the Son and perfecting *in* the Spirit."[22] It is clear that Basil believes that the Spirit is a co-worker with the other persons in creation. It is also clear that his usual way of understanding what is specific to the Spirit in creation is the Spirit's work of constituting angels and humans as spiritual creatures. Obviously Basil is assuming an ancient worldview in which angels and humans both appear at the beginning of the story of creation. Today we must ask the question: What was the Spirit's role with regard to the universe in the fourteen billion years before the appearance of modern humans?

Basil gives clear indications that he does think of the Spirit as involved with the creation of the nonhuman universe. In his *On the Holy Spirit* he insists that the Spirit is a transcendent creative power at work in and through everything that exists.[23] Toward the end of his life, he discusses the creative role of the Spirit in a series of sermons on the six days of creation, called the *Hexaemeron*. In his reflection on the wind of God that swept over the waters (Gen. 1:2), Basil tells us that he shares the interpretation he had learned from a Syrian theologian: the Spirit of God hovers over the water like a bird covering eggs with her body, enabling them to come to life through the warmth she imparts. The Spirit, like a mother bird, warms and "fosters" the waters, "preparing the nature of water for the generation of living beings."[24] Clearly he sees the Spirit as fostering and enabling the emergence of a universe of creatures.

In the *Hexaemeron*, Basil delights in the diversity of creation. He discusses in extraordinary detail the varieties of plants, fish, birds, and land animals and their behavior, making use of the science of his day and his own observations. He speaks of the fertile Earth as a mother, made beautiful by the great trees and colorful and fragrant flowers that adorn her.[25] He sees God as Creator, Craft-worker and supreme Artist. God cares for each creature in the vast array of living things. Basil tells us that God's providence embraces even the little sea urchin, which, in the wisdom of God, knows when a storm is coming and hides under a rock. He sees God as "present everywhere," as "watching over" all creatures, and as "giving to each being the means of its preservation."[26] Basil thinks of the immense variety of creatures as reflecting the Wisdom of God. Wisdom brings the wonderfully diverse things that make up the universe into a harmonious whole. He speaks of the "symphony" of creation.[27] The diversity of creatures is brought into "communion (*koinōnia*) and harmony" and united in a mutual "sympathy" by the divine Artisan.[28]

About the same time, Ambrose of Milan developed a clearly articulated theology of the Creator Spirit. In 378 the emperor Gratian had asked Ambrose to write a treatise on the Holy Spirit. Soon afterward, in 380, Ambrose attended a council in Rome where the main topic was the defense of the divinity of the Holy Spirit in opposition to the Macedonians. Ambrose published his own work *On the Holy Spirit* in 381, writing in Latin and making use of, among others, the Greek works of Athanasius, Basil, and Didymus the Blind.[29] He insists that the Spirit is the one who brings life to all creatures. With the Father and the Son, the Spirit is the Creator of all things.[30] Ambrose sees the grace and beauty of creation as the gift of the Spirit:

> So when the Spirit moved over the waters, there was no grace in creation, but after the creation of this world also received the operation of the Spirit, it gained all the beauty of that grace with which the world is illumined. Finally, the prophet declared that the grace of the universe cannot abide without the Holy Spirit, when he said: "Thou

shalt take away their breath, and they shall fail, and shall return to
the dust. Send forth thy Spirit and they shall be created, and thou
shall renew the face of the earth." Not only did he teach that all creation cannot stand without the Spirit, but also that the Spirit is the
Creator of all creation.

And who can deny that the creation of the earth is the work of the
Holy Spirit, whose work it is that is renewed? For if they desire to
deny that it was created by the Spirit, since it cannot be denied that it
must be renewed by the Spirit, they who desire to sever the Persons
must maintain that the operation of the Holy Spirit is superior to that
of the Father and the Son, which is far from the truth; for there is no
doubt that the restored earth is better than it was created.[31]

Ambrose sees the Spirit as the creator of the whole universe, as the one
who brings beauty and grace to creation, and as the one who enables it to
exist at every moment. The Spirit continually sustains the process of ongoing creation. He assumes that all will agree that it is the Spirit's role to bring
about the regeneration of all things in Christ, and he argues from this to
the absurdity of excluding the Spirit from the work of creation. The Spirit's
work is both the creation of the world and the renewal of the world.

Ambrose's most powerful and interesting argument is from the incarnation. In a form of Spirit Christology, he points out that the Creator Spirit
is the author of the incarnation. Luke 1:35 and Matthew 1:18-20 proclaim
that "the fruit of the womb is the work of the Spirit."[32] If the Spirit is
responsible for the incarnation, then this suggests that there is nothing that
the Spirit has not created. He argues that if we are right to think of the
humanity of Jesus as the work of the Creator Spirit, then we can rightly
conclude that the whole of creation is the work of the Holy Spirit. The
Spirit of God is the author of both: "So we cannot doubt that the Spirit is
Creator, whom we know as the author of the Lord's incarnation."[33]

Ambrose sees the Spirit as the author of the Christ event, the author of
creation, and the author of the life of grace.[34] He thus has a line of thought
about the Spirit that anticipates the line of thought developed in this book:
the Breath of God is the life-giving Creator Spirit at work in creation,
grace, the incarnation and, of course, the church.

THE SPIRIT AS THE IMMANENT SOURCE
OF THE NEW IN AN EMERGENT UNIVERSE

In what follows, then, I will work with the biblical image of the Holy
Spirit as the Breath of God; and I will propose that this Breath of God can
be thought of as breathing life into the universe in all its stages: into its laws
and initial conditions, its origin and its evolution. As the universe expands
and evolves in an emergent process, it is the Breath of God that empowers

and enables the whole process from within. The Spirit enables the emergence of the new at every stage from the first nuclei of hydrogen and helium, to atoms, galaxies, the Sun, bacterial forms of life, complex cells, the wonderfully diverse forms of life on Earth, and human beings who can think and love and praise.

With Irenaeus, I will see Word and Spirit, the two hands of God, as reciprocally interrelated in the one great act of ongoing creation. With Athanasius, I will think of God as creating *through* the Word and *in* the Spirit. I will see it as particular to the Spirit to be the immanent presence of God in creation. With Basil, I will see the Spirit, always in the Communion of the Trinity, as dwelling in all the diverse creatures of the universe and so enabling them to exist from the divine Communion. This *is* the relationship of ongoing creation. The Spirit dwelling in all things already brings them into the communion of creation, and promises them their eschatological completion in God. With Ambrose, I will think of the Holy Spirit as the Creator Spirit, the author of creation, who is also the author of incarnation.

Some scientific thinkers challenge the idea of an upward movement or of progress in evolutionary history. Stephen Jay Gould, for example, admits that there is a phenomenon of increased complexity in life's history, but he flatly denies that progress defines the history of life or even exists as a general trend at all.[35] Ernst Mayr takes a different approach from Gould. While he finds no scientific evidence for the existence of any intrinsic drive toward upward evolution, he insists that it is legitimate to talk of progress in the series of evolutionary steps from the prokaryotes to eukaryotes, vertebrates, mammals, primates, and human beings.[36] I believe that it is both possible and important to trace the emergence of the new in evolutionary history. But it is also important to acknowledge that the emergence of the new does *not* define the evolutionary strategy of a great deal of life. Bacteria, Gould's favorite example, not only survive but flourish. Many species of fish seem perfectly adapted to succeed as they are. The movement toward the new that exists in some creatures must be seen in the context of relative stability in others. Gould is certainly right to call for an honoring of "all life's bursting and bustling variety."[37] But, granted this, I think he underestimates the dynamic evolution toward the new that coexists with and depends on the foundation afforded by bacteria and other forms of life.

There is a movement to the new, in the particles formed in the first part of the first second of the Big Bang, in the hydrogen nuclei formed in the first few minutes, in the assembly of atoms a few hundred thousand years later, in the stars that synthesize further elements, in the DNA molecule, in the first nucleated cells, in multicellular creatures, and in the neurons that fire in human brains. At every stage in this process, and at many points along the way, something that is genuinely new occurs. And while the new is completely dependent on its preexisting components, it is not reducible to its components. As Philip Clayton says, in an emergent universe "genuinely new properties emerge which are not reducible to what came before, although they are continuous with it."[38] The information contained in DNA is simply not there in amino acids. Nancey Murphy and George Ellis defend the concept of an emergent universe. They describe emergent order as "the appearance of properties and processes that are only describable by means of irreducible concepts, concepts that are simply inapplicable at the lower levels of order." They describe complex hierarchical systems in which both emergent order and top-down effects can be found.[39]

Arthur Peacocke has long championed a view of reality that is emergentist. Peacocke argues that the natural sciences provide a picture of the world as a series of levels of organization, in which each level can be understood as a *whole* made up of constituent parts. He argues that there is an emergence of higher-level properties that cannot be reduced to the sum of the parts. There is downward causation of the whole as well as causation from the bottom up. Peacocke speaks of *whole–part influence* to describe the way in which the whole acts as a causal factor in relationship to its constituent parts.[40] Clayton and Peacocke both argue for an emergentist monist approach to the relationship of the mind to the brain. Mental properties are understood as dependent on physical properties, but as irreducible to them. They see personal life, being a person in relation to others, as an irreducible and emergent property of the human.

Holmes Rolston III insists that in nature—above all in the history of life on Earth—*more* regularly comes from *less*.[41] There is a prolific fertility of life, a generativity in which there is seemingly endless novelty. He sees the genes as central in creating, storing, testing, and transmitting the new discoveries that make the evolution of life possible. He insists that human culture is rooted in biology, but culture exceeds biology as biology exceeds physics and chemistry. There is genuine novelty in culture that emerges out of the wildness of nature. He argues that both genes and culture are fundamental in the genesis of information and value, and he traces the history of science, ethics, and religion as emergent phenomena in culture.

If more comes from less, how can this be understood? It is important to distinguish two levels of explanation, the level of science and the level of theology. At the level of science, scholars like Stuart Kauffman are convinced that they can point to self-organization at work in complex systems.[42] Paul Davies has reviewed attempts to model complex structures in physics, chemistry, biology, astronomy, and ecology that point to patterns of self-organization at work in nature. This leads him to suspect that there are organizing principles over and above the known laws of physics that are yet to be discovered.[43] While he allows that the specific details of emergence depend on the myriad accidents of evolution, Davies contends that the general trend of matter–mind–culture is written into nature at a fundamental level.[44] Davies believes that the acid test of his thesis is the question whether there is life, especially intelligent life, in other parts of the universe.

If we are not alone, he says, life on Earth can be understood as the natural outworking of universal laws.

The theologian will leave it to scientists to test the viability of what Davies has called the emerging paradigm of a self-organizing universe. Theology's task is to deal with the issue of the emergence of the new in evolutionary history at another level—that of a revised and developed theology of creation. At the heart of the Christian theology of creation in its classical formulation is the profound idea that the universe, and everything in it, exists at every point because God holds it in existence. God holds things in being over the abyss of nothingness. I believe that this theological position is both fundamental and in need of significant development if it is to be able to deal with an evolutionary view of reality. Karl Rahner has made an important contribution to a revised theology of creation with his theory of active self-transcendence. Rahner sees the biblical God as the *Absolute Future*—the future not only of human beings but also of all creation. He insists that the discovery that we are part of an evolving world demands a new understanding of reality, a transformed metaphysics and theology. The tradition articulated by Aquinas and others needs to be developed so that God is understood not simply as the dynamic cause of the *existence* of creatures, but as the dynamic ground of their *becoming*.

In evolutionary history, Rahner tells us, we can find instances when what *is* clearly becomes something altogether *new*. The two most obvious examples are the emergence of life and the emergence of self-conscious human beings. Rahner argues that we need to think of the divine act of ongoing creation, then, not simply as the divine "conservation" and "concursus" of all things, but as the enabling of creation to become what is radically new.[45] He calls this process whereby God empowers creation itself to produce something radically new "active self-transcendence." It is a capacity that nature itself has. Rahner insists that evolutionary emergence has its own autonomy and its own explanation at the level of science. It is to be explained by the laws of nature. But at the deepest metaphysical and theological level, it is God who enables and empowers this becoming. God is the inner power of evolutionary emergence. In Rahner's view, God cannot be thought of as intervening from outside; rather, God empowers the whole process of ongoing creation from within by constantly giving to creation itself the capacity to transcend itself and become more than it was.[46]

Rahner has further developed this line of thought in his evolutionary Christology, where he presents Jesus in his humanity as a product of the evolutionary universe. Jesus is understood as both the self-transcendence of the universe to God and the self-communication of God to the universe.[47] Rahner's thought needs further articulation precisely as a trinitarian theology of the Spirit of God. The immanent source of the creation's capacity for self-transcendence is more precisely seen as the Spirit of God breathing life into the whole process of an emergent universe. It is the Spirit who is the immanent divine principle that empowers the new, enabling creatures to transcend themselves. It is the empowering Spirit who draws things toward the future, who enables more to come from less.

It is the Spirit dwelling in creatures who enables them not only to *exist*, but also *to become what is new*. Elizabeth Johnson beautifully captures this boundless energy of the empowering Spirit:

> The Spirit is the great, creative Matrix who grounds and sustains the cosmos and attracts it toward the future. Throughout the vast sweep of cosmic and biological evolution she embraces the material root of existence and its endless new potential, empowering the cosmic process from within. The universe, in turn, is self-organizing and self-transcending, corresponding from the spiralling galaxies to the double helix of the DNA molecule to the dance of her quickening power.[48]

It will be the task of the rest of the book to develop further these biblical, patristic, and contemporary insights into a theology of the Creator Spirit. I will conclude this chapter with seven points that are meant to summarize key ideas from this chapter and open out toward the rest of the book.

1. The Spirit can be thought of in biblical terms as the Breath of God, breathing life into a universe of creatures. The biblical tradition offers the image of the Breath of God breathing life into human beings and other creatures. This points to the divine act of *creatio continua* that enables a world of creatures to exist and to evolve. Along with the image of breath, the new life experienced in the Spirit can be expressed in symbols like wind, fire, and streams of living water. These images suggest an understanding of the Spirit in nonanthropomorphic terms, as all-encompassing yet immanent in all things, as unimaginably powerful yet gentle and subtle, as unpredictable and wild yet creative and life-giving. The Spirit's life-giving power embraces not only living things but the whole of the universe that gives rise to life. There is a deep and interior connection between the hydrogen that comes from the Big Bang, the nuclear processes in stars, and the elements that make up the bodies of the living creatures of Earth. Everything is interconnected. It is the Breath of God who breathes life into the whole process.

2. The Breath of God and the Word of God act together in creation. One of the theological advantages of the image of the Spirit as Breath of God is that it makes an easy and natural connection between the breath and the word. With this image as central, the ancient patristic tradition kept Word and Spirit together. Irenaeus, Athanasius, Basil, and Ambrose all gave a central place to the words of Psalm 33:6 in their theology of creation: "By the word of the Lord the heavens were made, and all their host by the breath of his mouth." Irenaeus influenced the whole tradition with his image of God creating and redeeming through the two hands of the Word and the Spirit. Word and Spirit accompany each other. The image of the two hands suggests a reciprocal relationship between Word and Spirit, something I will take up as one of the central themes of this book.

3. The Spirit of God is the Source of the new in an emergent universe. The movement to the new occurs throughout the whole history of the evolution of the universe—from the first quarks to the first stars, from the first appearance of life on Earth to the emergence of modern humans. At every stage in this process, something that is genuinely new occurs. And while the new is completely dependent on its preexisting components, it is not reducible to its components. Emergent properties cannot be simply reduced to the sum of the parts. The Creator Spirit is not to be thought of as simply sustaining the universe, but must be thought of as enabling and empowering the genuinely new to occur. The Spirit can be understood as the immanent divine power that enables evolutionary emergence, continually giving to creation itself the capacity to transcend itself and become more than it is. The Breath of God breathes life into the whole process of an emergent universe. The Holy Spirit is the immanent divine principle drawing creation toward an open future.

4. Creation is a relationship—a relationship between each creature and the divine Communion. As Basil's theology makes clear, God *is* Communion. This is a communion in which distinctiveness, uniqueness, and integrity of the Persons flourish. Creatures exist only because God, who is Communion, enables them to be. Creation means that each creature exists at every moment in relationship to the divine Communion. All things exist from Communion. Thomas Aquinas described creation as a relationship between each creature and the Creator as the principle by which the creature exists.[49] In a trinitarian theology, creation can be understood as the relationship between each creature and the divine Communion by which creatures exist and become in an interrelated and evolutionary universe. If God's being is being-in-relationship and the existence of each creature is a being-in-relation to the divine Communion, then this suggests that relationality is at the very core of being. Being-in-relation can be thought of as defining the whole of created reality as well as the divine life. This will become the theme of chapter 9 of this book.

5. The Spirit is the Communion-Bringer, the indwelling creative presence that relates each entity with the divine Communion. It is the Three-in-Communion that enables a world of creatures to exist and holds them in being at every moment, but this one act of the Trinity involves the distinctive roles of the Three. Creation comes from the Source of All, through the Wisdom of God, in the Spirit. Within the one act of creation it is the role of the Spirit to be the immanent presence of God, bringing all things into communion with God, enabling them to exist and to reach their completion in God. As John V. Taylor puts it, the Holy Spirit is "that unceasing dynamic communicator and Go-Between operating upon every element and process of the material universe, the immanent and anonymous presence of God."[50] In chapter 8, I will take up the discussion of the distinctive and proper role of the divine persons in creation. At this stage I simply want to propose that it is faithful to the biblical and patristic tradition to see the Spirit as the indwelling one, as the interior presence that empowers being and becoming, always in communion with the eternal Word and with the Source of All.

6. *In the Creator Spirit, God is present to each creature, embracing each in love.* The Spirit dwells in every creature of the universe, in all its galaxies, stars, animals, and plants. This presence of the Spirit by which a creature exists is an act of love (Wis. 11:26-12:1). What I want to propose at this point is that this love embraces individuals. It is not a love that embraces only humans, or only species of other creatures, or only the whole process. As Basil points out, God watches over every creature, lovingly providing for each. Every sea urchin is precious. If this is to have meaning today in the light of what we know from biology, then it requires serious reflection on the place of pain, death, and extinctions in the process. It is not possible to say without qualification that creation is harmonious. In chapter 7, I hope to make the case that the Spirit is present in love with each creature as a faithful companion and midwife to new creation, groaning with groaning creatures in the birthing of the new.

7. *Through the indwelling Spirit, creatures of the universe are brought into communion with one another.* The Spirit of God not only embraces individuals but enables them to exist in an interrelated world of creatures, bringing them into the circle of divine love and leading them to their completion in God. Ambrose sees the Spirit as bringing beauty and grace to the whole of creation. Basil speaks of the Creator as an Artist who creates a world of wonderfully diverse creatures that reflect and express the Wisdom of God. He sees the divine Artist as bringing creatures, in spite of their diversity, into a mutual *sympathy*. He tells us that they are brought into a communion that is like a *symphony* of creation. This line of thought can provide an important direction toward an ecological theology. One of the themes that I will continue to explore is the idea that the same Spirit dwells in clams, in eucalyptus trees, in kangaroos, and in human beings, being with them in ways that are appropriate to each and directing each to their fulfillment in God. Human beings who are open to the grace of the indwelling Spirit are called into a kinship with the other creatures of Earth and with the universe itself. To be made a child of God by the Spirit of God is to be called to share the divine passion for trees, birds and stars.

The work of the Creator Spirit embraces not only ongoing creation but also the work of grace, the theme of the next chapter. In both creation and grace, it is the Spirit of God who makes all things new.

FOUR

Enfolding Human Beings in Grace

If the first part of the story of the Spirit concerns creation, the second involves the Spirit's work in the grace that transforms human existence. Grace precedes the Christ event. I believe that this order is important. It is helpful to see not only the great sweep of the Spirit's work in creation but also the universal gracious presence of the Spirit to human beings *before* moving on to what is for Christians the center of the story—Jesus of Nazareth. Many Christians have assumed that the saving work of the Holy Spirit begins after the Christ event. In this chapter I will put the case that, while Christians see this work of the Spirit as salvation in and through Christ, they can also see the Holy Spirit as *always and everywhere* graciously present in self-offering love to human beings.

One way of beginning a reflection on this issue is to think of the inhabitants of my own country, Australia. Archaeological evidence suggests that human beings have been present in Australia for more than fifty thousand years. A mere four hundred years ago, in 1605, Pedro Fernandez de Quiros, a Portuguese in the service of Spain, set off to discover the great south land, *terra australis*. He believed that he had been called to bring saving faith to the inhabitants of the place he called the South Land of the Holy Spirit, *Australia del Espiritu Santo*. De Quiros was convinced that the inhabitants of the south land were children of God, but he imagined them living in the darkness of unbelief. He hoped to bring them the good news of salvation in Christ. The indigenous peoples of Australia had certainly not heard the gospel, but what does this mean in terms of a Christian theology of salvation? Did salvation arrive only with the European missionaries, or was it already at work in Australia? Was the Spirit present only when the gospel was preached, or was the Spirit present and active among the people of Australia for fifty thousand years before Europeans saw their first kangaroo?

These same questions can be asked of the indigenous inhabitants of all lands. They can also be asked of the first humans. Did they emerge in a world of grace? Richard Leakey points out that we have little evidence about the consciousness of early humans. The first evidence of deliberate burial is that of a Neanderthal of a little more than one hundred thousand years ago. Leakey sees Neanderthals as having a reflective consciousness, but one that would have been less developed than that of modern humans, who have benefited greatly from the emergence of modern language. What about the self-awareness of *Homo erectus*? Leakey suggests that it would be surprising if late *Homo erectus* "did not have a level of consciousness significantly greater than that of chimpanzees." He says of *Homo erectus* that their "social complexity, large brain size, and probable language skills" all point to a developed level of consciousness. But he acknowledges that we are not certain that they possessed a form of spoken language, and we cannot be sure that they possessed a form of humanlike self-awareness.[1]

Clearly there is not enough evidence available to pinpoint when our ancestors first had the capacity for religious experience, but I will argue for the idea that whenever humans emerged with the capacity for self-awareness and God-awareness, the Spirit of God was already present to them in gracious self-offering. The Holy Spirit was present in self-offering love to human beings long before Pentecost, long before the ecstatic utterances of the prophets of ancient Israel and long before the call of Abraham and Sarah. The Spirit was with the people of Australia fifty thousand years ago. The Spirit of God was present in the very emergence of the human, not simply as enabling the process of evolution from within but as surrounding and embracing early humans in self-offering love. Humans evolved into a world of grace. The Spirit of God was the ambience for the emergence of the human. The theological story of the emergence of the human is the story of emergence into a gracious universe.

In presenting this line of thought I will build on insights developed in Karl Rahner's theology. I will presuppose what is accepted by much of the Christian tradition and has become the formal and explicit teaching of the Roman Catholic Church on the work of the Holy Spirit *beyond* the church. I will begin by arguing that the experience of the Spirit is shared by all human beings. Then, in a second step, I will ask about the relationship between the universal experience of the Holy Spirit and the Christian conviction about salvation in Christ. Finally I will offer some brief reflections on a Christian approach to other religious traditions.

EXPERIENCE OF THE HOLY SPIRIT

Can we human beings experience the Spirit of God? This is clearly a fundamental question for theology. I do not think the answer to this question is completely obvious. On the one hand, there are Christians who testify to ecstatic, charismatic, or mystical experiences of the Spirit. On the other hand, critical thinkers point to the linguistic and conceptual limitations of human experience. They rightly insist that God, by definition, radically transcends our minds. God can never be grasped as one object among others of our experience. They point to cultural conditioning and to the dangers of mistaken interpretation, self-deception, and delusion in claims about religious experience.

What is clear is that cultural and psychological factors necessarily play a significant role in the interpretation of experience. This suggests at least a cautious approach to claims about the experience of the Spirit of God. What is claimed to come from the Spirit will always be, at least in part, the product of a human imagination. It will be interpreted with the aid of pre-existing language and concepts. Cultural and personal biases will always play a role. The experience will be expressed only in the limited images and words that are available. It is always possible that a person claiming to experience the Holy Spirit may be deluded. To say all of this is not to deny the possibility of religious experience but to argue that it is always filtered through the personality of its recipient. It can find expression only by way of the human imagination and in human words and symbols. These are always limited and sometimes misleading. They may be pathological. This means that a critical stance is required, above all when a person claims to have a message from God that they expect others to accept or follow. While a cautious and critical stance is essential, it does not of itself rule out a theological claim that we can and do experience God's Spirit.

Karl Rahner has articulated such a claim. Furthermore, he insists that the experience of the Spirit occurs in a fundamental way in ordinary human experience of the world. It is not reserved for religious elites. It is something that exists among human beings of all times and places. It is an experience of the Spirit at the heart of daily life. Rahner insists that, when we speak of the experience of the Spirit, the experience in question is not of the same order as the experience of created objects, like a door, a book, or a tree. It is a much more global experience of transcendence, of openness to the infinite, an experience that occurs as the context and background for our more specific everyday experiences.

Rahner points out how this experience of transcendence, of "going beyond" the ordinary and everyday, occurs precisely *in* ordinary everyday knowing. Human beings ask questions. Every specific answer opens up further questions. There is a restless, ceaseless searching of our minds that cannot rest in any specific result. Our questions have no end. They open out toward endless infinity. Whenever our minds move to grasp an individual object of knowledge such as a flower, we come to know it only in a wider context. What is known and named as an individual object is known against a background of other possible objects. This background is usually unnamed and known only implicitly. It involves the range of possible knowledge. It has no boundaries, reaching out toward the infinite. We can bring this context to explicit awareness, but only by making it concrete and specific. It always escapes our concepts. It is like the horizon that forms the context for our journey, but which, if we focus on it and move toward it, always springs up again beyond our grasp.

We know specific objects only against a horizon that has no limits. Rahner offers two beautiful images for the experience of infinite mystery that occurs as the horizon for our everyday knowing. His first image is of an island seen against a vast sea. He says that the object of explicit awareness is like a tiny island in the boundless ocean of the nameless mystery that surrounds it. His second image is of a light seen against the darkness of the night. The things that we can grasp with our minds are like little lights, and the nameless mystery that surrounds them is like the night that alone makes visible our little lights and gives then their brightness.[2]

This experience of openness to mystery occurs not only in human knowing but also in the free acts of the human will. In all of our specific commitments there is an implicit invitation to give ourselves into a love that is unconditioned. Above all, this implicit invitation is found in the experience of love of another person. Even in the deepest and most satisfying experiences of loving dear friends we come up against limitation and loneliness. We recognize that there are hungers of the heart that no human being can finally fill. The partial fulfillment we experience in love of another opens out toward a love that has no limits. It points to the seemingly endless restlessness of human desire and to the unlimited capacity of the human heart.

There is a boundless expanse to the human mind and heart, and this boundless expanse is always there as the context of ordinary knowledge and love. Rahner sees the Spirit of God as dwelling in this openness of the human person, but he insists that this is known as the Spirit of God only through revelation. *Philosophically*, on the basis of reason, all we say is that there is an unlimited openness of the human spirit, and we may hope that God is the goal of this movement. But, *theologically*, on the basis of the revelation of God's universal salvific will, we can say that it is the grace of God, God's self-communication in the Spirit that surrounds and sustains the human person. On the basis of Christian revelation, the dynamic openness of the human person can be understood as openness toward the Spirit of God present in self-offering love.

This experience is often obscured by preoccupation with the specific things that engage our attention. It can remain implicit, preconceptual, and unnamed—like the light of the Sun which we may not see directly because we are concerned with the objects made visible only by its light.[3] We can avoid attending to the mystery that surrounds our conscious activity, but we can also attend to it and open our minds and hearts to this silent mystery that surrounds us. We can learn to dwell in this open place of the Spirit.

Rahner points out that alongside the experience of transcendence in ordinary knowing and loving, there are also particular moments when this ever-present experience of the Spirit is brought more clearly to the forefront of conscious experience. These are moments that are commonly thought of as religious experiences. They occur when the individual objects of our attention serve to bring to mind the accompanying experience of the Spirit. Particular aspects of everyday experience draw our attention to the ever-present but not always noticed experience of the Spirit.

This can happen when the object of our experience in its beauty, good-ness, or mystery points toward the Spirit of God who sustains it. An every-day reality can seem to become transparent to the light of the Spirit shining through it. A person can be captivated by a single flower, can ponder the exuberance of life in a rain forest, can gaze at the stars on a moonless night, and can find in the experience a sense of wonder, mystery, and gracious presence. A moment of shared friendship can come as a pure gift, a gift that cannot be controlled or held too tightly, but which brings a sense of being immensely blessed. A newborn child can bring the parents to absolute won-der and be received as a mysterious gift. There are moments of creativity in cooking, writing, gardening, building, painting, teaching, parenting, and relating, when we can experience the breakthrough to the new as simulta-neously from ourselves and as a gift that comes from beyond ourselves.

There are also negative and sometimes extremely painful moments that lead us into mystery, when the everyday realities with which we are con-cerned break down. There are times when all that supports our deepest commitments seems to disappear and we find ourselves called to go on in trust and in hope against hope, and, perhaps, to come to know that this is a moment of God's Spirit in our lives. There are times when loneliness takes hold in our hearts, when love is unrequited, when those we love seem far away, when all we feel is absence and emptiness, and yet we find this empti-ness giving way to a solitude where there is a silent presence. There is the experience of being badly damaged by another, when in spite of bitterness and disappointment, we find ourselves with the freedom to forgive and know this freedom as grace. There is the death of those we love, times when loss and grief leave us unspeakably desolate, when, eventually, we may come to know we are upheld in what seems absolutely hopeless and unendurable.

Rahner's argument is that in the light of the God revealed in Jesus, Christians can see in these kinds of experiences the presence of God in the Spirit. They can understand what they experience as "the love of God poured into our hearts by the Holy Spirit that has been given to us" (Rom. 5:5). Paul, of course, was talking about the experience of those who are jus-tified by faith and "have peace with God through our Lord Jesus Christ." This raises the important question of the relationship between the experi-ences of the Spirit and salvation through Christ. If all human beings live in a world of grace, if they experience the Spirit in some way in everyday life, how is this experience connected to the salvation that Christians see as mediated to the world in the life, death, and resurrection of Jesus Christ?

THE GRACE OF THE SPIRIT
AND SALVATION THROUGH CHRIST

The Christian tradition has long struggled with the relationship between the universality of God's saving will and salvation in Christ. The early Christian community was convinced that the boundless love of God revealed in the Christ event is a universal love that breaks through all boundaries and embraces the whole world. At the same time, they believed that this saving love is given through Jesus Christ, in his life, death, and resurrection. These two aspects of Christian theology are both represented in the Christian Scriptures. The conviction that salvation comes through Christ is expressed in texts such as these: "For as in Adam all died so also in Christ shall all be made alive" (1 Cor. 15:21), "I am the way and the truth and the life. No one comes to the Father except through me" (John 14:6). "There is salvation in no one else, for there is no other name under heaven given among mortals by which we must be saved" (Acts 4:12). "For there is one God; there is also one mediator between God and humankind, Christ Jesus, himself human, who gave himself a ransom for all" (1 Tim. 2:5).

God's universal saving love finds its real expression in the whole person of Jesus Christ, rather than in specific texts. It also finds expression in the biblical figures of both testaments who are neither Jewish nor Christian but are moved by God and open to God. Cornelius was a favorite example for writers in the patristic period. Cornelius is a devout and good Gentile whose prayers and almsgiving are well pleasing to God long before his conversion and baptism (Acts 10). In Acts 17, we find Paul reflecting explicitly on God's presence to non-Christians: "What therefore you worship as unknown I proclaim to you . . . the God who made the world and everything in it . . . made all nations to inhabit the whole earth . . . so that they would search for God and perhaps grope for him and find him—though indeed he is not far from each one of us. For '[i]n him we live and move and have our being'; as even some of your own poets have said, 'For we too are his offspring'" (17:23-28). God's universal will to save finds its classic expression in the words from First Timothy: "God our Savior desires everyone to be saved and to come to the knowledge of the truth" (1 Tim. 2:4).

These two insights, that salvation is through Christ and that God wills all people to be saved, have stood in some tension throughout Christian history. At times the stress has been on the possibility of universal salvation. Justin Martyr (ca. 100-165) writes of Jewish people who obeyed the Mosaic Law: "since they who did those things which are universally, naturally, and eternally good are pleasing to God, they shall be saved in the resurrection."[4] In response to the question whether Gentiles can be saved, he comments that "Christ is the *Logos* of which all humankind partakes" and that those "who lived according to reason (*logos*) were really Christian."[5]

Clement of Alexandria (ca. 150-215) insists that God is "the Savior of all" and "as each was disposed to receive it, God distributed his blessings, both to Greeks and barbarians."[6] Origen (ca. 185-254) teaches that in every age God wanted human beings to be just and "always provided human beings endowed with reason with occasions for practicing virtue and doing what is right." He appeals to a beautiful text from the Wisdom of Solomon: "In every generation she [the Wisdom of God] passes into holy souls, and makes them friends of God and prophets" (7:27).[7]

Alongside this tradition was one that insisted that salvation is given through Christ and the church and to willfully reject either was to reject God. This found expression in the saying of Cyprian (ca. 200-258), taken up by Augustine (354-430) and others: "Outside the church, no salvation." This was affirmed by the Fourth Lateran Council (1215), the Council of Florence (1442) and the bull *Unam Sanctam* of Pope Boniface VIII (1302). This negative formulation, however, was not understood to be an absolute denial of salvation for those who were not Christian. Thomas Aquinas pointed to the possibility of salvation through an explicit or implicit desire for baptism. Dominican theologians from the Salamanca school, such as Domingo Soto (1494-1560), and Jesuits from the Roman school, such as Francisco Suarez (1548-1619), responded to the European discoveries of countless non-Christian peoples with a theology of the possibility of salvation through implicit faith.

In one of its most decisive and most important theological clarifications, the Second Vatican Council taught a positive approach to the theology of salvation outside the church. The Dogmatic Constitution on the Church (*Lumen Gentium*) says:

> Those too can attain eternal salvation who, through no fault of their own, do not know the Gospel of Christ or his church, yet sincerely seek God, and, moved by grace, try in their actions to do God's will as they know it through the dictates of conscience. (§16)

This text insists that salvation can come to those who do not know the gospel and are outside the church. It comes through the gift of God's grace, which finds expression in fidelity to conscience. Salvation exists beyond the confines of the church. That this salvation is the work of the Holy Spirit is taught explicitly in a parallel text in the Pastoral Constitution on the Church in the Modern World (*Gaudium et Spes*). The context is a description of the way Christians participate in Christ's death and resurrection through the indwelling of the life-giving Spirit. The text goes on to describe how non-Christians also share in Christ through the Spirit:

> All this holds true not only for Christians but also for all people of good will in whose hearts grace works in an invisible way. For since Christ died for all, and since the final vocation of humankind is in

fact one and divine, we ought to believe that the Holy Spirit offers to all, in a way known only to God, the possibility of being associated with this paschal mystery. (§22)

The Spirit of God is thought of as offering saving grace to *all* people, and this grace is understood as participation in Christ's death and resurrection. Many think of salvation as being available not only through the death of Jesus but also *after* it. But according to the teaching of the Second Vatican Council, salvation is universally available in the self-giving of God to us in the Holy Spirit. This can only mean thinking of salvation as possible throughout the whole history of modern humans going back perhaps 150,000 years, and to any of their ancestors capable of responding to God's self-offering love. Whenever there has been a human person open to the mystery of God, there the Spirit of God has been present as self-offering love.

If the Spirit is present in self-offering to every human being, and if what is offered is already the grace of Christ, does this mean that this grace is something that is natural to human beings, something that is due to us? Rahner answers no. He insists with the great Christian tradition that grace is not due to us. It is unearned. It is far beyond anything to which we have a right. It is a sheer gift. But, Rahner insists, it is not a restricted gift. It is a gift that God freely offers to every human being. This self-offering is always there. Because of God's free choice, it forms the ever-present context of our human existence in the world.[8] God has freely chosen that we should live in a world of grace. We can freely choose to say yes to this grace in the way we live our lives, and in this way embrace God's saving love. We can also explicitly or implicitly reject God's self-offering and choose to live in sinful alienation from God.

But there remains a fundamental question: How can the salvation of, for example, a woman who lived fifty thousand years ago in Australia, be related to Jesus of Nazareth? Karl Rahner offers a response to this question. He points out that the Spirit who is at work in grace throughout human history is always the Spirit directed toward Christ. The meaning and purpose of the Spirit's work are expressed in God's self-giving to the world in Jesus Christ. Christ and the Spirit are radically interrelated. It is the Spirit of God who brings about the incarnation, and in this sense the Spirit is the efficient cause of the Christ event. But the whole history of the Spirit's presence in grace is directed toward Jesus Christ. In this sense Christ is the final cause of the Spirit. The Spirit is oriented toward God's explicit self-giving in Christ. The Spirit always bears this goal of the Christ event within. Rahner speaks of this as an intrinsic *entelechy* of the Spirit.[9] This expression from Aristotelian philosophy refers to the inner ordering that directs an entity to its natural goal or completion. The Spirit has an inner ordering and direction toward the goal of God's self-giving in the Word made flesh.

Christians have understood salvation as coming through the cross of Christ. How can we envision today the causal relationship between the cross and the salvation of people who lived before as well as after Christ? Jesus' life lived in compassionate love finds its ultimate expression in his self-giving death and its culmination in the resurrection. God's saving love is expressed in all of this. The whole Christ event is contained in the central symbol of the cross. Rahner sees traditional ways of talking about salvation—such as satisfaction, substitutionary atonement, and sacrifice—as legitimate when properly understood, but as time-conditioned attempts to communicate something more basic, the mystery of what God has done for us in Jesus. They are secondary and derivative with regard to the primary experience of salvation in Christ. He sees them as in danger of giving the false impression that something happens in the cross that changes God's mind. Rahner insists that the cross does not cause a change of mind in God. It does not change God from being a God of wrath to being a God of grace. God does not need appeasing. God is to be understood as the cause of salvation. It is God's eternal will to save that finds expression in the cross. The death and resurrection are not in any sense a cause of God beginning to love sinners. They are the consequence, expression, and embodiment of divine love.

Rahner suggests an understanding of the death of Jesus as the symbolic or sacramental cause of our salvation. Jesus' life of self-giving love finds its climax in his surrender to God in death. This is both the symbol and the accomplishment of God's eternal saving love.[10] In this event, salvation receives its explicit expression and embodiment in human history. God's saving grace, present throughout the whole of human history in the Spirit, has always been the grace of Christ. The saving grace that is already mysteriously present and active in the Spirit is both symbolized and realized in Jesus' life, death, and resurrection. The cross is the primary sacramental sign of grace. This specific efficacious *symbol* of grace and the *universal reality* of grace are intrinsically interconnected. The sign, the Christ event, belongs to the essence of grace. In the cross, grace finds historical expression. In this sense, the cross, understood as the whole Christ event, is the cause of the salvation which it signifies.

The Christian, then, can see Jesus Christ as the sacrament of the salvation of the world. I embrace this theology that comes from Rahner as a Christian way of understanding the saving action of God. But, as will become clearer in the next section, I believe in taking up and witnessing to this Christian understanding in a humble way. It ought not be taken up in a way that excludes other religious traditions or religious figures. Christians can believe that Christ has a unique role as sacrament of salvation while being prepared to listen to and enter into honest and authentic dialogue with others about their beliefs concerning salvation and its mediations in our world.

A woman living in Australia fifty thousand years ago already lives in a world of grace. This grace is nothing else than the Spirit of God surrounding her, present to her in the openness of her own heart and mind. Because God has freely chosen to come to us, to embrace our existence, and to offer us love, this woman lives in a graced universe. She, like every human being, can respond to this divine self-offering positively or negatively. She can accept or reject the Spirit. To accept the Spirit is to receive the gift of justifying grace through a form of faith. It might be an implicit faith that finds expression in her care for her children and her compassion for those around her. It may find expression in her fidelity to the promptings of the Spirit in the depths of conscience.

Her response might also be a sinful rejection of the Spirit. In any case, her existence is touched not only by the gracious presence of the Spirit, but by the cumulative weight of human sin that enters into the place of her free decision. Over and over again human beings have chosen to reject love. Sin has been with the human from the beginning. Every human being is born into a world that is not only a world of grace but also a world of sin. In addition to being born into a world of sin, human beings inherit genetic tendencies from their evolutionary ancestors. These tendencies, such as the impulse to self-defense, are not evil. They are part of good creation. They lead to evil only when human beings—who are called into a rich human cultural world in which love for others and love for God become real possibilities—refuse the way of love. They become evil only when human beings refuse growth toward other-centered love and choose to function only at the level of basic orientations, such as those to self-protection, territoriality, possessiveness, and satisfaction of appetites.[11] As Holmes Rolston III puts it, human beings "fall" into evil rather than rise to their destiny. They refuse to embrace their humanity. They choose to live in selfishness. It is not that their animal nature is selfish, but rather that "trying to become human without emerging from the animal nature results in selfishness."[12] Sin is the choice to refuse to be human before God.

Both sin and grace are part of human experience. The early Australian woman I described above experienced the pull of sin as well as the invitation of grace. In spite of the inclination to evil that is part of all human existence, this woman lives her life with an always-present experience of the Spirit as the horizon of everyday experience. And, in grace, she may well embrace this self-offering of love and find her salvation. From the point of view of Christian faith, when she embraces the Spirit she embraces the Christ-directed Spirit.

THE SPIRIT OF GOD
AND THE RELIGIOUS TRADITIONS OF HUMANKIND

In many theological circles, then, including those associated with my own Roman Catholic tradition, it is not in any way controversial to claim that the salvation of Jesus Christ is offered to all people of every age through the ever-present Spirit of God. In fact this is the explicit and formal teaching of Pope John Paul II, who writes:

> The universality of salvation means that it is granted not only to those who explicitly believe in Christ and have entered the Church. Since salvation is offered to all, it must be made concretely available to all. But it is clear that today, as in the past, many people do not have an opportunity to come to know or accept the Gospel or to enter the Church. The social and cultural conditions in which they live do not permit this, and frequently they have been brought up in other religious traditions. For such people salvation in Christ is accessible by virtue of a grace which, while having a mysterious relationship to the Church, does not make them formally part of the Church but enlightens them in a way which is accommodated to their spiritual and material situation. This grace comes from Christ; it is the result of his sacrifice and is communicated by the Holy Spirit. It enables each person to attain salvation through his or her own free cooperation. (*Redemptoris Missio* §10)[13]

But if salvation is indeed understood as universal in outreach, then this raises the further question of how a Christian theology might view the role of other religions in mediating salvation. The Second Vatican Council addresses other religious traditions positively, as a "preparation for the gospel" and as containing "seeds of the Word" (*Ad Gentes* §§3, 11). It expresses respect for all that is "true and holy" in these traditions and sees them as often "reflecting a ray of that Truth that enlightens all people" (*Nostra Aetate* §2).

John Paul II has made a further contribution by his emphasis on the presence and work of the Holy Spirit in non-Christians and in their religions. In his first encyclical, *Redemptoris Hominis*, he speaks of beliefs of non-Christian religions as being an "effect of the Spirit of truth" operating outside the visible confines of the Christian church (§6).[14] He challenges missionaries to respect everything "wrought in the human being by the Spirit, 'which blows where it wills'" (§12).[15] He said, in a radio broadcast to the peoples of Asia: "I have come to Asia to be a witness to the Spirit who is active in the history of peoples and of nations." Reflecting on the Day of Prayer for Peace at Assisi with leaders of religious traditions, he states: "every authentic prayer is called forth by the Holy Spirit, who is mysteriously present in the heart of every person."[16] In his encyclical on the Holy Spirit, *Dominum et Vivicantem*, he again speaks of the universality of the Spirit's presence and action. He says that to understand the Spirit's work we need to go back behind the last two thousand years: "We need to go further back, to embrace the whole of the action of the Holy Spirit even before Christ—from the beginning, throughout the world, and especially in the economy of the Old Covenant" (§53).[17] Finally, in his encyclical letter on mission he returns to this theme of the universal presence and action of the Spirit:

> The Spirit, therefore, is at the very source of the human being's existential and religious questioning, a questioning which is occasioned not only by contingent situations but by the very structure of his or her being. . . . The Spirit's presence and activity affect not only individuals but also society and history, people, cultures and religions. Indeed the Spirit is at the origin of the noble ideals and undertakings which benefit humanity on its journey through history. . . . Again, it is the Spirit who sows the "seeds of the Word" present in various customs and cultures, preparing them for full maturity in Christ. . . . Thus the Spirit, who "blows where he wills" (cf. John 3:8), and who "was already at work in the world before Christ was glorified," and who has "filled the world, holds all things together (and) knows what is said" (Wis. 1:7), leads us to broaden our vision in order to ponder his activity in every time and place. I have repeatedly called this fact to mind, and it has guided me in my meetings with a wide variety of peoples. (*Redemptoris Missio* §§28, 29)

The church's relationship with other religions is to be governed by a respect for the action of the Spirit. This body of Christian teaching might be summarized in the following six points: (1) The Spirit of God is at work universally in all times and places and for every person; (2) this Spirit is always the Spirit of Jesus Christ; (3) the Spirit offers every person salvation, an offer that each person can accept or reject; (4) the Spirit is present and active not only in individuals, but in societies, cultures and religions; (5) the Spirit sows the "seeds of the Word" that are present in various cultural and religious practices; (6) Christians are called to discern and ponder the presence and action of the Spirit in other religious traditions.

Clearly, what we encounter in another tradition may be the gift of the Spirit. Does this mean that such an aspect of the tradition may be thought of by Christians as a mediation of salvation? While this question is not answered by John Paul II, he states: "Although participated forms of mediation are not excluded, they acquire meaning and value *only* from Christ's own mediation, and they cannot be understood as parallel or complementary to his" (*Redemptoris Missio* §5). This raises the question: Is it appropriate for one who believes that salvation comes through Christ to understand that non-Christian religious figures or institutions may constitute participatory forms of mediation in salvation? I believe that the answer to this question can only be yes. As Karl Rahner points out, once it is granted that a non-Christian shares in salvation, then one cannot deny that such a person's religion may have a positive contribution to make to salvation without understanding salvation in "a completely ahistorical and asocial way."[18] Salvation is always a gift of God, but if it is to have an impact on humanity then it has to find embodiment in history and community. The experience of saving grace will arise, in some cases, in and through religious figures, texts, and rituals. It will find expression in the language and practices of one's religious tradition. Religious figures, texts, or rituals may be both revelatory and a means of salvation, because they may give expression to the presence and action of the saving Spirit of God.

I believe that this theology of the Spirit, particularly when combined with a Wisdom Christology, offers an important foundation for a Christian approach to interreligious dialogue. I find the traditional typology of approaches to this dialogue (exclusive, inclusive and pluralist) of little help in the contemporary situation.[19] In a recent book, Paul Knitter has offered an improved fourfold typology. He speaks of the *replacement* model (Christianity as the one true religion), the *fulfillment* model (Christianity as the fulfillment of the many religions), the *mutuality* model (Christianity as one of many true religions that point to the Real), and the *acceptance* model (Christians called to accept enduring differences between the religions).[20] He does a fine job of bringing out the strengths of each model and the problems associated with each. I find, however, that my own views do not fit exactly with any one model. I embrace key ideas in the work of Karl Rahner, Jacques Dupuis, and Gavin D'Costa, who are included under the fulfillment model. I also find fundamental insights in the work of scholars like Raimon Panikkar, Michael Amaladoss, and Aloysius Pieris, who are included in the mutuality model. I find myself in disagreement with some of those who adopt pluralist positions, particularly when these involve a priori judgments about what is common to the religions. I believe that it is important to insist on respect for the proper specificity and otherness of the traditions. What the other has to say should be discovered in the dialogue. My own, still tentative, position on this complex issue can be summed up in the following four points:

1. Interreligious dialogue ought to proceed not in an a priori fashion but in a tradition-specific fashion that respects the otherness and integrity of the dialogue partner. Christians, for example, ought not to decide in principle and before the dialogue has taken place that their partners can be accounted for in some preexisting overarching framework. Dialogue, if it is to be genuine, must be tradition-specific. Christianity is committed to the belief that God's self-revelation and salvation are irrevocably given to the world in Jesus Christ. But there is no reason from within Christian faith to suggest a priori that Jesus either excludes or includes other religions as such. Of course, specific beliefs and practices of another religion may be found to be congruent or incongruent with one's Christian or Hindu faith, but this is a matter to be discovered in dialogue, not decided prior to genuine conversation.

2. Because of its theology of the Holy Spirit, Christianity is committed to the real possibility that the Spirit of God might be addressing Christians in a new way from the otherness of another religious tradition. If a Christian is to enter into interreligious dialogue, then he or she can do so only on the basis of the living Christian tradition. But at the heart of this tradition is the trinitarian understanding of the Holy Spirit. In the Christian doctrine of the Spirit there is a commitment to the idea that the Spirit is like the wind, blowing where she wills (John 3:8). Christians believe that the Spirit cannot be contained within the confines of the Christian church. This means that the Spirit may well challenge Christians from outside Christianity. The Spirit may speak to Christians from what is *other* in another tradition in a way that appears new and confronting. As Gavin D'Costa and also Jacques Dupuis point out, this provides a trinitarian basis for a Christian position of genuine openness in dialogue to another tradition.[21] This is a truly radical position. The Spirit of God may be addressing the Christian community in a prophetic way from another religious tradition. The Spirit may have something to say to the Christian from the side of the other that is not obvious or taken for granted within the Christian tradition. The Christian church, if it is to be faithful to its own identity as a Spirit-led church, cannot fail to be attentive to what the Spirit has to say from the side of the other tradition. It will need to attend to what the Spirit is saying through the rituals, prayers, practices, and traditions of the other partner. This commitment to listen for the Spirit leads to a stance before other religions that is both "critical and reverential."[22] It will involve a genuine discernment of spirits that cannot be done in the abstract or in principle, but only in the concrete engagement of humble and patient tradition-specific dialogue.

3. In a theology of Jesus as the Wisdom of God, Christians can humbly affirm their conviction that God's saving love finds a unique and liberating expression in the life, death, and resurrection of Jesus. In Jesus, Christians find the Wisdom of God revealed in the midst of humanity. They understand this Wisdom of God as radically with us in the specificity and uniqueness of Jesus' person—his liberating words, his prophetic deeds, his life, death, and resurrection. Jesus is the sacrament of God's saving love. Jesus is the human face of God. Christians see the action of God in creation and grace as directed toward this presence of divine Wisdom in Jesus. This does not rule out the possibility of the presence and saving action of God finding unique expression in other religious persons and traditions. Nor does it stop Christians who are engaged in interreligious dialogue from proposing a unique presence of God in Jesus. Aloysius Pieris, for example, insists that what is unique about Jesus is not simply incarnation itself but the *kind* of incarnation we find in Jesus—Jesus is found like a slave, among the poor, the victims, and the oppressed. Jesus expresses God's covenant with the poor of the world.[23] Michael Amaladoss finds what is special and different about Jesus primarily in four elements: the *cross* of Jesus; Jesus as a person *engaged in history* with the struggle of poor and the oppressed; Jesus as the *Sannyasi* who shows people the *Way* to liberation and wholeness; and Jesus as *within* us as a source of life and communion.[24]

4. If Jesus is understood as the Wisdom of God, other religious persons, texts, and traditions may also be understood as authentic expressions of this same Wisdom of God. The concept of holy Wisdom can be a bridge with other religious traditions. Many religious traditions relate to the language of Wisdom. The biblical notion of Wisdom was not particular to the Hebrew people but was widely shared by cultures of the Middle East. The same is true today. Speaking from India, Michael Amaladoss says: "Jesus the Wisdom of God will interest all the Asians."[25] But Wisdom language about Jesus is important for dialogue not only because it is language that is meaningful in many different traditions but also because it invites Christians to a nonexclusive view of what God is doing in Jesus. Christians may well see Jesus as Wisdom in our midst, as Wisdom incarnate. But they will not be inclined to see Jesus as exhausting the presence of Wisdom in our world. They will not be inclined to exclude the possibility that the same Wisdom of God might find radically different expression in the teachings of the Buddhist tradition. They may well see a Hindu saint like Mahatma Gandhi, and his teaching of nonviolence, not only as inspired by the prophetic Spirit but also as constituting an expression of divine Wisdom that challenges the Christian churches. It can be seen as something that relates closely to the teaching of Jesus yet is received in its unique radicality and integrity as a gift of the Spirit given to Christianity from another tradition.

Christians may believe that the Spirit is always directed to the Wisdom made flesh in Jesus of Nazareth. But this does not exclude other Spirit-directed expressions of divine Wisdom. In dialogue with other religions, Christians may well find that the Spirit finds expression in an explicit way in holy persons, rituals, and texts of the other traditions. These may be understood as a Spirit-given Wisdom from God, a Wisdom that Christians may be able to understand in relation to their own view of Jesus as Wisdom incarnate.

CONCLUSION

The story of the Spirit that begins with creation continues as the story of grace. The Creator Spirit who fills the universe is from the very beginning the Sanctifier, the bringer of grace. From the beginning, the Spirit is present to human beings in self-offering love. The Spirit of God who graciously accompanies and celebrates the emergence of every form of life delights in the emergence of human creatures who can respond to the divine self-offering love in a personal way. They are offered the gift of transforming grace. A grace-filled universe awaits their arrival. Alongside this story of grace there is also a tragic story of the willful rejection of grace. Human beings are born into a world of grace, but are also drawn toward violence and evil. In the midst of such a world, the Spirit offers freedom and salvation in a way that Christians understand as anticipating, and as directed toward, the Christ event.

FIVE

Bringing About the Christ Event

The Life-Giving Breath of God, who enables the universe of creatures to evolve and who enfolds human beings in grace, brings about the event to which both creation and grace are directed—the Christ event. The divine Breath transforms and sanctifies the humanity of Jesus so that he might be the Christ of God. As Ambrose says, in a text to which I referred earlier, the Holy Spirit is "the author of the Lord's incarnation."[1] It is by the action of the Spirit that Jesus of Nazareth is constituted as the Son of God and the eternal Wisdom of God in our midst.

To ponder the Spirit's role as author of the incarnation is to do a form of Spirit Christology. There is nothing new in this. It is as old as the affirmations that Jesus was "conceived of the Holy Spirit" (the Apostles' Creed) and that he became incarnate "by the power of the Holy Spirit" (the Nicene-Constantinopolitan Creed). It goes back behind the creeds to the infancy narratives of the Gospels of Matthew and Luke, which both attribute the conception of Jesus to the Holy Spirit (Matt. 1:18, 20; Luke 1:35). But the Spirit's role in Christology has long been neglected. It is being rediscovered in a number of recent Spirit Christologies. I will describe some of these below and attempt to contribute to this work of retrieval and renewal. In this chapter I will begin with a sketch of the way that the four Gospel writers connect the identity and saving mission of Jesus with the work of the Holy Spirit. Then I will describe some recent approaches to Spirit Christology before outlining my own approach.

MARK: JESUS AS ONE ON WHOM THE SPIRIT DESCENDS LIKE A DOVE

Mark's portrait of Jesus begins with Jesus as an adult being baptized in the Jordan by John the Baptist. Even before Jesus appears on the scene, his saving mission is described in terms of the Spirit. John the Baptist declares of this coming one: "he will baptize you with the Holy Spirit" (1:8). This can only mean that he will be the bearer of the promised eschatological Spirit (Isa. 44:3; Ezek. 39:29; Joel 2:28). As Lyle Dabney points out, Mark and the other evangelists thus define the salvation that Jesus brings in terms of the Spirit. This baptism with the Spirit will come through the ministry of Jesus, which culminates in his death and resurrection. Mark will make it abundantly clear that there is no understanding Jesus or the baptism of the Spirit he brings without the cross. By announcing Jesus as the one who brings this baptism of the Spirit, Mark and the other evangelists "sum up all the ministry of Jesus as a mediation of the Spirit."[2]

The baptism of Jesus marks the arrival of a wonderful new era. Morna Hooker says that John's baptism "marks the eleventh hour," while Jesus' baptism with the Holy Spirit "is a sign of the arrival of the eschatological era."[3] When Jesus is baptized, three motifs make it clear that this is a unique event of divine revelation. First, the heavens are "torn apart," symbolizing the new era of communication between heaven and earth (Isa. 64:1; Ezek. 1:1). Second, the Spirit descends in a "dovelike" way on Jesus, possibly referring to the hovering of the wind of God over the waters of creation.[4] Third, the voice from heaven declares "You are my Son, the Beloved; with you I am well pleased" (Mark 1:10-11).

There are echoes in these words of Psalm 2:7, where God declares at the enthronement of the king: "You are my son; today I have begotten you." There are also echoes of Isaiah 42:1-2: "Here is my servant, whom I uphold, my chosen in whom my soul delights; I have put my spirit upon him; he will bring forth justice to the nations."[5]

Clearly, the anointing with the Spirit is a key event for Mark, an event in which Jesus' messianic identity as God's beloved Son is established. In the tradition of Israel, the Spirit had been conferred by anointing (1 Sam. 10:1; Isa. 61:1), and Jesus is now understood as the anointed one. The Hebrew word *mashiach*, "messiah," and the Greek word *christos*, "Christ," both mean "the anointed one."[6] Jesus is anointed by the Spirit as beloved Son of God. As Michael Trainor says, in the Markan baptismal event, the Spirit both discloses Jesus' true identity and authorizes his ministry.[7]

In the light of the later debate over Jesus' identity as eternal Son of God, it is natural for contemporary readers to ask whether Mark thought of Jesus as becoming the Son *only* at his baptism. Was Mark thinking of Jesus as being adopted at his baptism? This does not seem to be a question that Mark addressed. Eduard Schweizer is surely right to insist that Mark is not concerned with the issue of whether Jesus is to be thought of as an eternal or as an adopted son, but with presenting the baptism of Jesus as a *divine epiphany*. This epiphany reveals the dimension in which everything told about Jesus must be viewed. Jesus is revealed as the conclusive act of God that is to bring salvation to the world.[8]

Immediately after the baptism, the Spirit "drives" Jesus out into the wilderness, where he is tempted by Satan. This picture of the Spirit-driven

Son of God doing battle with Satan in the wilderness sets the pattern for Jesus' liberating ministry. He will have extraordinary authority over evil spirits (Mark 1:27). He will be the stronger one, who confronts the prince of demons and plunders his house (3:22-27). Jesus returns from the wilderness to announce the good news of the reign of God and to embody this reign of God in his parables, his liberating exorcisms, his healing ministry, his practice of an open table, and the formation of a community of disciples. He comes into conflict with the authorities and is accused of driving out demons through Beelzebul (3:22). In this context, we are told that sinners can be forgiven, but not one who "blasphemes against the Holy Spirit" (3:29). Presumably this refers to the willful refusal of the Holy Spirit, who is present and manifest in the ministry of Jesus. Joel Marcus comments: "In the Markan context, blasphemy against the Spirit means the sort of total malignant opposition to Jesus that twists all the evidence of his life-giving power into evidence that he is demonically possessed."[9]

Jesus promises his community that they will be sustained by the Holy Spirit in the time of trial and that the Holy Spirit will speak through them (13:11). As Jesus was sustained by the Spirit in his temptation and trials, so the community of Jesus will be empowered by the same Spirit in times of persecution and struggle. Mark points in an uncompromising way to the death of Jesus. Jesus' identity, already established in the outpouring of the Spirit at the beginning of the Gospel, is not fully revealed until his death on a cross (15:39). Here God is revealed in the midst of a suffering world, bringing the promise of marvelous life: "He has been raised; he is not here. Look, there is the place they laid him. But go, tell his disciples and Peter that he is going ahead of them into Galilee; there you will see him just as he told you" (16:6-7). The baptism of the Spirit promised at the beginning of the Gospel is experienced as the risen one goes ahead of his disciples, bringing healing and hope in the midst of the everyday sufferings, struggles, and challenges of discipleship.

MATTHEW:
JESUS AS CONCEIVED FROM THE HOLY SPIRIT

If, as many biblical scholars think, Matthew builds on Mark, then it is a matter of interest to see where Matthew differs from Mark on the Holy Spirit. In fact, Matthew takes over Mark's theology of the Spirit and builds on it in a few significant places. One of the most important of these is in Matthew's infancy narrative. Here he makes it clear that Jesus' profound connection with the Spirit can be traced back to his conception and birth. He tells us that Mary "was found to be with child from the Holy Spirit" (Matt. 1:18). Joseph is told by the angel: "Do not be afraid to take Mary as your wife, for the child conceived in her is from the Holy Spirit" (1:20).

In Matthew's baptismal scene, John the Baptist announces Jesus as one who will baptize "with the Holy Spirit and fire" (3:11). What does "with fire" mean? And which is more original, Mark's "with the Holy Spirit" or Matthew's and Luke's "with the Holy Spirit and fire"? These questions have been much debated. A number of commentators think that Matthew understands "with fire" as referring to judgment.[10] James D. G. Dunn argues that the linkage of Spirit and fire may well go back to John the Baptist himself. He thinks it may have been John who connected the hope of the outpouring of the eschatological Spirit with the Spirit-anointed Messiah. And it may have been John who, on the basis of his own baptismal rite, described the Messiah's gift of the Spirit as a baptism in Spirit and fire. Dunn thinks that this would have had elements of both warning and promise—warning of judgment to the stiff-necked and promise and grace to the penitent.[11]

Matthew has the Spirit of God not only descend on Jesus "like a dove" but also "alight" on him at his baptism (3:16). Jesus is "led" into the desert by the Spirit (4:1) rather than being driven there as he is in Mark. He gives his disciples authority over unclean spirits (10:1) and promises them that "the Spirit of your Father will speak through you" (10:20). In chapter 12, Jesus is celebrated as the Spirit-endowed servant spoken about in Isaiah, "who will not break a bruised reed or quench a smoldering wick" (Matt. 12:15-21). Jesus casts out demons "by the Spirit of God" (12:28) and proclaims that "whoever speaks against the Holy Spirit will not be forgiven" (12:31-32). Finally, in a text that presumably reflects the baptismal practice of Matthew's community and will later be of central importance in the emergence of the doctrine of the Spirit's divinity, the risen Christ commands the disciples to baptize "in the name of the Father and of the Son and of the Holy Spirit" (28:19).

LUKE-ACTS:
JESUS AS ANOINTED WITH THE HOLY SPIRIT

Luke is unique among the Gospel writers in that he offers us two volumes, the Gospel and the Acts of the Apostles. His interest in the Spirit is apparent even to a casual reader of the Gospel, and in Acts the Spirit is presented as at the center of the story of the emerging church. Joseph A. Fitzmyer, S.J., points out that, while Mark has six references to the Spirit, Matthew twelve, and John about fifteen, Luke has seventeen or eighteen references in his Gospel and fifty-seven in Acts.[12]

Luke sees Jesus as one who is anointed with the Holy Spirit. In Peter's speech in the house of Cornelius, we find a succinct version of the Lukan story of Jesus:

That message spread throughout Judea, beginning in Galilee after the baptism that John had announced: *how God anointed Jesus of*

Nazareth with the Holy Spirit and with power; how he went about doing good and healing all who were oppressed by the devil, for God was with him. We are witnesses to all he did both in Judea and in Jerusalem. They put him to death by hanging him on a tree, but God raised him on the third day and allowed him to appear, not to all the people, but to us who were chosen by God as witnesses, and who ate and drank with him after he rose from the dead. (Acts 10:37-41)

The anointing of Jesus with the Holy Spirit and with power leads him to the praxis of "doing good and healing." His fidelity to the Spirit leads ultimately to his death and resurrection.

Fitzmyer points out that Luke introduces the Spirit at the beginning of key stages of the narrative of Luke-Acts.[13] Thus, the Spirit appears seven times in the infancy narrative, six times at the beginning of Jesus' ministry, four times in chapters 10-12 near the beginning of the journey to Jerusalem, and very often in the first sixteen chapters of Acts. There is no reference to the Spirit in the last part of the Gospel and relatively few references in the later chapters of Acts. Luke makes it clear that each stage in the story of salvation is initiated under the influence of the Holy Spirit.

In the infancy narrative the creative presence of the Spirit is found everywhere. All the faithful representatives of Israel gathered in the infancy story are Spirit-led: John the Baptist is presented as "filled with the Holy Spirit" from his mother's womb (Luke 1:15) and as one who will be a "prophet of the Most High" (1:76); Elizabeth (1:41) and Zechariah (1:67) are "filled with the Holy Spirit"; Simeon is described as one on whom the Holy Spirit "rests" (2:25), as one who has a revelation from the Holy Spirit (2:26), and as one guided by the Spirit (2:27); Anna is described as a prophet who never left the temple, worshiping there with fasting and prayer night and day (2:36-37). In the midst of all this abundance of the Spirit, we are told of the Holy Spirit coming upon Mary. Like the cloud of God's presence in Exodus (Exod. 40:34-38), and like the overshadowing cloud of the transfiguration (Luke 9:34), the Holy Spirit, as God's creative presence, comes upon Mary and overshadows her, so that her child will be holy and will be called "Son of God" (1:35).

Jesus' ministry begins with a further outpouring of the Spirit. John the Baptist announces the coming of one who will baptize not with water but with "the Holy Spirit and with fire" (3:16). In the Lukan context, this points toward the Spirit and the fire of Pentecost.[14] In Luke's version, it is while Jesus is in prayer *after* the baptism that he experiences the descent of the Spirit and the words from heaven, "You are my Son, the Beloved; with you I am well pleased" (3:21-22). Luke insists that the Spirit descends *in bodily form* like a dove—apparently to stress the reality of this extraordinary experience of the Spirit. Even though Jesus' identity before God is already established by the infancy narrative, Luke maintains the story of the baptism and shows how the ministry of Jesus begins under the influence of the Spirit.

In contrast to Mark, who tells of Jesus being "driven" by the Spirit into the wilderness, Luke writes: "Jesus, *full of the Holy Spirit*, returned from the Jordan and *was led by the Spirit* in the wilderness, where for forty days he was tempted by the devil" (4:1-2). After the temptation, Luke continues the story: "Jesus, *filled with the power of the Spirit*, returned to Galilee" and "began to teach in their synagogues and was praised by everyone" (4:14-15). Luke offers his readers a unique insight into the meaning of Jesus' anointing with the Spirit in the programmatic statement that Jesus makes in the synagogue at Nazareth. He reads from the scroll of the prophet Isaiah:

> The Spirit of the Lord is upon me,
> because he has anointed me
> to bring good news to the poor.
> He has sent me to proclaim release to the captives
> and recovery of sight to the blind,
> to let the oppressed go free,
> to proclaim the year of the Lord's favor. (Luke 4:18-19)

At the end of the reading, Jesus tells his hearers: "Today this scripture has been fulfilled in your hearing" (4:22). The meaning of Jesus' Spirit-anointing is specified in terms of human liberation—as good news for the poor and as freedom for the oppressed (see Isa. 61:1-2; 58:6). The rest of Luke's Gospel tells the story of the Spirit-anointed Jesus as he announces God's priority for the poor and powerless, brings healing to those who are ill and bent over with life's burdens, liberates those who are in bondage to evil, invites outcasts and public sinners to an open table that celebrates the coming reign of God, and celebrates the unthinkable generosity of God in parables such as the Good Samaritan (10:30-37), the Great Supper (14:16-24), the Lost Sheep (15:4-7), the Lost Coin (15:8-10), and the Prodigal Son (15:11-32).

Further direct references to the Holy Spirit occur only in 10:21 ("Jesus rejoiced in the Holy Spirit"), in 11:13 ("how much more will the heavenly Father give the Holy Spirit to those who ask"), in 12:10 ("whoever blasphemes against the Holy Spirit will not be forgiven"), and in 12:12 ("the Holy Spirit will teach you at that very hour what you ought to say"). The Gospel culminates in Jesus' life poured out to the point of death, his resurrection, and the consequent outpouring of the Spirit at Pentecost. At the end of the Gospel, the risen Christ tells the disciples: "I am sending upon you what my Father promised; so stay here in the city until you have been clothed with power from on high" (24:49).

In his second volume, Luke presents the Holy Spirit as the "Spirit of

Jesus" (Acts 16:7), continuing the pattern of Jesus in the church. His account of Pentecost (Acts 2:1-42) creates a narrative connection between the Spirit's work in Jesus and the Spirit's work in believers. He speaks of the Spirit as "the Father's promise" not only at the end of the Gospel (Luke 24:49) but also at the beginning of Acts (1:4). This divine promise involves baptism with the Holy Spirit (Acts 1:5). This promise is kept in the wind and fire of Pentecost. As Peter's speech makes clear (Acts 2:17), this event is the fulfillment of the prophecy of Joel: "I will pour out my Spirit upon all flesh; your sons and daughters shall prophesy" (Joel 2:28).[15] In Luke's view, the Holy Spirit poured out at Pentecost is the same Spirit who was promised by the prophets, who overshadowed Mary, and who anointed Jesus and led him in his ministry to his death and resurrection.[16] In Peter's Pentecost sermon we are told that now the risen Christ, "having received from the Father the promise of the Holy Spirit," has "poured out this that you may both see and hear" (Acts 2:33).

The Spirit poured out at Pentecost initiates something new in salvation history. God is now present with God's people in a new way—precisely as the Holy Spirit in the life of the Christian community. Luke sees this Spirit as behind every aspect of the emergence and development of the church. In Acts we find five distinct accounts of the outpouring of the Spirit on the believers (2:1-4; 4:31; 8:15-17; 10:44; 19:6). These mark the geographic progress of the Word of God.[17] The missionaries are described as "filled with the Spirit" (4:8; 5:32; 6:3; 7:55; 11:24; 13:9).

Luke Timothy Johnson points out that in Acts we find the Spirit actively intervening in the story, speaking, acting, empowering, enabling, and guiding the community (Acts 8:29, 39; 10:19; 11:15; 13:2; 15:28; 16:6; 20:22; 21:4, 11).[18] The work of the Spirit is revealed not simply in "speaking in tongues and prophesying" (2:4; 10:44-46; 13:2; 19:5-6; 21:9), not simply in the missionaries' proclamation and wonder-working, but above all in their ability to follow Christ in suffering (5:41; 7:59; 9:16; 12:4; 14:22; 16:23; 20:19, 22-24, 35; 21:11-14). Johnson says, "by establishing a narrative role for the Holy Spirit, Luke has taken a significant step towards the eventual theological recognition of the Holy Spirit as a 'person.'"[19]

JOHN:
JESUS AS THE ONE ON WHOM THE SPIRIT RESTS

In John's Gospel, Jesus is the Word made flesh (1:14) and the Son sent by God into the world (3:17). He is the Wisdom of God in our midst, the one who proclaims: "I am the bread of life. Whoever comes to me will never be hungry, and whoever believes in me will never be thirsty (6:35). With such a "high" Christology, it is sometimes assumed that John has little to contribute to a Spirit Christology, but I do not think this is the case. John's view of Jesus as eternal Word and divine Son is accompanied by a conviction that Jesus is the one in whom the Spirit "abides" or "remains" (*menein* in Greek).

At the beginning of the Gospel, immediately after the opening hymn celebrating Jesus as the Word made flesh, John the Baptist testifies to Jesus as the Lamb of God. The Baptist explains how he knows the true identity of Jesus: "I saw the Spirit descending like a dove and it *remained* on him" (1:32). He had already been told by God: "He on whom you see the Spirit descend and *remain* is the one who baptizes with the Holy Spirit" (1:33). Having seen this descending and resting of the Spirit on Jesus, John the Baptist knows that Jesus is the one who will baptize with the Spirit and can testify that he is the Son of God (1:34).

The word *menein* is a key word in the Gospel of John. It describes not only the presence of the Spirit with Jesus but also the mutual indwelling between Jesus and his Father and the disciples' participation in this shared life (6:56; 8:31; 14:2-24; 15:4-11). It can be translated as "to remain with," "to abide with," or "to rest with." Because Jesus is the one in whom the Spirit abides, Jesus will not only baptize with the Spirit (1:33), he will give the Spirit without measure (3:34). This giving of the Spirit without measure will take place only through the glorification of Jesus in his death and resurrection (7:38-39; 20:22).

The Spirit that Jesus brings is a renewing and regenerating Spirit. In his exchange with Nicodemus, Jesus tells him that no one can enter the kingdom of God without being born anew. When Nicodemus queries this, pointing out that we cannot return to the womb, Jesus replies:

> Very truly, I tell you, no one can enter the kingdom of God without being born of water and Spirit. What is born of the flesh is flesh, and what is born of the Spirit is spirit. Do not be astonished that I said to you, "You must be born from above." The wind blows where it chooses, and you hear the sound of it, but you do not know where it comes from or where it goes. So it is with everyone who is born of the Spirit. (3:5-8)

What is required is not a return to the womb of one's human mother, but a new birth of the Spirit. We can become part of the reign of God only by being born of the wild and uncontrollable Spirit. Only the mysterious, motherly Spirit can bring us to birth in the new life of God. Jesus invites Nicodemus further into the mystery, pointing out that the Son of Man must be lifted up so that whoever believes in him may have this new and eternal life (3:15).

In his encounter with the woman at Jacob's well, Jesus declares: "Everyone who drinks of this water will be thirsty again, but those who drink of the water that I will give them will never be thirsty. The water that I will give will become in them a spring of water gushing up to eternal life" (4:13-14). Jesus tells the woman that God is spirit, and those who worship God must worship in spirit and in truth (4:24). Later, on the last day of the festival of Tabernacles, Jesus cries out, "Let anyone who is thirsty come to me, and let the one who believes in me drink. As the scripture has said, 'Out of the believer's heart shall flow rivers of living water.'" The author of the Gospel explains that this living water is the Spirit: "He said this about the Spirit, which believers in him were to receive; for as yet there was no Spirit, because Jesus was not yet glorified" (7:37-39).

In the Last Supper discourse of the Gospel, there are five passages where we hear of the sending of the *Paraclete* (14:15-17, 26; 15:26-27; 16:7-11, 12-14). This word means "one called alongside of" and can be translated as "advocate," "helper," "witness," or "comforter." The Paraclete promised by Jesus is called *"another* Paraclete," presumably because Jesus himself is the first Paraclete (14:16). In First John, the exalted Christ is explicitly named as Paraclete (2:1-2). The promised Paraclete's role will be to dwell in the disciples, to guide them, to teach them, and to prove the world wrong. The Paraclete is called the Spirit of Truth (John 14:17; 15:26; 16:13) and is explicitly identified as the Holy Spirit (14:26).[20] In words that would later become crucial in the development of the theology of the Spirit, the Paraclete is described as the "Spirit of truth who *proceeds (ekporeue-tai)* from the Father" (15:26). The disciples will be given the Spirit of Truth as an inner teacher, who will guide them into all truth. This is not to be thought of as a new or different truth, but as the truth that the Father has given to Jesus: "He will glorify me because he will take what is mine and declare it to you" (16:14).

The Spirit is given only in and through the glorification of Jesus (7:39), and this glorification occurs in the lifting up of Jesus' death and resurrection (3:14). As Jesus dies, we read the words: "He bowed his head and gave up his spirit" (19:30). This is interpreted in different ways. Francis Moloney is among the commentators who argue that its meaning is not simply that Jesus is giving up his spirit in death, but that he is handing over the Spirit to his followers.[21] A few verses later we read: "One of the soldiers pierced his side with a spear, and at once blood and water came out" (19:34). Again the interpretation of this text is disputed, but it is worth remembering that the narrator has earlier identified living water welling up from within as the Spirit (7:39).

Finally, the risen and glorified Christ formally and unambiguously gives the Spirit to his disciples with the words:

> "Peace be with you. As the Father has sent me, so I send you." When he had said this, he breathed on them and said to them, "Receive the Holy Spirit. If you forgive the sins of any, they are forgiven them; if you retain the sins of any, they are retained." (20:21-23)

The gift of the Holy Spirit is symbolized as the Breath of the risen Christ. The Spirit, given in the glorification of Jesus through his death and resurrection, constitutes the community of disciples as a church that brings forgiveness of sins. The Spirit rests on Jesus, and the gift of the Spirit, the living water that Jesus brings, is poured out upon the world "without measure" through the lifting up of Jesus in his death and resurrection. This is the baptism with the Holy Spirit that Jesus brings, the saving outpouring of the Spirit announced by John the Baptist in the opening chapter of the Gospel (1:33).

CONTEMPORARY SPIRIT CHRISTOLOGIES

As this brief survey makes clear, in Mark, the Spirit descends on Jesus at his baptism, and in this same event he is declared to be God's "beloved Son." In Matthew and Luke, Jesus is conceived of the Holy Spirit and thus is called "Son of God" (Luke 1:39). In John, Jesus is the eternal Word and Son of God and, at the same time, the one in whom the Spirit abides and the one who will give the Spirit without measure. In each of the Gospels, the Spirit is profoundly connected to Jesus' identity as Son of God. Clearly, the Holy Spirit is central to the Christologies of the four Gospels. But many of the dominant Christologies, particularly in the West, have been Son-of-God and Word-of-God Christologies that have largely ignored the role of the Spirit.

In recent years, I have been among those who have argued for the importance of recovering a Wisdom Christology as one form of contemporary Christology.[22] Feminist theologians have pointed out that understanding Jesus as *Sophia* contributes to a life-giving and inclusive Christology.[23] In my view, it also provides an important foundation for an ecological Christology. But more and more it has become clear to me that a fully ecological Christology must *also* be a Spirit Christology. There are other important reasons for retrieving Spirit Christology. One of them is that some form of Spirit Christology seems required by a responsible interpretation of the gospel traditions concerning Jesus. Another is that for many people today a plausible Christology will best begin *from below* as a Spirit Christology. Finally, if we are to pursue the much-needed retrieval of the Spirit in the theology and praxis of the Western church, this can only be based on a proper assessment of the role of the Spirit in Christology. A renewed Spirit Christology is clearly required, but as this project is beginning in contemporary theology, a fundamental question has emerged. Is a Spirit Christology to be conceived of as an *alternative* to a Wisdom/Word/Son-of-God Christology? Or do we need a Spirit Christology that is also a Son-of-God or Wisdom Christology?

The question was not put this way in the pre-Nicaean church, where a number of Spirit Christologies emerged. Some early Jewish Christian groups known as Ebionites held adoptionist views. They saw Jesus as called to sonship through the Holy Spirit and as the last of the bearers of the Spirit or *Shekhina* (the presence of God). Some Jewish Christians held an angel Christology, in which Jesus was identified as the angelic being coming at the end of the age. At times the Word and the Spirit were identified with angels such as Michael or Gabriel.[24] In the Second Letter to the Corinthians, wrongly attributed to Clement, a second-century author sees the Spirit as the preexistence of Christ.[25] In the *Shepherd* of Hermas, it is said that God makes the preexistent Spirit who creates all things and then this Spirit dwells in the flesh in Christ.[26] In this period, there is often no clear distinction between Christ and the Spirit; nor is it always clear when the word *spirit* is referring to the human spirit, to God in an undifferentiated way, or to one of the trinitarian persons.

A stream of recent Spirit Christologies has raised questions about the traditional trinitarian understanding of the Spirit. In his exegetical work, the New Testament scholar James D. G. Dunn sets the scene for some of these questions. He offers the basis for a Spirit Christology with his argument that Jesus was conscious of the Spirit as powerfully at work in his own life and ministry.[27] But in his interpretation of Pauline theology, Dunn suggests an identification of the risen Christ and the Holy Spirit.[28] Other Pauline scholars acknowledge the very close relationship between the Spirit and the risen Christ in Paul, but challenge the idea that they are to be simply identified.[29]

Geoffrey Lampe takes a radical stance with his Christology of the Spirit's inspiration, indwelling, and possession in Jesus. He dispenses with the distinction of persons in the Trinity and demythologizes the christological traditions of preexistence, incarnation, and resurrection.[30] James Mackey also demythologizes New Testament and conciliar statements about Jesus and rejects preexistence and inner-trinitarian speculation. He develops a binary theology of Jesus and the Father: the Spirit is understood as the one divine being that is in the Father and that is also the presence of God in Jesus and the church.[31]

In a different approach, the systematic theologian Piet Schoonenberg has argued for a Spirit Christology that can take its place alongside a Logos Christology. He insists that Jesus is a human person. He sees him as anointed with the Spirit and radically Spirit-filled. But he finds both Word and Spirit at work in Jesus: Word and Spirit make Jesus Son. Schoonenberg holds that the Word and the Spirit become persons only in the event of the incarnation and Pentecost.[32] He does not deny the preexistence of Word and Spirit or the fact that they come forth from the Father in eternity. But they became fully personal, in relation to each other and in relation to creation, only in the Christ event. While the Word becomes personal as the Son, the Spirit becomes personal in another way—in a way that involves indwelling in the church and its members. In the Christ event, the Father too becomes a person in a new way, in relation to creation, and in relation to the Son and the Spirit. Only in the Christ event can God be described as a communion of persons.

Rosemary Radford Ruether proposes a feminist Spirit Christology. She seeks a liberating Christology that gets beyond the identification of the maleness of Jesus with a male Logos. She argues for a Spirit Christology that begins from the message and the praxis of the Jesus of the Synoptic Gospels. She sees Jesus in iconoclastic and prophetic terms. She writes: "Jesus as the Christ, the representative of liberated humanity and the liberating Word of God, manifests the *kenosis* of patriarchy, the announcement of the new humanity through a lifestyle that discards hierarchical caste privilege and speaks on behalf of the lowly."[33] She supports a Spirit Christology that affirms that Christ continues to be disclosed today through Spirit-led persons of both sexes. She affirms that, in the language of early Christian prophetic movements, "we can encounter Christ *in the form of our sister.*"[34]

Jürgen Moltmann's *The Way of Jesus Christ* is developed as a Spirit Christology that is also an ecological theology. He sees the history of Jesus as the Christ as beginning with the Spirit. The story of Jesus is a Spirit-history: "the coming, the presence, and the efficacy of the Spirit in, through and with Jesus, is the hidden beginning of the new creation of the world."[35] He proposes a messianic Christology, a Christology from below, from the perspective of Israel. Moltmann understands Spirit Christology as interconnected with Wisdom and Son-of-God Christologies, not as opposed to them. The Gospels present Jesus as in relation to both the Spirit and to the one he called *Abba*. Because of this, Moltmann sees Jesus' history as at heart a "trinitarian history of God." He believes that Spirit Christology can point to a unique action of the Spirit in Jesus, while at the same time being open to the presence of the Creator Spirit beyond Jesus. Moltmann speaks of a *kenōsis* of the Spirit in the life of Jesus and sees the suffering of Jesus on the cross as also the suffering of the Spirit. In the event of the cross, the Father and the Son suffer such a separation that the direct relationship between them is broken, while the Spirit remains the bond that unites them.[36]

Roger Haight, in his *Jesus Symbol of God*, sets out to articulate the meaning of Jesus plausibly in a pluralist and postmodern context, while remaining faithful to the broad Christian tradition. He consistently works from below and argues that biblical phrases such as "Word of God," "Wisdom of God," and "Spirit of God" are to be understood as symbolic expressions that arise from the experience of God at work in Jesus and in the economy of salvation. They are not to be understood as providing information about divine hypostases or persons. At the end of his reconstruction, he concludes that both a revised Logos Christology and a renewed Spirit Christology can be meaningful in today's context. In his articulation of a Spirit Christology, he opts for one that would be inclusive and open to other christological approaches. But he sees the symbol of the Spirit of God as referring to God's very self. This appears to set Haight apart from those, like Moltmann, who see the Spirit as referring to one of the trinitarian persons. Haight's form of Spirit Christology makes the ontological claim that from the beginning nothing less than God was at work in Jesus, so that "Jesus is the reality of God."[37]

David Coffey, building on the work of M. J. Scheeben, Heribert Mühlen, and particularly Karl Rahner, has developed a Spirit Christology in a series of articles and books that culminate in his recent book *Deus Trinitas*. In his writings he argues for a "bestowal" model, a Christology from below, in which Jesus is anointed to divine sonship with the Holy Spirit. He argues that the divinity of Christ is realized in his humanity and not alongside it.[38] Coffey proposes that his ascending bestowal model of Spirit Christology is a necessary correlate of a descending Son-of-God or Logos Christology. Coffey's bestowal model successfully articulates the inner relationship between Christology and the theology of grace. The same Spirit who anoints Jesus as divine Son of God in a unique way also unites believers in grace as sons and daughters of God. Coffey builds on the western idea that the Spirit can be understood as the mutual love of the Father and the Son. This "mutual love theory" means not only that the Father and the Son mutually bestow the Spirit upon each other but also that the Son's sending of the Spirit enables human beings and finally all of creation to participate in the communion of mutual love.[39]

Ralph Del Colle, in his *Christ and the Spirit*, offers a systematic overview of various Spirit Christologies, reflects at length on Coffey's work in relation to other theologies, and develops his own approach to Spirit Christology. He argues consistently for the nonidentity and the inseparability of the trinitarian persons. The event of the incarnation involves both the Spirit and the eternal Word/Son, clearly distinct from each other but profoundly interrelated. He holds, with Coffey, that Jesus is anointed as divine Son by the Spirit. He sees this Christology as grounded not only in the accounts of Jesus in the Synoptic Gospels but also at the primary level of Christian experience, in that it is only in the Spirit that Christians confess Jesus doxologically as Son of God and Word of God.[40]

My own position is in broad agreement with those who find it necessary to speak not only of the presence and action of the Spirit in Jesus, but also of the divine identity of Jesus as the Word of God, Son of God or Wisdom of God. In developing my own proposal for a Spirit Christology below, it will be clear where I differ from some of the views described above and where I gratefully adopt them. In the course of outlining this proposal, I will bring into the discussion ideas on Spirit Christology from three further theologians—Karl Rahner, Yves Congar, and Walter Kasper.

JESUS AS THE SPIRIT-ANOINTED WISDOM OF GOD

Since my own preferred way of speaking of Jesus' divine identity is as the Wisdom of God, I will propose a trinitarian theology of Jesus as the

Spirit-anointed Wisdom of God, a Spirit Christology that is at the same time a Wisdom Christology. I will outline this position briefly in a series of steps.

1. A Spirit Christology proceeds from below. Spirit Christologies begin from below, in the sense that they begin with Jesus of Nazareth, who is anointed by the Spirit. Roger Haight is right to argue that a Christology that hopes to be plausible in a postmodern context will proceed from below. He proposes three senses in which a Spirit Christology might be characterized as from below. First, it would begin with a historical consideration of Jesus and would remain faithful to this history in subsequent interpretation. Second, it would trace the historical genesis of the various interpretations of Jesus. Third, it would appeal to the Christian experience of grace as an analogy for understanding what is going on in Christology.[41] I would add another. A Spirit Christology ought to be from below in the sense that Jesus would be understood not only in relation to human beings and their experience of grace but also as a product of evolution. Jesus, like us, is to be seen as part of the evolutionary emergence of life on Earth and in relation to the life-bearing universe.

A Christology cannot be *only* from below. Christology is always a claim that God is at work in Jesus Christ. As such, Christology is not only from below but also in some way from above. It must be able to affirm that what is experienced below is truly from God. Christology is situated within the context of Christian faith, tradition, community, and worship. In a suffering world it seeks to articulate a theology of liberation and healing that comes from God. It is always a claim about the divine meaning of Jesus. In this sense, Christology is also always from above; but it is my contention that it best begins from below, in what is experienced of Jesus, his preaching, praxis, and person. It begins from Jesus as one who is radically open to God's Spirit.

2. The same Spirit who is the Life-Giver, empowering the emergence of the universe, and the Grace-Bearer, enfolding human beings throughout history, now anoints and rests upon Jesus of Nazareth. In chapter 3, I outlined the story of the Spirit as the Breath of Life empowering the emergence of our universe through the Big Bang, in the evolution of the first galaxies, the formation of our solar system, and the 4.8-billion-year history of life on Earth—"By the word of the Lord the heavens were made, and all their host by the breath of his mouth" (Ps. 33:6). In chapter 4, I traced the story of the universal presence of the Spirit to human beings in gracious self-offering love. For Christians this story is a story that is directed toward Jesus and goes on in him. The life-giving, grace-bearing Spirit is now poured out upon Jesus of Nazareth, so that he might be the Wisdom of God in the midst of creation, the one who brings healing and liberation.

As Walter Kasper points out, the Spirit of God acts in the whole of human history: "The Spirit of God is not only at work in nature, however, but also in civilization, in agriculture, architecture, jurisprudence and politics; all human wisdom is a gift of God's Spirit."[42] In a particular way, Christians see this Spirit of God at work in the sacred history of the people of Israel. This same Spirit, who had once led the judges, Moses, and David, would come to rest on the promised Messiah: "The Spirit of the Lord shall rest upon him" (Isa. 11:2). God's Spirit would descend upon the chosen servant of God: "Here is my servant, whom I will uphold, my chosen, in whom my soul delights; I have put my spirit upon him; he will bring forth justice to the nations" (Isa. 42:1). The Christian community sees Jesus as the Spirit-anointed one, the Christ, in whom these promises are fulfilled (Mark 1:10-11).

The Spirit of God, present in every aspect of the emergence of our universe fourteen billion years ago, with every atom, and every distant galaxy, with every living creature from bacteria to dinosaurs, present by grace to all human beings and leading the people of Israel throughout their sacred history, now works creatively in Jesus, sanctifying and transforming his humanity, enabling him to be the Wisdom of God in our midst.

3. The Christ event is brought about "by the power of the Holy Spirit."
The Christian sources testify that Jesus' unique relationship with God is the work of the Holy Spirit. So, in the Gospel of Luke, the angel says to Mary: "The Holy Spirit will come upon you, and the power of the Most High will overshadow you; therefore the child to be born will be called holy; he will be called Son of God" (1:35). Matthew twice testifies that Mary the mother of Jesus "was found to be with child from the Holy Spirit" (1:18, 20). The creeds that emerged in the early church point to the central role of the Spirit in the incarnation. In the Apostles' Creed, the Christian community says of Jesus: "He was conceived by the power of the Holy Spirit and born of the Virgin Mary." The Nicene-Constantinopolitan Creed states: "By the power of the Holy Spirit he became incarnate."

The work of the Holy Spirit in the Christ event was not developed in the scholastic theology of the medieval period. It tended to attribute the grace of union (*gratia unionis*) between the divine and human in Christ simply to the Logos.[43] This has been corrected in some more recent theologies. Walter Kasper, for example, sees the Holy Spirit as the freedom and excess of divine love within the trinitarian life of God, who makes all of God's action toward creatures possible, and who is the creative and sanctifying principle at work in the incarnation. The Spirit sanctifies the humanity of Jesus, making it possible for him to be God's loving self-communication in person. Kasper sees this as the meaning of Jesus' anointing with the Spirit (Luke 4:21; Acts 10:38). He sees Jesus as the one in whom the Spirit finds acceptance in a unique and undistorted way. This means that Jesus' Spirit-transformed humanity can be the receptacle for God's self-communication in the Word. The Spirit sanctifies the humanity of Jesus "in such a way as to enable him, by free obedience and dedication, to be the incarnate response to God's self-communication."[44]

Kasper's view that the Holy Spirit brings about the Christ event echoes Ambrose, who, as I pointed out in chapter 3, sees the Holy Spirit as "the author of the Lord's incarnation."[45] I have already mentioned Rahner's technical but succinct summary: the Spirit of God brings about the saving event of the incarnation, and so the Spirit can be understood as the *efficient cause* of the Christ event; but the whole history of the Spirit's presence in grace is directed toward Jesus Christ, and in this sense Jesus Christ is the *final cause* of the Spirit.[46] In this kind of Spirit theology, Word and Spirit are understood as reciprocally related in the one economy of salvation.

4. There is a true history of the Spirit in the life, death, and exaltation of Jesus. Jesus is led by the Spirit in every aspect of his life and ministry. This means that he needs to invoke the Spirit in specific circumstances and that he is led by the Spirit in new ways as he confronts particular situations. There is a true history of the Spirit in the life of Jesus. This has not always been the way that theologians have understood the work of the Spirit in Jesus. Yves Congar points out that, for Thomas Aquinas, the work of the Spirit is accomplished in Jesus once for all at his conception. All that occurs after this is a manifestation to others of what had already happened. Congar seeks a more biblical and historical understanding. While maintaining that Jesus was the Son of God from his conception, Congar attempts to do justice to the successive stages in the history of the Spirit that occur in the life, death, and resurrection of Jesus

As the human Servant of God, Jesus is led by the Spirit in a series of events that are situated in time and that provide something new when they occur. They are "authentic qualitative moments in which God's communication of himself in Jesus Christ and in a very real sense also to Jesus Christ was accomplished."[47] Congar points to successive comings of the Spirit in the story of Jesus. These include his conception, baptism, temptation, proclamation of the reign of God in word and deed, death on the cross, resurrection, exaltation, and sending of the Spirit. The resurrection involves a new and ultimate stage in the union between the humanity of Jesus and the Spirit, so that from this profound union the risen Christ sends the Spirit upon his disciples.[48]

Congar takes seriously the New Testament texts that apply the words of Psalm 2:7—"You are my Son, today I have begotten you"—to a particular moment in the history of Jesus. These words are applied to Jesus not only at the annunciation (Luke 1:35) but also at his baptism in the Jordan (Mark 1:11; Matt. 3:17; Luke 3:22), and particularly at his resurrection (Acts 13:33; Heb. 1:5; 5:5). According to Congar, these are moments of the Spirit in which Jesus is not only proclaimed as Son but actually becomes the Son in a new way.[49] Above all, in the union between the humanity of Jesus and the Spirit in the resurrection, Jesus enters into a new stage of his existence. Jesus, who was Son of God in his life and death as Servant of God, becomes in his resurrection the firstborn of many Spirit-filled sons and daughters.

As Jesus is constituted Son of God from the beginning, but still has to grow into who he is through fidelity to the Spirit, so we too may be already God's adopted children (Gal. 4:6; Rom. 8:14-17), but still have to grow into who we are through fidelity to the Spirit. Congar insists that a more historical view of the work of the Spirit in the life of Jesus demands a more historical view of the work of the Spirit in the church. The concept of the Spirit as given to the church once for all at the beginning can all too easily lead to complacency. If the Spirit comes to us in history, then the Spirit needs always to be invoked anew.[50]

5. The Spirit transforms the negativity of the cross into an event of liberation. Jesus' fidelity to God and to the demands of love leads to his death. But the Spirit stays with Jesus in his death, enabling him to give his life in love and transforming a brutal and ugly death into life for the world. This is what theology calls the paschal mystery, the mystery of new life coming through the life, death, and resurrection of Jesus. Luke speaks of this paschal event as Jesus' exodus (9:31). It culminates in the outpouring of the Spirit at Pentecost. This is the baptism of the Spirit that Jesus had come to bring (Acts 1:5). In John's account, this baptism is accomplished when Jesus is lifted up. In his death he hands over the spirit (19:30), water flows from his side (19:34), and as the risen one he says to the disciples: "Receive the Holy Spirit" (20:22).

In an important theological reflection, Pope John Paul II sees the Holy Spirit as profoundly involved in the death of Jesus. On the journey from Gethsemane to Golgotha Jesus opens himself totally to the Spirit-Paraclete. This means that the Spirit who already fills the depths of Jesus' humanity, can now transform the humanity of Jesus into a perfect sacrifice in love. Hebrews 9:14, a text whose interpretation is disputed, speaks of Jesus as offering himself to God "through the eternal spirit." John Paul II sees the Spirit as radically with Jesus in the event of the cross, entering into human and cosmic suffering with a new outpouring of love. The Holy Spirit acts in Jesus' self-giving, transforming suffering into redemptive love. The Spirit of God is the fire that works in the depths of the mystery of the cross. Because the cross is also an act proper to Christ, John Paul II sees Christ in his passion as radically receiving the Spirit. It is this same Spirit that the risen Christ will give to the church and world. The Holy Spirit is revealed as "the Love that works in the paschal mystery, as the source of the salvific power of the cross of Christ, and as the gift of new and eternal life."[51]

The Holy Spirit is *with* Jesus in his suffering and death, transforming suffering into redemptive love and bringing life out of misery and death. This line of thought can be taken further. I believe it is important to insist that the cross itself cannot be thought of as directly willed by God. God does not plan or want the evil act of crucifixion. This was an arbitrary, ugly, and sinful act performed by a number of human beings against one who was innocent. In this way it was like many other murders and executions then and now. God does not will any such horrors. This is why Edward Schillebeeckx can say that "first of all, we have to say that we are not redeemed thanks to the death of Jesus but despite it." He insists that it is only in the overcoming of the evil, in its transformation by God that we can think of being saved through the execution of the innocent one.[52] The Spirit of God transforms the brutal and wicked act of crucifixion into an event that brings healing and liberation. God brings new life, freedom, and healing through the cross, because the destructive act of crucifying Jesus is transformed by the power of the life-giving Spirit into the vehicle of resurrection life.

Christians find here a basis for hope. There is a promise that the Spirit who was present with Jesus in his experience of utter abandonment will be radically with us in our moments of struggle and death (Mark 13:11). The Spirit groans with us in our struggle, upholds us as a faithful companion in our experiences of abandonment and ultimately transforms these experiences from within. We are given reason to believe that when, in our own experiences of grief and darkness, we find that something enables us to hang on seemingly against all odds, we may be able to recognize this as the presence of God's healing Spirit. When we find that there is a place where some kind of life begins to emerge, we may recognize this as the place of the transforming Spirit of God in our lives.

6. *There is an inner relationship between the anointing of Jesus by the Spirit and the Spirit's work in us by grace.* In the theology of grace outlined in the last chapter, human beings are understood as transformed by the gracious presence of the Holy Spirit, surrounding them at every moment, offering forgiveness, healing, and life. According to Rahner, human nature in its very essence is oriented toward absolute Mystery. We are truly human insofar as we give ourselves into this absolute Mystery. It is in openness to the ever-present grace of the Spirit of God that we are most human. What happens in Jesus can be understood as the instance where the Mystery of God is received by one human being in complete and radical openness. Because Jesus is a human being who is fully receptive to the Spirit, he is human in the fullest sense. Because he is totally open to the Spirit of God, he is one with God in such a way that we can say that he is the Wisdom of God, the Son of God.[53]

The same Spirit who transforms the humanity of Jesus transforms human beings by grace. As David Coffey points out, with a Spirit Christology it becomes clear that the same Holy Spirit is the agent of both incarnation and grace. What makes the case of the incarnation distinct, he says, is that the Holy Spirit is bestowed on the humanity of Jesus "in an act by which at the same time that humanity was created, sanctified and united in person to the divine Son."[54]

While Jesus is uniquely related to God, there is an inner relationship between what happens in Jesus and what happens in us through grace. Through the anointing of the Spirit, the humanity of Jesus is transformed and he is rightly called Son of God (Luke 1:35; Matt. 1:20). Through the outpouring of the same Spirit in grace, we are regenerated and transformed and rightly called adoptive children of God (Rom. 8:14-17). The sanctifying Spirit of God who transforms us by grace is the same Spirit who sanctifies and transforms the humanity of Jesus in the "grace of union." In Jesus, the anointing of the Spirit constitutes him as the Christ, the anointed one, the Son of God, and the Wisdom of God. In us, the grace of the Spirit makes us into the Body of Christ, adopted daughters and sons of God.

7. There is a twofold structure in Jesus' relationship with God. While the developed doctrine of the Trinity is not found in the New Testament, there is evidence of a twofold structure in Jesus' relationship with God. In the baptismal text in Mark, Jesus is anointed by the Spirit and a voice from heaven declares that he is God's Son (Mark 1:10-11). This suggests two closely connected but distinct divine relationships—with the Spirit and with the one who says to Jesus "You are my Son, the beloved." Jesus has a relationship with the Spirit that enables another relation to exist—his filial relationship with the one he called *Abba*. This is a consistent pattern in the New Testament.

In Paul, the experience of the Spirit and the experience of the risen Christ are very closely related, but it is not suggested that the Spirit is *who* Jesus is. As Joseph Fitzmyer says: "Though Paul comes to identify Christ with the power and wisdom of God, he never calls him explicitly 'the Spirit of God.'"[55] In the Gospels, Jesus is given a wide range of titles to express his identity, but never that of Spirit.

Jesus is overshadowed by the Spirit, led by the Spirit and finally gives the Spirit. The Spirit constitutes Jesus in his divine identity—as messianic Son of God. In the Spirit, Jesus addresses God as *Abba*. Ralph Del Colle comments: "Jesus anointed by the Spirit for mission also calls upon God as 'Abba.' Both of these elements appear in the oldest strata of the synoptic christologies." Del Colle insists that both relations are essential to Jesus' entire mission: from his baptism to Gethsemane, Jesus is *both* Spirit-led and faithful to the God who is Abba.[56]

On a broader level, the New Testament not only claims that God is with us in Jesus of Nazareth but also that the Spirit of God has now been poured out on the disciples. The claim is twofold—"In Christ, God was reconciling the world to himself" (2 Cor. 5:19) and "God's love has been poured into our hearts through the Holy Spirit that has been given to us" (Rom. 5:5). The religious experience of the first Christians was focused on the living memory of Jesus—his words and deeds, his life, death, and resurrection—but it occurred as an experience of the presence of the mysterious, life-giving Spirit. These two dimensions of the life of faith provide the experiential ground for what would come to be called the missions of the Word (associated with the incarnation) and the Spirit (associated with Pentecost), and for the development of the doctrine of the Trinity.

New Testament Christians saw God as really present to us tangibly and historically in the Christ event and as poured out in another, more mysterious way in the Spirit given at Pentecost. Postresurrectional Christians had a threefold relationship with God—with the risen Jesus, with the Spirit, and with the Abba/God who sent Jesus and the Spirit. James Dunn acknowledges this trinitarian structure of the experience of believers, while rightly seeing it as quite distinct from a later metaphysical theology of the Trinity.[57] While I agree with this, I would add, with the classical Christian tradition, that the development of a more explicit doctrine of the Trinity in the period after the New Testament can be understood not only as legitimate and appropriate, but as Spirit-led.[58]

CONCLUSION

The kind of Spirit Christology that I have been proposing is one in which Jesus is anointed by the Spirit and in this anointing is constituted as the Wisdom of God. I think that the application of Wisdom language (and Son-of-God language) to Jesus would have begun with the experience of first-century Christians—*from below*. The Sophia story, the story of Wisdom as God's companion in creation who now makes her home among us and invites us to her table, found in texts such as Proverbs 8-9, certainly tells of a visitation from above.[59] But it is a story that attempts to account for the ecstatic doxological experience of the first Christians—the experience that they had of Christ in the Spirit. This doxological experience found expression in hymns based on Wisdom, such as those that gave rise to texts such as John 1:1-18, Colossians 1:15-20, and Hebrews 1:1-3.

The Breath of God inspires Jesus in new and transforming ways in the successive stages of his life, ministry, death, and glorification. The anointing of Jesus with the Spirit at his baptism establishes Jesus in his identity and mission. The Spirit leads Jesus out into the desert and then inspires him to return to take up his vocation as prophet of the reign of God. Faithful to the Spirit, Jesus witnesses to the coming reign of God in his preaching, his healing, his open table, his priority for the poor and for sinners, and his formation of a community in which there is to be no lording it over one another. He lives a life of radical openness to the Spirit, an openness that reaches its climax in the unknowing and abandonment of the cross. The Spirit does not abandon Jesus, but remains with him in brutality, terror, pain, and finally death. What was a vicious and savagely evil act becomes in the transforming power of the Breath of God an event of liberation and life. Jesus gives his life in the Spirit only to be taken up into a glorification that involves a new stage of radical union with the Spirit. Filled with the eschatological Spirit he pours forth this same Spirit upon the community of disciples, constituting them as church.

SIX

Poured Out on the Church

The Holy Spirit who empowers the evolving universe, who in grace is present to all human beings as self-offering love, who anoints Jesus as the Wisdom of God, is now poured out on the community of disciples in the Pentecost experience, constituting them as the church of Jesus Christ. I will begin this chapter by pointing to some places where I think that the action of the Spirit can be discerned in the contemporary experience of being church in the world. Then I will build on insights from Congar to suggest that what is needed in the theology and praxis of church is a real reciprocity between Word and Spirit. This leads to a consideration of a second fundamental reciprocity, between local and universal church. This, in turn, will lead to a proposal for a third reciprocal relationship, between synodality and ordained ministry.

CHARISMATIC AND PROPHETIC MOVEMENTS
OF THE SPIRIT

A theologian of the Spirit might well be asked to point to what he or she considers to be examples of the Spirit's work. Talk of the Spirit must be grounded. Are there signs of the Spirit at work in the life of the church? Are there empirical examples of the Spirit's action? Are there visible movements of the Spirit? In an attempt to ground my own theology of the Spirit, I will offer a brief sketch of some movements in which I think the Spirit of God can be discerned. These involve not only the life of the church but also the "signs of the times" that are far wider than the church. I will point briefly to three examples of the Spirit at work in the life of the church and three further examples of the Spirit at work in the wider human community.

The Pentecostal movement is an obvious place to start. In its contemporary form it had its origin at the beginning of the twentieth century. Key events in its foundation were a revival that began at Charles Parham's

Bethel Bible School in Topeka, Kansas (1901), and the work of the Holiness preacher William J. Seymour at the Azusa Mission in Los Angeles. Pentecostal revival meetings were soon held throughout North America and in Asia, Latin America, Africa, and Europe. By the end of the twentieth century the Protestant Pentecostal movement involved more than four hundred million people, most of them in the developing world. The movement is centered on faith in Christ as Savior rather than directly on the Holy Spirit. A core conviction is that the gifts of the Spirit—healing, prophecy, and speaking in tongues—remain central for Christian life today. The movement is extremely diverse, involving more than fourteen thousand denominations.[1] It appears to respond to the need felt by many people for a more affective spirituality. In the shape of the charismatic movement it has had a major impact within the Episcopalian, Protestant, Roman Catholic, and Orthodox churches since the 1960s. The Roman Catholic charismatic movement, for example, seems to have begun with the formation of a charismatic prayer group at Duquesne University, Pittsburgh, in 1967. Charismatic prayer groups bring a dynamic life of prayer to many Christians while allowing them to maintain the doctrinal commitments of their own church traditions.[2] In many cases, this leads to deeper appropriation of spirituality and worship, to meditative and contemplative as well as charismatic styles of prayer, and to engagement in action on behalf of justice.

A second movement that I find to be clearly of the Spirit is the twentieth- and twenty-first-century ecumenical movement. One of the key moments of this movement was the missionary conference in Edinburgh (1910) where the delegates confessed that "our divisions were contrary to the will of Christ." In 1920, the Orthodox Ecumenical Patriarch called for a permanent institution of fellowship and cooperation between the Christian communities. The first Faith and Order conference was held in Lausanne in 1927. The World Council of Churches (WCC) was set up in 1948. The Catholic Church became an observer at the World Council in 1961 and a full member of its Commission on Faith and Order in 1968. A number of important multilateral and bilateral dialogues were set up at that time. Important gains have been made on central issues in the agreed statements that have come from these dialogues. They include the WCC document *Baptism, Eucharist and Ministry* (1982), the Anglican/Roman Catholic *Final Report* (1981), and the Lutheran/Roman Catholic *Joint Declaration on the Doctrine of Justification* (1999), where real progress has been made on the major issue that divided the churches at the Reformation. This movement, faithful as it is to the will of Christ expressed in the Scriptures, can only be seen as the work of the Spirit. It is not only a gift but also a radical challenge to the churches, demanding of them a far more faithful and committed response.

The Second Vatican Council (1962-1965) represents a movement of a different order. It is an event in the life of one Christian church, but one that has had effects on the wider Christian community. Among other things, it has definitively committed the Catholic Church to the ecumenical movement. It is part of, and perhaps can symbolize, the wider movement of church renewal to which other Christian churches have been called. In convoking the council, Pope John XXIII prayed that the Spirit would come down upon the church as in a new Pentecost. The result was a shift from the defensive stance that had characterized much of Catholic church life since the Reformation. Instead of seeing the Catholic Church itself as a "perfect society," the council offered a vision of the church as the People of God, as the sacrament of salvation, and as a communion in love that lives from the divine trinitarian Communion. Through the council, the Catholic community was led to a clearer sense of God's grace at work beyond the boundaries of the church, to a renewed focus on the biblical Word of God, to a recovery of the importance of the local church, to a theology of the collegiality of bishops, to a new respect for the call to mission and holiness of all the baptized, to a rediscovery of the charisms of all the baptized, and to the renewal of liturgical life. When this movement of renewal is considered in the light of Christ's promise to send the Advocate to be with the church and to lead it into truth, I believe that it can be thought of as the work of the Spirit.

None of these movements is in any way exempt from human limitation, failure, and sin; but I would argue that in their basic orientation they can be understood in the light of the biblical promise to be gifts of the Spirit. If this is so, then this suggests that these movements can help us to know something of the Spirit, and working creatively and critically with these movements can be considered a faithful response to the Spirit. On the other hand, it would also suggest that willful resistance to these movements may "grieve" the Spirit (Eph. 4:30).

On the much larger stage of the global community, I believe that the Spirit can be discerned in the movements that seek to promote authentic justice for the poor of the earth. The Breath of God breathes life into the struggle of the poor to find freedom from oppressive and corrupt political structures and from all colonial mentalities. José Comblin has explored the theme of the Holy Spirit at work in human liberation. He sees the specific work of the Spirit in history as "to bring freedom and speech to the poor." He points out that with the gift of speech the poor begin to act in history.[3] The Spirit of God cries out in protest at every form of exploitation of the poor. The Spirit is grieved by every racist thought and by every discriminatory word or act. The Spirit is at work in all the small and large movements that bring hope and life. Solidarity with the poor is the place of the Spirit. A Christian spirituality, Gustavo Gutiérrez points out, involves a lifelong conversion to the side of the poor: "The solidarity required by the preferential option for the poor forces us back to a fundamental Christian attitude: a grasp of the need for continual conversion."[4] The place of the Spirit is the place where the humanity of the other is respected, in the space that allows the other to be other. The place of the Spirit is the place of freedom and genuine reconciliation. I believe that we can find the Spirit, who anointed Jesus to bring good news to the poor, revealed in diverse ways in the witness of people like Mahatma Gandhi, Martin Luther King, Dorothy Day, Mother Teresa, Oscar Romero, and Nelson Mandela.

A second contemporary human movement that I would point to as a clear sign of the times and a gift of the Spirit to the church and the world is the movement that promotes the full and equal humanity of women, the feminist movement.[5] Anne Clifford describes feminism as a "social vision, rooted in women's experience of sexually based discrimination and oppression, a movement seeking the liberation of women from all forms of sexism."[6] She sees it as a perspective on life that colors all of a person's hopes, commitments, and actions. She describes the three waves of recent feminism. The first is the nineteenth- and early-twentieth-century struggle for women's political rights. The second is the women's movement that began in the 1960s, which took liberal, cultural, radical, and socialist forms. The third wave involves attention to difference, in the experiences of womanist, *mujerista,* and other forms of feminism. It also embraces an ecofeminist commitment to the good of nonhuman nature.[7] I believe that Sister Spirit can be discerned in this developing feminist consciousness, which longs for the good of the whole of humanity and for the good of the Earth community. As Sandra Schneiders has said, feminist consciousness has deepened and the agenda has widened "to an ideal of recreating humanity itself according to patterns of eco-justice, that is, of right relations at every level and in relation to all of reality."[8]

This comment points to a third movement, one that needs to be understood as interrelated with the struggle for justice and with the feminist movement. The wild Spirit, who blows where she wills, has stirred up in human beings a passion for creation. Human beings have been led to share in the divine love for all Earth's creatures. They have begun to see the need to defend the earth itself, its atmosphere, its seas, its rivers and lakes, with all its plant and animal life. Earth is wounded by human greed. It suffers from ruthless and unrestrained exploitation. It is in need of healing. Paul points to the *groaning* of suffering creation (Rom. 8:18-29). While wanting to uphold the transcendence of the divine Spirit, I think it can be said with Mark Wallace that the Spirit so feels with suffering creation that we can speak not only of a wounded creation but also, in some sense, of a "wounded Spirit."[9] Certainly it can be said that the damage done to God's beautiful and good creation "grieves" the Spirit (Isa. 63:10; Eph. 4:30). This theme will be taken up in the next chapter. If the church is to respond to the Spirit's pleas on behalf of creation, it will need to use all its theological resources on behalf of creation. As Rosemary Radford Ruether points out, this will involve both a *covenantal* approach (the broadly Protestant tradition of the search for an ecological ethics in response to God's covenantal self-giving) and the *sacramental* tradition (the broadly Catholic tradition of

God's presence and self-manifestation in creation).[10] Both need to be embodied in the preaching and the praxis of the Christian community.

In naming these six movements I am not meaning to suggest that they are the only movements that are Spirit-led. The Spirit blows where she wills. I am simply naming some that I see as undeniably of God in the light of our biblical heritage. I believe that it is essential to respond to these as interrelated movements of the one Spirit. There is no way, for example, of being effectively committed to the poor of the earth, without a commitment to women, who are caught up in multiple forms of oppression. And the poor suffer most from ecological degradation. More fundamentally, I see these movements as interconnected in the one Spirit of God. I am not suggesting that these movements are always places of clear thinking and virtue. On the contrary, I think that they are all places of failure and sin as well as of grace. But they *are* places of grace. To find where one locates oneself in any one of them requires a good deal of discernment.

I think it is clear that the Spirit of God has found expression in our time in the search for authentic spirituality that finds expression in the Pentecostal movement, in the invitation and challenge of the ecumenical movement, and in the church renewal movements such as the Second Vatican Council. Equally, I would argue that there is something transparently of the Spirit in the hunger for social justice, in the struggle for full equality for women, and in the search for ways of respecting the intrinsic value of all God's diverse creatures. If this is so, then these movements give insight into the characteristics and priorities of the Spirit of God in our time.

To be faithful to the Spirit, the church will need not only to respond to the hunger for spirituality, for Christian unity, and for church renewal, but also to play its part, both within the church and without, in the interrelated movements concerned with justice, gender, and ecology. I believe that the church can be faithful to its mission only by rediscovering the place of the Spirit in its life and ministry. The church in the West has attempted to be faithful to the gospel and to the authentic tradition of Jesus Christ. But it has not always given a full and proper place to the Spirit. I will propose that the church in the West is in need of a *radical reorientation toward the Spirit in theory and practice.*

RECIPROCITY OF WORD AND SPIRIT

As the new century begins, the Christian community faces serious issues. In many parts of the world, congregations are becoming smaller and older. In my own tradition, the ordained ministry is in crisis, local churches seem overwhelmed by centralist policies and tendencies, and the participation of women in ministry is a cause of pain and division. The issue of authority polarizes the church—with some holding absolutist views and others appearing to reject any form of authority. The ecumenical movement continues to make some gains, but it has come up against obstacles on many fronts. Issues such as these cannot be resolved simply by recourse to the authority of the Word, whether it be that of church tradition or the Bible. The Word will remain the criterion for those who attempt to follow the way of Jesus, but the church is called to listen to the Spirit in radically new situations. Only a proper balance between Word and Spirit will free us to allow the Spirit to call us into God's future.

Yves Congar was right to insist that the Western churches have got the balance wrong. We have tended to give priority to the Word and to neglect the Spirit. We have a tendency toward what Orthodox theologian Nikos Nissiotis has called *Christomonism*—a focus on Christ to the exclusion of the Spirit.[11] In Roman Catholicism this tendency takes the form of the Catholic emphasis on the tradition of authoritative teaching that it traces back to Jesus Christ. In Protestant traditions it takes the form of a focus on the Christ who speaks in the biblical Word. I do not accept that there has been anything like a deliberate or a complete exclusion of the Spirit in these churches, and contemporary theology has once more begun to address the theology of the Holy Spirit. The World Council of Churches has encouraged a return to a living theology of the Spirit. The Second Vatican Council gave a significant place to the work of the Spirit in its theology of communion, even though observers from the Orthodox tradition still found it deficient. Liturgical reforms since the council have restored the *epiclesis*, the invocation of the Spirit, in the Eucharist and other sacraments. I agree with Congar that the process of restoring the place of the Spirit is already under way.[12] But I agree with him too that much needs to be done to restore a proper balance. Needed are a theory and practice of church that involve a mutual and reciprocal relationship between Word and Spirit.

One of the truly attractive things about Congar is that he continued to develop his theology throughout his life. He was not afraid to admit mistakes and was always open to new insights. In 1971, when he was sixty-seven, he was prepared to say of his own theology of church: "I have gradually corrected my vision which at first was principally and spontaneously clerical."[13] An important part of this correction was to locate ordained ministry not apart from or above the members of the church, but within the communion of the baptized. His emphasis at the end of his journey was on the Spirit of God raising up ministries on the basis of charisms which the Spirit gives to all members of the church.

Three key principles sustain Congar's thinking about the role of the Spirit in the church. The first relates the theology of the church to Christology: *Spirit Christology is the foundation for a Spirit theology of church*. I pointed out in the last chapter that Congar insists on the historical nature of the work of the Spirit in the life and ministry of Jesus. The Holy Spirit comes to Jesus in successive stages—in his conception, his baptismal anointing, his ministry as God's servant, his death on the cross, and his resurrection and exaltation. Jesus, who has received the Spirit and has been sanctified by the Spirit, is in his resurrection constituted by the Spirit as Son of God in power (Rom. 1:3-4).[14] The risen Christ can now pour out this same Spirit on the disciples, constituting them as the church. This historical perspective on the work of the Spirit in the life of Jesus sets the stage for a view of the church in which the Spirit acts not only in its foundation but in a concrete and historical way in its life. The same Spirit is now at work in the diverse charisms of the whole community and in the Word, the sacraments, and the ministry. The church lives always from the free action of the Spirit. At every point the church needs to invoke the Spirit.

A second principle concerns reciprocal relations between Word and Spirit: *The Word and the Spirit do God's work together.*[15] Congar clearly distinguishes Word and Spirit but refuses to separate them. He appeals to the ancient tradition captured in Irenaeus's image of the Word and the Spirit as the two hands of God, working together in creation and salvation. A theology that is exclusively focused on the Word will not only rightly stress what comes from Christ, such as his words, the Eucharist, and the apostolic mission, but will also have a tendency to overemphasize the visible and structural side of church life. It may run the risk of becoming authoritarian and centralist. It may tend to be closed to what is new and to resist the voice of prophecy. On the other hand, a church that is exclusively Spirit-centered will have a tendency to overemphasize the experiential side of church life. It may lead to individualism and a negative attitude to all authority. It may tend to lose sight of the value of the Christian tradition and end up rejecting the very structures that enable the Gospel message to be passed on in the life of the church.

In his later work, Congar came to express what can be thought of as a third fundamental principle of this theology of church: *The charisms of the Spirit are a basis for the whole life of the church.* It is not that Congar sees a charismatic element existing *alongside* an institutional one in the church. There is not an institutional zone running parallel to a charismatic one. He explicitly rejects an idea that he had himself taught in 1953, in *The Mystery of the Church,* that there is a kind of "free zone" reserved for the Holy Spirit alongside the instituted structures and means of grace of the church. Congar insists in his mature work that in both the charisms and in the structural means of grace, Word and Spirit act together.[16]

A theology of the church in which the Spirit is given a proper place will involve an understanding of the charisms as central to the life of the church. Congar insists that we need a properly "pneumatological" ecclesiology: "Pneumatology should, I believe, describe the impact, in the context of the vision of the Church, of the fact that the Spirit distributes his gifts where he wills and in this way builds up the Church."[17] He understands charisms as gifts of nature and grace given for the fulfillment of the mission of the church—such as those of preaching, teaching, healing, music, art, peacemaking, and prophetic words and deeds on behalf of human liberation. He points out that a charism such as prophecy can be found not only inside the church but also outside it.[18] Congar insists that charisms are given to all members of the church. Because of this, the church is open to the Spirit only when it is open to the charisms of each member: "The Church receives the fullness of the Spirit *only in the totality of gifts made by all her members.*"[19]

Congar attempts to keep a balance in his theology of church between charisms and the ordained ministry. On the one hand, he continues to give a proper place to the ordained ministry and to the structural side of the life of the church. On the other hand, he sees the charisms of the Spirit as part of the church's constitution and as a principle of its order.[20] He sees the institution as based on the charisms. It is the operation of the charisms that produces the institution.[21]

While Congar had always thought of the Spirit as the animator of the life of the church, by the time he wrote his three-volume *I Believe in the Holy Spirit*, he had come to see the church as made by the Spirit. Word and the Spirit coinstitute the church.[22] Together they establish the church in its charismatic reality and together they establish the means of grace—the Word, the sacraments, the apostolic ministry. Congar further develops the significance of the Spirit's role as foundational for the church by offering reflections on the Spirit as principle of the church's unity, catholicity, apostolicity, and holiness.

The Spirit is the principle of unity in the church because the Spirit who is given to individuals is also the Spirit of communion. The New Testament presents the Spirit as given both to individual persons and to the community. This leads Congar to see the Spirit as both a personal principle and as a principle of unity.[23] As personal principle, the Spirit is given to individuals in charismatic and prophetic freedom. As principle of unity, the Spirit makes the church one body, the Body of Christ. The one Spirit is the author of both the charisms of the individual and the unity of the community. Thus, it is this same Spirit who can bring both into harmony. The Spirit enables diversity to flourish in unity. Congar believes that, in the modern era, "excessive emphasis has been given in the Catholic Church to the role of authority, and there had been a juridical tendency to reduce order to an observance of imposed rules and unity to uniformity."[24] This has led to a distrust of the expression of the personal principle so that those with something to say have been marginalized or silenced. But with the contemporary emphasis on individual freedom, Congar sees a danger of overreaction in the opposite direction. Proper authority is devalued or rejected. Only the Spirit can bring these diverse elements of contemporary experience together. Congar defends the idea that the Spirit is at work in the pastoral leadership of the church. But he insists that the Spirit's way of bringing about communion is not by using pressure or by reducing the whole of the church's life to a uniform pattern, but "by the more delicate way of communion."[25] The way of the Spirit cannot be reduced to a recipe. It can be discovered only through prayer, discernment, and loving relationships.

In his reflection on *catholicity*, Congar points to the Spirit as the source of the church's vocation to be both universal and particular—and he believes that it is "the task of the Spirit to contain and resolve this fertile tension between the particular and unity."[26] I will take up this issue in my next section. He goes on to point out that the Spirit keeps the church *apostolic*. The very Spirit who was in Christ, sanctifying him in his humanity is also *in us*, the church. The Holy Spirit is therefore the ultimate principle of the identity of the saving work of God. Congar thinks of apostolicity not only as fidelity to the *past* but as openness and fidelity to the *future*. The Spirit keeps the church faithful both to its origins and to its future—to Christ as the church's beginning and as its end, its Alpha and Omega. The inspiration of the Spirit that keeps the church faithful is given to the whole church, and in a specific way to ecumenical councils and to the pastoral leadership of the church. Congar recognizes that the role of the Spirit has often been presented in an automatic and institutional way. He insists that the Spirit cannot be reduced to an automatic juridical principle. The Spirit needs to be invoked. We need to await and to expect the Spirit's action in all pastoral and sacramental ministries of the church.[27]

Like the whole tradition, Congar sees the Spirit as the principle of holiness in the church.[28] The church is a church of sinners. We can "grieve" the Spirit (Eph. 4:30), "quench" the Spirit (1 Thess. 5.19), and "resist" the Spirit (Acts 7:51). But we can also cooperate with the Spirit. Congar sees individual Christians, the saints, as in some way revealing the Spirit. We possess this same Spirit, and the Spirit is the principle by which we can participate in the communion of saints. Congar's insight into the work of the Spirit leads him directly into a spirituality. In Congar's work, as Denis Doyle has said, "the line between ecclesiology and spirituality dissolves in practice."[29] In a recent article, Elizabeth Groppe shows how Congar's theology of the Spirit is always simultaneously a theology of the human being before God (anthropology) and a theology of church (ecclesiology).[30] While the indwelling Spirit is certainly a gift given to individual persons, these persons are always understood as persons-in-relation-to-others. The Spirit transforms individual persons, making them daughters and sons of God, but they are transformed precisely as persons-in-communion, as members of the church, the Body of Christ. The work of the Spirit *is* communion.

In all of this Congar has offered a fundamental corrective to the theory and practice of church. A theology that holds together Word and Spirit will be a theology that listens for the promptings of the Spirit in the "signs of the times" and does this specifically in the light of the tradition of Jesus Christ. It will be a theology that finds ways to listen to the Spirit at work in the *sensus fidei* of the whole People of God as well as in the teaching

office of the church. It will value both the charisms of every member and
the ministry of the ordained. Congar's theology of the church offers a
proper foundation for dealing with a number of issues that confront the
church today. One of the most important of these is the relationship
between local churches and the universal church.

RECIPROCITY OF LOCAL CHURCH
AND UNIVERSAL CHURCH

The Second Vatican Council returned to the ancient understanding of
the church as a communion in which the universal church exists "in and
from" the particular or local churches (*Lumen Gentium* §23). In the theology of the council, the one church of Jesus Christ truly exists in the local
church, above all in the gathering of the local church for the celebration of
the Eucharist. But the church of Christ is present in each of the local
churches, not in isolation but as they are linked to one another in the communion of the universal church. Individual churches exist in their proper
fullness only in this communion, and the universal church exists in and
from the local churches.

The council sees the bishop as the focus of the communion of the local
church. The bishop is "the visible principle and foundation of unity" in a
particular church. The bishops of the universal church form a college in
union with the bishop of Rome. Each bishop represents the local church,
but all of them together in union with the bishop of Rome, represent the
universal church, "joined in the bond of peace, love and unity" (*Lumen
Gentium* §23). The bishop is not a delegate of the pope but a representative of Christ. The bishop's power, which is always that of a servant, is
"proper, ordinary and immediate" (*Lumen Gentium* §27). The local church
is not a province or department of the universal church. Nor is the universal church simply a federation of local churches. The universal church has
no existence apart from its presence in local churches. At the same time, a
local church can exist only in the communion of the universal church.

This was a return to a vision of the church as communion that was
shared by East and West in the first millennium. It was a return to a biblical view, in which Paul could speak, for example, of "the church of God
that is in Corinth" (1 Cor. 1:2). Within Roman Catholic circles, it was seen
as balancing the work of the First Vatican Council. This council had been
cut short by the Franco-Prussian War and, instead of its proposed document on the church, which was to include fifteen chapters, it produced only
four chapters on the papacy. It was hoped that the teaching of the Second
Vatican Council would fill out what was left incomplete at the First Vatican Council and would act as a corrective to monarchical and centralist
tendencies within Roman Catholicism.[31]

Forty years later, there is a good deal of evidence that the proper balance has not yet been achieved. The appointment of bishops is more centrally controlled than in any other period of church history. The norms that control synods of bishops limit their power and their capacity to respond to urgent pastoral needs. There are no effective mechanisms to respond to extremely serious issues that confront local churches, such as lack of ordained ministers and the consequent lack of the Eucharist. Some curial officials interfere in issues that clearly fall within the competence of local bishops. It is difficult for local bishops to deal with complex pastoral problems when lobby groups can use their influence to have a bishop overruled by curial officials. Senior figures in the Roman Catholic Church, including archbishops and cardinals such as John R. Quinn, Franz König, Carlo Maria Martini, and Walter Kasper, have pointed out that the relationship between the universal and local church has become unbalanced.

Restoring the balance between the local and the universal church is not only essential for the life and mission of the Roman Catholic Church; it is also at the heart of the impasse that confronts the ecumenical movement. The goal of the ecumenical movement is not uniformity but a unified church existing in a communion of reconciled diversity. As Walter Kasper points out, ecumenical partners can contemplate full communion with the Roman Catholic Church only if it is clear that unity in communion does not mean suppressing the individual church with its unique tradition, but guaranteeing it a space of legitimate freedom. He insists that the ecumenical challenge facing the Roman Catholic Church is for it to become a shining example of how the universal church and the local church exhibit "unity in diversity and diversity in unity."[32] This would provide some hope to ecumenical partners that unity in diversity is a real possibility for a reunited church.

A recent debate in the Roman Catholic Church illustrates key dimensions some of the key issues. In 1992, the Congregation for the Doctrine of the Faith published a document on the theology of the church as communion, in which it is stated that in its essential mystery, the universal church is "a reality ontologically and temporally prior to every individual Church."[33] This statement has been challenged by Walter Kasper. He rightly insists that this is not Catholic doctrine, but one position within Catholic theology. Cardinal Joseph Ratzinger has defended the position taken by the Congregation. This has brought a fuller treatment of the issue from Kasper and a further response from Ratzinger.[34] Other theologians have since joined in this discussion.[35] At the heart of this important debate is Ratzinger's argument for the ontological primacy of the universal church on the basis of the biblical and traditional idea of the *preexistence* of the church (Gal. 4:6; Heb. 12:22-23). Kasper embraces the idea of the preexistence of the church and locates it in the mystery of God's eternal will to save. But he holds that this eternal will is directed to the actual church embodied in the world rather than to some abstract and ideal preexisting reality. In this line of thought, the idea of the preexistence of the church supports not the ontological priority of the universal church but rather the idea that the universal and local churches exist simultaneously.[36]

I believe that Walter Kasper is right to insist that that there is no ontological or temporal priority of the universal church over the local church. Wherever the church exists, it exists in a local church. Wherever a local church exists, it exists only in the communion of the universal church. There is a *perichoresis,* a mutual indwelling of universal and local, a relation of mutual presence and reciprocity.

Congar's vision of the Spirit in the life of the church supports this line of thought. The Spirit poured out on the church at Pentecost already gives the church a vocation to universality. But, Congar insists, the church "was born universal by being born manifold and particular."[37] The church can be universal only because it is particular. Congar sees this reciprocity between universal and particular operating through the Spirit in two related aspects of church life. First, at the level of charisms, the Spirit gives gifts to individuals but only for the good of the whole. The charismatic nature of the church means that the particular and the universal are always interrelated. Second, at the level of the local and universal church, the Spirit is the source of the local church with its own particular gifts and at the same time the source of unity for the whole church. There is a Spirit-given tension between the local and the universal. Congar sees it as "the task of the Spirit to contain and resolve this fertile tension between the particular and the local."[38]

If Congar is right, then this suggests that there can be no recipe for resolving this tension. What is clear is that it is disastrous to collapse this tension by centralist policies, extreme legalism, and coercion. It is equally disastrous to collapse in the other direction by exclusive emphasis on the local church or by an excessively ethnocentric view of church. There are no short cuts. The way forward can only be in the discernment of the Spirit by pondering the Word in the midst of the reality in which the church finds itself. Authority is important in a Spirit-led church because it enables the church to be united in its diversity. But it can only be an authority that looks to Jesus, who emptied himself (Phil. 2:7) as its model. Such an authority rejects all power over others, and all lording it over others (Mark 10:42-45). An authority based on the cross can be only a persuasive authority, one that cannot enforce its will and therefore remains vulnerable.

RECIPROCITY OF SYNODALITY
AND ORDAINED MINISTRY

Where there is a proper balance between Spirit and Word in the theology and praxis of church, there will also tend to be a reciprocal relationship between two essential dimensions of the church's communion that I will call the synodal and the ministerial.

The term *synod* comes from the Greek *syn-hodos*, which means a common *way*.[39] It points to the whole community of disciples who follow the way of Jesus. It indicates the whole church that is called to walk together in Christ. In the Gospel of Mark, the disciples follow Jesus along the *way* (10:52). In John's Gospel, Jesus himself is proclaimed as the *Way* (14:6). In the Acts of the Apostles, belonging to the community of disciples is called belonging to the *Way* (9:2). The Holy Spirit forms and maintains this communion, this common way, of each local church. This synodality finds its most profound expression in the Eucharist of the local church. The spirit works through all members of the community, using the gifts given to each for the good of all. The whole community shares in the common way, and the whole community is the bearer of the tradition of Jesus.

Each believer, by the grace of the Spirit, inherits the faith of the church and passes it on. By his or her sense of the faith (*sensus fidei*) each believer is called to recognize and receive the truth of faith handed on to them. This *sensus fidei* can be described as "an active capacity for spiritual discernment, an intuition that is formed by worshiping and living in communion as a faithful member of the church."[40] The exercise of this gift by each member of the church contributes to the formation of the *sensus fidelium* of the whole community. This *sensus fidelium* "contributes to, receives from and treasures" the ministry of those called to be bishops of the church.[41] Historically, synodality, the participation of the whole community of believers in the life of the church, found expression not only in the Eucharist but also in the election of bishops, in the sharing of goods, in the exchange of visits and letters between churches, and particularly in local, regional, and ecumenical councils or synods.

In a theology of the church as communion, this participation of all is not opposed to but intimately related to ordained ministry. The bishop is called to be a sign and agent of communion within the local church and to represent the local church in communion with other local churches. As Greek Orthodox theologian John Zizioulas points out, ordination is essentially a relational matter: it relates the ordained person profoundly and existentially to the community. For the ordained, he tells us, "a person's existence is determined by *communion*."[42] He insists that ordained ministry, understood in relation to communion, can only be described in terms of love. The Second Vatican Council says something similar when it points to the centrality of pastoral love in the lives of priests. Ordained ministers are also called to foster the living memory of the tradition. This has been described as the "ministry of memory." Through this ministry, "the Holy Spirit keeps alive in the Church the memory of what God did and revealed, and the hope of what God will do to bring all things into unity in Christ."[43]

Ordained ministry can exist and function only within the community of the whole church. Elizabeth Groppe, in her study of Congar's theology of the Holy Spirit, points to two key insights of his later work. First, Congar insists that the capacity of the ordained minister to mediate grace is dependent not just on institution by Christ but also on the continuing activity of the Holy Spirit. Every act of the ministry calls for an invocation of the Holy Spirit (an *epiclesis*). Second, the activity of the Spirit is mediated not by the ordained minister alone, but by the minister in relation to the whole community in whom the Spirit dwells and through whom the Spirit works.[44] Ordained ministry always involves the communion of the faithful; and synodality, the common way of the communion of the faithful, always involves the ordained ministry. Ministry and synodality belong together. They are reciprocally interrelated. As the Anglican–Roman Catholic agreed statement *The Gift of Authority* puts it, "the *sensus fidelium* of the people of God and the ministry of memory exist together in reciprocal relationship."[45]

In the Roman Catholic tradition, particularly since the Reformation, there has been an emphasis on ordained ministry at the expense of synodality. In the period since the Second Vatican Council, more attention has been given to synodality. There has been new insight into the *sensus fidelium*, to the theology of reception, to the importance of consultation and collaboration in the whole life of the church. Synodal institutions have been set up, including the Synod of Bishops and national conferences of bishops. There are diocesan synods, diocesan pastoral councils, councils of priests, and parish pastoral councils.

These emerging structures are an important beginning in the restoration of balance, but they are only a partial and inadequate beginning. We need to find creative and imaginative ways to facilitate participation of the community in synodal structures. Women's voices are not heard at all in many assemblies. They are excluded from all major decision-making processes. We live in a democratic age, and there is a widespread desire for a more participatory style of government in the church. This consciousness is surely a positive gift of the Spirit, a gift that this age can give to the church. While the church can never simply identify itself with any secular system, there is every reason to learn from the experience of our contemporaries about participatory forms of organization.

At the deepest level, the need for participatory structures comes from the *nature* of the church. The church has always been called to the way of communion. In spite of all its evident failures, it has been called from the very beginning to function in a synodal way (Acts 4:32-35). The fundamental reason for seeking participatory structures is because the Spirit of God dwells in all the baptized and gives charisms to each for the good of all (*Lumen Gentium* §12). The church receives the fullness of the Spirit only when it is open to the gifts given to all its members. It is only by encouraging the participation of all God's people that the church can be open to the Spirit of God.

THE LIFE OF THE CHURCH
AS ONE LONG INVOCATION OF THE SPIRIT

The heading of the last chapter of Congar's three volumes on the Holy Spirit is called "The Life of the Church as One Long Epiclesis."[46] He rejoices in the restoration of the invocation of the Holy Spirit to the liturgical rites of the Roman Catholic Church. The invocation of the Spirit stops us thinking that it is the ritual itself, or the action of the church, that produces the divine effect of divinizing grace. It shows us that grace is given only as the free gift of the Holy Spirit. He insists that every action performed in the name of the church calls for an invocation of the Spirit. He says that "Orthodox Christians are right when they say that the life of the Church is entirely epicletic."[47] In a little article published in 1973, Congar sums up his position on the Spirit and the church with five points.[48] They are adapted here by way of summary of this chapter:

1. The church is not ready-made. It is always in the process of being built by the Spirit.

2. The church receives the fullness of the Spirit only by receiving the totality of the gifts of all the members of the church.

3. The charisms are constitutive and foundational for the church. They give rise to a variety of ministries in the church. The ordained ministry has its place among the charisms of the Spirit and has a role in the ordering of the charisms.

4. The church is to be understood in trinitarian terms as a community of the faithful in whom the Spirit dwells, rather than as a hierarchical monopoly that dispenses gifts from above.

5. While the church holds to what is already given in the Christ event, the Spirit draws us into the new, into the openness of God's future. The Spirit thus appears as "God-before-us," the God of the future, the one who makes all things new.

PART 3

Exploring the Theology
of the Creator Spirit

SEVEN

The Spirit as Midwife and Companion as Creation Groans in Giving Birth

There are times when the earth seems to be a Spirit-filled place. Sitting in the shade of a eucalyptus tree watching the play of light in a creek bed, being brought alive by the colors of spring in a backyard garden, walking on the beach on a long summer evening—in these and many other moments there can be a sense of the presence of the Spirit of God. But there are other times when the world seems cold, empty, and alien. The Spirit appears to be absent or, at least, hidden. When a genetic mutation distorts a young body, when one creature is preyed upon by another, when we are confronted with the death of a friend, it is not easy or, perhaps, appropriate to speak in an unqualified way of the Spirit's presence.

The movement of tectonic plates and changing weather patterns, along with tides and seasons, create the endless array of evolutionary niches that leads to the glorious diversity of living things. But the same processes give rise to deadly earthquakes and tidal waves. Random mutations provide the novelty that enables better adaptation to evolutionary niches, but they also bring damage and suffering. Life has flourished on Earth in seemingly endless novelty and beauty, but it has been at the cost of massive extinctions of species, like the extinction of 248 million years ago, when more than nine-tenths of the wondrous variety of marine species were lost, and that of 65 million years ago, when the dinosaurs along with 65 percent of the Earth's species were wiped out.

Our bodily existence involves feeding off other creatures and death. Predation cannot be removed from the story of life. Human beings and other animals have to eat other living creatures. We can eat in a way that values other forms of life and acknowledges our dependence on them respectfully and thankfully—attitudes inculcated by a number of ancient indigenous religious traditions. But living from others is built into biological life. We are inescapably part of the food chain. Some Christians have understood death not as part of creation but as a deformity that arises as a result of human sin. Sin clearly has deadly effects on the biosphere. Sinful exploitation and greed contribute to the destruction of Earth's rain forests, the extinction of uncounted species, and the pollution of the global climate. However, I believe that to attribute biological death in itself to human sin is a mistake, based on a misunderstanding of our biological natures and on a few slim biblical references taken too literally. Death, whether it be that of a dinosaur, a butterfly, or a human being, is part of the pattern of biological life.

Although there is beauty and harmony in nature, the biological world is not simply a place of ecological harmony or balance. Celia Deane-Drummond points out that ecological science today is not so much about stability as about chaos. It takes account of fire, wind, pests, and drought that disturb and disrupt ordered systems. A contemporary look at ecology reveals not simply an ordered whole but patchwork quilts of interrelating species. While ecology is ordered at one level of description, there is a good deal of disorder at another level.[1] What is needed, Deane-Drummond argues, is a scientifically and theologically informed attitude of wisdom. This would involve a stance before the natural world of profound and loving attention to detail. It would also involve taking into account chaotic elements, refusing to dismiss what does not fit, and a continual openness to further insights.[2]

Creation can seem unrelentingly harsh and bloody. Cats drag home small birds and animals. White sharks prey on seals. Birds attack other birds straying into their territory. Where is the Spirit of God in this kind of natural violence? The temptation is to deny the blood and to escape into a romantic view of nature. Jay McDaniel suggests that an authentic response to struggle in nature must involve facing reality honestly and compassionately. It is not a matter of being caught up in guilt, but it does mean facing up to suffering rather than hiding from it. It involves trusting that "the very Heart of the universe suffers with each and every living being that suffers" and being inspired toward "a nonviolent way of living that shares with the world the non-violence of God."[3]

Christian theology has no theoretical answer to the issue of pain and death in nature. It simply has to face the fact that this is the way things are in this finite, limited, and evolving world. All Christian theology has to offer is its witness to the death and resurrection of Jesus. Here divine love is revealed as unthinkable compassion. The cross reveals a God who enters into the pain of the world, who suffers with suffering creation. In the resurrection and the outpouring of Spirit, new life is promised and in some way already given. Those who live in the power of resurrection life are convinced that forgiveness, liberation, and new creation have already taken hold at the heart of this world.

While a theology of the Spirit cannot explain suffering in nature, it must attempt a response to it. One part of such a response, I believe, needs to deal with Christian teachings that have intensified the problem of evil by presenting divine power as the absolutely unqualified capacity to do anything no matter how arbitrary. In what follows, then, I will begin by redefining divine power as the power to love, a love that involves free self-limitation. Then I will suggest that the Spirit can be seen as the midwife of a new creation. This will lead to the idea of the Spirit as the faithful companion who accompanies each creature in love.

SELF-LIMITATION IN LOVE IN THE WORK OF CREATION

I have been proposing that the Holy Spirit can be understood as the life-giving Breath of God who empowers the emergence of the universe and all that makes it up. How is the power exercised by the Creator Spirit to be understood? I would propose that the only source for a fully Christian understanding of divine power is found in the cross and resurrection of Jesus. The cross reveals divine power as self-emptying, limitless love. The resurrection reveals a God who brings life from defeat and death. The cross and resurrection tell us that the divine capacity for love involves boundless generosity, incomprehensible vulnerability, free self-limitation, and the capacity to bring life out of a violent death.

Christians confess in the creed that God is "almighty." They understand God as the one whose immense power and love create and sustain the universe and bring it to liberation and fulfillment. I accept these as fundamentals of Christian faith. What needs further questioning is the *kind* of power we attribute to the Creator. What is meant by divine omnipotence?

The cross defines the power of God in a very particular way. What it reveals is an omnipotence in love, a power to love that involves a divine capacity for loving self-limitation. I am convinced that Christians have often got this issue wrong and that there is an urgent need to redefine divine power. Behind much thinking about divine power, there lurks an idea of the kind of power exercised by human tyrants, an oppressive and dominating power. It is assumed that God's power is the power to do anything at all, regardless of the consequences. A God with this kind of power could arbitrarily overrule human freedom and the laws of nature. This assumption about divine power is revealed when Christians, in the face of tragedy or difficulty, say: "Why is God doing this to me?" It is revealed as well in the all too common response: "It is God's will." If one has this view of God's omnipotence, then it is natural enough to see God as capricious and cruel in not acting to stop evil. But I would argue that this view of divine power comes not from what we find at the heart of the gospel, but from transferring to God the kind of notions of sovereignty and power that appear in the worst excesses of human emperors, kings, presidents, and dictators. God is being understood as the great lordly individual able to do and to command absolutely anything no matter what the consequences.

The Christian Scriptures portray a different view of divine power. In Mark's Gospel, for example, we find that the identity of Jesus is radically connected to the cross. Mark presents Jesus as messianic Son of God, but will not allow us to understand Jesus as a messiah who wields dominating power. Jesus comes to serve and to give his life. Those who follow him are called to identify with the slaves, the poor, and the children. His true identity is revealed only in his death. Only those who know the mystery of the cross can know the meaning of Jesus. It is this vulnerable, defeated, and humiliated one who is proclaimed as messianic Son of God (Mark 15:39). It is this "Jesus of Nazareth who was crucified" who is raised up by God to go before the disciples into Galilee (Mark 16:6).

In First Corinthians, Paul describes this same Christic pattern of divine power in response to disputes in the Christian community at Corinth. Again the cross defines God's power:

> For Jews demand signs and Greeks desire wisdom, but we proclaim Christ crucified, a stumbling block to Jews and foolishness to Gentiles, but to those who are the called, both Jews and Greeks, Christ the power of God and the wisdom of God. For God's foolishness is wiser than human wisdom, and God's weakness is stronger than human strength. (1 Cor 1:22-25)

Christ crucified is not only the Wisdom of God in our midst but also the shape of divine power at work in the world. Divine power is the power of love. This is the "foolishness" that is so radically beyond human wisdom. The same pattern is revealed in the christological hymn in Philippians (2:6-11). Here Christ Jesus is proclaimed as the one "who did not think of equality with God something to be exploited, but *emptied himself*, taking the form of a slave" (Phil. 2:7). This self-emptying (*kenōsis*) refers to Christ. Paul is pointing to the mind of Christ that he wants his hearers to take upon themselves. Many commentators have thought that Paul had preexistence in mind and was referring to a letting go of divine status in Christ. Some others see him as referring to Christ's earthly existence and view the text as contrasting Adam's attempt to claim divine status with Jesus' self-emptying. In either case, Paul is seeing self-emptying as both characteristic of Christ and as revelatory of God.

Each of these early Christian texts insists that the kenotic love revealed in Jesus is to be lived out in the Christian community. In Mark, Jesus absolutely forbids "lording over" others in the Christian assembly (Mark 10:42-45). Dominating power is excluded from the Christian community. In First Corinthians, Paul tells the community that he did not approach them in a superior way but in humility: "I decided to know nothing among you except Jesus Christ, and him crucified" (1 Cor. 2:1). In Philippians, the community is instructed that Christian life involves taking on "the same mind that was in Christ Jesus" (Phil. 2:5). In these and many other New

Testament texts, such as the foot-washing of John (13:1-15), it is made clear that the pattern of kenotic love is to shape the Christian community.

If God is to be understood as consistent and faithful, then the Christic pattern of vulnerable and self-limiting love can be understood to govern not just the story of Jesus and the church but also God's creative presence to all creatures in the Spirit. It suggests that the kind of power exercised by the Spirit in ongoing creation will be consistent with the kind of power revealed in the cross and resurrection of Jesus. Creation will involve the self-limiting power of love. It is important to note that a self-limiting love may still be a transcendent love. In Jesus, divine transcendence is revealed as the capacity for kenotic love that is beyond all human possibilities. Moreover, in the work of creation, the capacity for free self-limitation in love is to be understood not as a diminishment of the transcendence of the Creator Spirit but as the real expression of this transcendence.

Because God is omnipotent in love, God can freely enter into the vulnerability of loving. In our ordinary experience of love we find that it involves not only self-communication to the other but also self-limitation. The lover needs to "make space" for the other. The lover allows the beloved to exist in difference and distinction. The lover allows the beloved to affect him or her and can suffer with the beloved. This involves a letting be of the other, a making room for the other, that is a form of self-limitation. The God revealed in the cross is a God who has a transcendent capacity to enter freely into the self-limitation and vulnerability of love, without compromising the proper autonomy and integrity of the creature. In Elizabeth Johnson's words, "Love grants autonomy to the beloved and respects this, all the while participating in the joy and pain of the other's destiny." It "vigorously cares for and works for and urges the beloved toward his or her own well-being but never forces."[4]

I believe that this describes the work of the Spirit in ongoing creation. The Creator Spirit relates with creatures in a compassionate, self-limiting love that respects each creature's proper nature and autonomy. The Spirit works with kenotic power in every creature, in every aspect of ongoing creation, and in every human event, even in events like Golgotha—above all there. As Patricia Fox says, this is not a denial of the omnipotence, but its redefinition. In this new gospel vision of relational power, "self-containment and absence of relationship do not represent an ideal but signify imperfection." And omnipotence is redefined as "the free unlimited capacity to make room within the self for the other."[5]

The power of the Creator Spirit is a power defined by love, a power that makes room for creatures to be their finite creaturely selves. It makes room for human freedom and the integrity of the laws of nature. It is a power that is self-limited because, in the freedom of love, it respects the otherness and autonomy of both human freedom and physical processes. Only a God whose power is absolute, unconditioned, and arbitrary would always be completely free to intervene to stop a tidal wave or to ensure that a dangerous mutation did not occur. A God who respects the otherness and integrity of creatures may not be.[6]

The power of the Creator Spirit is not an unqualified despotic power capable of doing anything regardless of cost. It is the supreme power to love, a love that involves a divine capacity to make room for the other. It involves a transcendent capacity to respect the identity, integrity, and autonomy of creatures and created processes. If this view of divine power is correct, it means that the Creator Spirit, because of divine free self-limitation that respects the otherness, the autonomy, and the integrity of creatures, may not be free to overturn the proper unfolding and emergence of creation.

THE SPIRIT AS MIDWIFE TO THE BIRTH OF THE NEW

Creation has an unfinished character. It is not yet what it will be. We are in mid-process. Do we have any idea of the whole? I believe that Ted Peters is right when he says that we do glimpse God's purpose for unfinished creation in the life, death, and resurrection of Jesus Christ. In Christ we see something of God's purpose for the whole. This is a single purpose that runs "from alpha to omega, from beginning to end." Peters argues that we can think of cosmic history as one act of God, one creative act with many sub-acts. Because God's creation has not yet come to its completion, it is not yet brought into wholeness. The future remains open. The whole is being determined in our history in "mutual reciprocity" between finite events and the overall divine purpose.[7]

The resurrection functions as a promise that creation has a future in God. The promise that Christians see encapsulated in the resurrection runs through all the biblical literature. In a recent study of the prophetic tradition, Carol Dempsey has shown how in diverse ways these books show that the "the eschatological hope of humanity's redemption is intrinsically linked to the restoration of all creation." The prophetic vision of salvation involves a relationship of harmony among God, humans, and all other creatures.[8] This promise finds beautiful expression in the vision of Isaiah: "The wolf will lie down with the lamb . . . the lion shall eat straw like the ox . . . the nursing child shall play over the hole of the asp . . . they will not hurt or destroy on all my holy mountain; for the earth will be filled with the knowledge of the Lord as the waters cover the sea" (Isa. 11:6-9). All through the ages, the Christian community has continued to cry out "Come Holy Spirit! Come Creator Spirit!" and it continues to pray: "Send out your Spirit and renew the face of the earth." The eschatological transformation of creation is thought of as *shalom,* as entering into the Sabbath of God. It is imaged as liberation from predation and death. This points to what is beyond imagining—the eschatological participation of all creatures in the dynamism of the divine life.

Paul understands the Spirit as the power of God's future already at work. In the Christian experience of the Spirit, he sees the beginning and the guarantee of the transformation of creation. Biblical scholar James D. G. Dunn points out that, for Paul as for Jesus, the Spirit is "the power of the new age already broken into the old."[9] Paul is convinced that for those who experience the Spirit, the future is already assured. The Spirit is the power of God's future already present. Paul sees this experience of the Spirit as the down payment and guarantee that God will complete what has been begun in Christ (2 Cor. 1:22; 5:5; Eph. 1:13-15). He thinks of the Spirit as the first installment of our inheritance of the kingdom (Rom. 8:15-17; 14:17; 1 Cor. 6:9-11; 15:42-50; Gal. 4:6-7; 5:16-24).[10] In a different image, he sees the Spirit as the firstfruits of God's harvest (Rom. 8:23).

For Paul, then, the experience of the Spirit always has an eschatological character. It is the tasting in anticipation of God's future for creation. The Spirit is the power of new life already at work in creation. Wolfhart Pannenberg sees the Spirit as "working creatively in all events as the power of the future." He understands the Spirit as "the power of the future that gives creatures their present and duration."[11] This concept of the Spirit as the power of the future encapsulates a central idea of the Pauline theology of the Spirit. This power of the Spirit, however, is not an overpowering or dominating force. It is the patient power of love that values and respects every creature. It is a power that is freely self-limiting because it makes room for the otherness of creatures. The Spirit works from within, enabling things to become what is new in a way that respects each creature's autonomy and integrity.

For the first Christians, the vivid experience of the Spirit's presence was a foretaste and pledge of the renewal of creation. It is the beginning of "new creation" (2 Cor. 5:17). In Romans 8, Paul contrasts the "sufferings of the present time" with the glory that is to come. In this context, he personalizes creation. He talks of creation waiting with "eager longing" for its liberation from "bondage to decay" and for "the freedom associated with the glory of the children of God" (Rom. 8:19-23). He sees the struggle and pain of creation as a bringing to birth: "For we know that the entire creation has been groaning together in the pangs of childbirth up till now" (Rom. 8:22).[12]

In his commentary on this passage, Joseph Fitzmyer says that Paul appears to be borrowing from Greek thinkers who compared the rebirth of nature each spring to a woman's labor in childbirth. However, Paul's focus is not on the yearly cycle but on the future of creation in God. He sees the labor and groaning of creation as expressing the eschatological expectation of the whole of creation.[13] Paul feels with the suffering of nonhuman creation. He interprets it as the pain of something being brought to birth. Creation is in bondage to death and under duress because of human sin. But it shares with Christians, who already have the firstfruits of the Spirit, in the hope of liberation from death and decay. Fitzmyer points out that Paul's talk of the corruption of nature rings true in a new way today. It has new significance in the context of the current ecological crisis, even though Paul did not have in mind what modern industry and corruption are doing to the earth.[14]

Another Pauline scholar, Brendan Byrne, notes that in Paul's argument in chapter 8 of Romans there are three interrelated groanings: in verses 19–22, creation groans in childbirth; in verses 23–25, we, who already have the first fruits of the Spirit groan while we await our adoption, the redemption of our bodies; and, in verses 26–27, the Spirit intercedes with groans too deep for utterance.[15] The Spirit groans for us, interceding on our behalf, with prayerful groaning that God's work in us might be brought to completion.

In Paul's explicit thought, the groaning of the Spirit is a groaning for and with human beings. But he certainly does see creation as groaning in the suffering of childbirth, human beings as groaning in anticipation of God's future, and the Spirit's prayerful groaning as related to the other two groanings. It seems entirely appropriate to build on Paul's thought to see the Spirit as groaning with suffering creation, suffering with creation in its labor. The Spirit can be thought of as the midwife who helps creation in its travail as it brings the new to birth. But the Holy Spirit is more than a mid-wife, because the Spirit also mysteriously empowers creation from within. The Spirit works patiently and lovingly in every aspect of nature as the power of the future, enabling creation to bring to birth a future beyond human imagination. This future is ultimately the unimaginable transfigu-ration of creatures as they participate in the divine Communion in their own specific and differentiated ways.

THE SPIRIT AS FAITHFUL COMPANION
ACCOMPANYING EACH CREATURE

I agreed above with Pannenberg's description of the Holy Spirit as "the power of the future that gives creatures their present and duration." But the Spirit is also far more than an impersonal power. The Spirit is the per-sonal presence of God and the faithful companion with every creature, accompanying each with love, delighting in each, suffering with each in its suffering, and promising each its future in God.

I see it as an important gain of contemporary theology to be able to say that the Holy Spirit suffers with suffering creation. The biblical God is a God of compassion, a God who can feel with the pain of others, a God of strong and rich feelings. But the patristic Christian tradition, rightly con-vinced of God's absolute transcendence, was concerned that God not be thought of as caught up in the creaturely world of suffering and decay. Because it wanted to preserve the otherness of God, it presented God as immune from suffering. In the medieval period, Thomas Aquinas developed a wonderful theology of creation as the intimate and immediate relation between each creature and God. From the side of the creature, Aquinas argues, it is a real relation of dependence between the creature and God, by which the creature exists. From the side of God, however, there could be only a logical relation between God and the creature, since in Aquinas's philosophical framework a real relation would seem to compromise divine transcendence.[16] For Aquinas and for much of the theological tradition, it has been considered inappropriate to speak of a suffering God.

Jürgen Moltmann is one among many contemporary theologians who have challenged this approach. Faced with the horror of Auschwitz, Moltmann says that "to speak here of a God who could not suffer would make God a demon."[17] He believes that God was a companion in suffering in the hell of Auschwitz: "The inexpressible sufferings in Auschwitz were also the sufferings of God himself."[18] A number of theologians resist this line of thought. Thomas Weinandy, for example, has argued against Moltmann, defending the traditional view with a good deal of care and learning.[19] He believes that it is absolutely fundamental to defend the biblical teaching of the total otherness of God and the patristic insight into the ontological distinction between God and the order of creation. He believes that talk of a suffering God undermines both. Only a God who is completely other can be a God who is immanent to creatures. Only a God who is completely other can bring healing and salvation.

Weinandy is right to insist on the radical otherness of God, but this does not necessarily rule out a theology of God suffering with creation. There is a way of speaking about God's suffering with creation that fully respects the transcendence and otherness of God. It builds on the very basic theological idea that all language about God is analogical. If the statement "God suffers with creation" is recognized as analogical language, then the statement is made on the understanding that God does not suffer with creation in a limited human way, but in the kind of identification with creation that is proper to God. God's capacity for being with creatures, God's capacity to love, God's capacity to feel with those who suffer, is *infinitely* beyond anything possible for human beings. Understood in this way, God's empathy and suffering with others are not to be thought of as diminishing God's transcendence. They are the very expression of God's infinite otherness.

In this sense Pope John Paul II is prepared to speak of the *pain* of God. He writes of a pain in the depths of the Trinity, a pain that comes from human sin and a pain that springs from God's compassion for suffering humanity. From this compassionate pain, the whole economy of redemptive love springs.[20] This kind of pain is not due to a deficiency in the divine being. It does not involve a lessening of God. It is a divine pain that springs from infinite compassion. *Pain* is being used of God in an analogical sense. The divine experience of compassionate love is beyond all human experiences and all human words. When we use the word *pain* of God, like any other word we might use, we need to be conscious of the absolute otherness of God and of the human limitations of our language. But we need words like *pain* to speak of God's feeling for creatures.

To do justice to the biblical revelation of divine compassion, it is important to be able to say that the Spirit of God suffers with suffering creation. The Holy Spirit suffers not out of necessity and not out of imperfection but in the active freedom of the divine love. This kind of suffering springs from the incomprehensible depths of divine compassion. The Spirit suffers with creation not to glorify suffering but in order to bring liberation and healing. The Spirit is the companion to each creature, loving it into being and opening up a future for it in God. She is the power of ongoing creation, the Life-Giver, precisely as the eschatological Bringer of Communion. It is because creatures are already brought into the communion of divine life by the Spirit that they exist. This relationship with the Spirit is creation. The power of the future, the power of creation, is nothing other than the power of love. God's eschatological future exerts its influence on the present in the Spirit, constantly, faithfully, lovingly in all events and in all creatures.

I think it is important to make the claim that the Spirit embraces each creature in love. As Michael Schmaus says, "Every creature has an indissoluble and indestructible value of its own, simply because it exists, and this individual value is continually created by God."[21] While scientific ecology rightly points to the importance of populations, species, and habitats, theology insists, as well, on God's respect and love for individuals. The Spirit is present to each creature here and now, loving it into existence and promising its future. Creation is an act of love. If creation is an act of love, then this can only mean that salvation begins in and with creation. I agree, then, with Ruth Page when she refuses to separate God's presence with creatures from God's salvation of them. God's presence involves both creation and redemption. She writes that "in relation to creation God's being there in freedom and love is already saving."[22] She insists that salvation is given *now* as "the divine presence companions each individual non-human creature." She writes: "the individual organism in its individual conditions, no matter how limited these look from a human point of view, is the outcome of God's gift of freedom and the subject of God's love."[23]

As I have indicated above, and here I differ with Page, I believe that the Spirit is also the power and the promise of God's future, a future in which all things will be taken up into the life of God. But I am convinced with Ruth Page that God is the faithful companion to every individual organism. I believe that this is the conclusion to be drawn from reflection on the doctrine of creation and on the nature of divine love revealed in the Christ event. The God of Jesus is a God who provides for all the plants and the birds (Matt. 6:26-29) and knows when every sparrow falls to the ground (Matt. 10:29). As Basil wrote, God's provident love embraced an individual sea urchin. The Creator Spirit, then, can be understood as companioning each creature with love that respects each creature's own identity, possibilities and proper autonomy. This conviction has immediate ecological consequences. It involves a claim that God knows and cares about each creature's experience. This can only mean that, in the words of Page, "God knows, as a fish or any other river creature knows, what it is like when poisonous effluent flows into its habitat."[24] Those who commit themselves to such a God commit themselves to something like the divine feeling for fish, and thereby commit themselves to fish habitats.

As Moltmann says, the discovery of the cosmic breadth of God's Spirit cannot but lead us to respect for the dignity of all God's creatures.[25] They are part of us and we are part of them, interrelated in one world, enlivened by one Spirit who holds all things together. The human experience of the Spirit leads to a compassion that embraces other creatures in their struggle for existence. As Jay McDaniel suggests, it can help us to feel the pain of the world, to accept our complicity in some of the violence, and to respond to the divine call to be peacemakers within creation.[26] It does not explain the pain of creation. But those who are convinced by the gospel claim that love is at the heart of all things, continue to place their trust in God without reaching understanding of why things are the way they are. For them, radical trust coexists with radical mystery.

The experience of nature leads into mystery at many levels. When we stand before nature at the level of quantum physics, we find that reality is completely counterintuitive and unimaginable. There is wave-particle duality, where an atom is understood as having wavelike and particlelike aspects depending on circumstances. There is the Heisenberg Uncertainty Principle, which tells us that one cannot know at the same time the precise position and momentum of a given particle—measuring the quantity of one rules out precise knowledge of the other. There is the principle of nonlocality, which tells us that once quantum entities have interacted with each other, they remain in fundamental relationship to each other no matter how widely they are separated. At the macro level of the universe, we find it easy to feel lost and completely insignificant. We are told that our own Milky Way galaxy contains more than a 100 billion stars and that there are about 100 billion galaxies in the observable universe. We find that at the heart of twinkling stars there are unimaginably powerful nuclear processes. We foresee the time, thankfully very distant from now, when our Sun will begin to run out of fuel, swell in size to become a giant red star, and eventually engulf nearby planets, including Earth.

In these and many other experiences we are confronted with nature as profoundly *other*. Common sense is revealed as a very unreliable guide to the real nature of reality. Ursula Goodenough reflects on this kind of experience from a naturalist perspective. She tells how as a young woman she looked up at the once-familiar night sky, and, seeing it in terms of the physics she had been learning, became overwhelmed with terror. She says: "A bleak emptiness overtook me whenever I thought about what was really going on out in the cosmos or deep in the atom." She goes on to describe herself finally moving beyond emptiness and nihilism by accepting the apparent pointlessness as the very locus of mystery: the mystery of why there is anything at all, the mystery of where the laws of physics came from, and the mystery of why the universe seems so strange. She speaks of coming to make her own "covenant with mystery," in which "nature takes its place as a strange but wondrous given." She points out that the "gasp" before mystery can terrify, but it can also emancipate.[27]

This covenant with mystery is also the shape of the most honest and searching of responses to the way things are in the biblical and theological tradition. It is the ultimate response found in the book of Job, when God addresses Job from the whirlwind, asking, "Where were you when I laid the foundation of the earth? . . . Have you entered into the springs of the sea, or walked in the recesses of the deep? . . . Can you bind the chains of the Pleiades or loose the cord of Orion? . . . Is it at your command that the eagle mounts up and makes its nest on high?" (38:4, 16, 31; 39:27). Job has no answers. He cannot comprehend or control the immensity of nature. He cannot deal with the forces of chaos, symbolized in the primeval monsters Behemoth and Leviathan (40:15-41:34). But Job encounters God in the mystery. He knows God, no longer simply by hearsay, but by experiencing the otherness of God in the very midst of incomprehension (42:5).

The experience of God's presence in creation and the experience of the radical otherness of creation can lead to worship and thanksgiving. In eucharistic liturgies, we bring the gifts of creation to the table and invoke the Spirit over them, praying that they might be sacramentally taken up into the divine communion, thus anticipating the final communion of all things in God. In taking such a eucharistic stance before the universe, human beings can be called, with Orthodox theology, "priests of creation." As John Zizioulas points out, the experience of the liturgy, in which all of creation is caught up in anticipation in the divine trinitarian life, can transform human perceptions of other creatures. A liturgical stance before creation leads to a profoundly Christian ecological "ethos."[28] In reflection on liturgy and prayer, we speak metaphorically of bringing creation to God. What we mean, I think, is that we bring creation to mind, *our* minds, in prayer and in praise and thanksgiving. We become conscious of other creatures and attend to them in the very place of our God-attentiveness. In our loving union with God we are drawn to love the creatures that God loves. We come to recognize with Aldo Leopold that God "likes to hear birds sing and to see flowers grow."[29] But we do not literally bring creation to God. The Spirit of God has been with all things and in all things as loving companion and midwife to the new long before the first spark of human consciousness appeared on Earth.

EIGHT

A Distinctive and Proper Role
of the Spirit in Creation

If the whole Trinity is involved in the action of creation, is it appropriate to talk about a *distinctive* role of the Holy Spirit? I have been proposing that the Spirit does have a distinctive role—that of being the immanent Life-Giver that enables all creatures to be and to become. In the first section of this chapter, I will explore this role of the Spirit more fully. There is, however, an important theological tradition which claims that the actions of the Trinity toward creation are undivided and one, and this has often been taken to mean that there is no *proper* role for any one of the trinitarian persons in creation. In the light of this, I will ask in the second section of this chapter: Can the role of immanent Life-Giver be described as proper to the Holy Spirit? I will conclude with some reflections on the ecological consequences of this theology of the indwelling Spirit.

THE IMMANENT ONE WHO CREATES THROUGH BRINGING
EACH CREATURE INTO DYNAMIC RELATIONSHIP
WITH THE DIVINE COMMUNION

According to the scientific story told in the opening chapter of this book, the visible universe has evolved over the last 14 billion years in a process that includes the momentous events of the first second, the formation of galaxies, the cooking of elements in stars, the appearance of the Sun and its solar system about 4.6 billion years ago, the emergence of bacterial life 3.8 billion years ago, the flourishing of life forms on Earth during the last 600 million years and the emergence of modern human beings in the last 150,000 years. None of the early Christian theologies of the Spirit had anything like this vast cosmic scenario in mind. Nevertheless, I have been proposing that, for one who stands in the Christian tradition, the Spirit of

God can be seen as the immanent power of becoming who enables this kind of life-bearing universe to emerge.

In chapter 2, I pointed to the biblical concept of the Spirit as Breath of Life: "When you send forth your spirit they are created; and you renew the face of the ground" (Ps. 104:30). The Breath of Life dwells in things, enabling them to exist and live. As the Wisdom of Solomon says, "God's immortal Spirit is *in* all things" (Wis. 12:1). Wolfhart Pannenberg sums up the ancient biblical tradition, "the Spirit of God is the life-giving principle, to which all creatures owe life, movement, and activity."[1] I pointed out that the Spirit is to be seen as Creator and Life-Giver, not just in the sense of biological life but in the wider sense of being the one who brings a universe to life. The Big Bang itself, the emergence of the great hydrogen clouds of the early universe, the cooking of carbon and other elements in stars, the formation of our solar system—all of this is the work of the Life-Giver.

For the ancient Christian tradition, it is the role of the Spirit to dwell *in* creatures. Athanasius encapsulates the ancient tradition when he writes: "the Father creates and renews all things through the Word in the Holy Spirit."[2] All divine action is *in* the Spirit. It is the Spirit who dwells in things, enabling them to be and to become what is new. This holy Breath is the ultimate source of the newness and freshness of creation. In the medieval period, Hildegard of Bingen (1098-1179) celebrated the Holy Spirit as the one who enables things to flourish. In her hymn to the Holy Spirit she sings:

> Holy Spirit, making life alive,
> Moving in all things, root of all creative being,
> Cleansing the cosmos of every impurity,
> Effacing guilt, anointing wounds,
> You are lustrous and praiseworthy life,
> You waken and re-awaken everything that is.[3]

The Spirit wakens and reawakens things from within. Hildegard had her own unique way of pointing to the vivifying effect of the Spirit. She used the Latin word *viriditas,* a noun that means "greenness." In her thinking, *viriditas* is associated with the freshness and vigor of life. It points to the fecundity of the Spirit at work in creation. It means "not only verdure or foliage, but all natural or spiritual life as quickened by the Holy Spirit."[4] Elizabeth Johnson builds on the tradition of Hildegard with her feminist theology of the Spirit at work in creation. She says of the Spirit: "she is the giver of life and lover of life, pervading the cosmos and all of its interrelated creatures with life." Johnson sees *connectedness* as the hallmark of the Spirit's touch. Because of her presence, the creatures of the universe are "mutually related and exist in an interplay of communion." Individual entities are given the gift of their own integrity, since the Spirit is at once "the source of individuation and community, of autonomy and relation."[5]

It is important to insist that the Spirit of God enables entities to exist in their individuality and creaturely otherness. This is a theme that will be further developed in the next chapter. The Spirit who brings a multidimensional universe to life respects the autonomy and integrity of individual creatures. The Spirit is not to be understood as a physical force. The Spirit is a personal divine presence, closer to individual creatures than they are to themselves. She is not to be associated with any form of "vitalism," as if her presence were some undiscovered ingredient of nature. She is not a power accessible to science. The Spirit is the presence of God in the divine relationship of ongoing creation. She is the hidden dynamism that brings the whole universe to life, continually sustains its existence, and enables it to evolve into an open future.

The Spirit is the Creator and Life-Giver who empowers creation to transcend itself so that what is new can emerge. The Spirit is the one who enables all the dynamism and fecundity of nature. Walter Kasper writes:

> Since the Spirit is divine love in person, he is, first of all, the source of creation, for creation is the overflow of God's love and a participation in God's being. The Holy Spirit is the internal (in God) presupposition of communicability of God outside of himself. But the Spirit is also the source of movement and life in the created world. Whenever something new arises, whenever life is awakened and reality reaches ecstatically beyond itself, in all seeking and striving, in every ferment and birth, and even more in the beauty of creation, something of the being and activity of God's Spirit is manifested.[6]

The role of the Spirit with each creature is a relational and personal one. The Spirit of God creates a relation between each creature and the divine perichoretic communion that enables a creature to be and to become. The Spirit is not simply an impersonal *power* but a *personal presence* interior to each creature, creating communion with all in ways that are appropriate for each of them. It is the presence of the Spirit that enables creatures to interact in their own creaturely patterns of relationship, at the level of particles, cells, organisms, evolutionary symbiosis, populations, ecological interactions, the planetary community, the solar system, the Milky Way galaxy and the universe.

In arguing for a personal divine presence to all creatures, I do not mean to suggest that the divine presence to a tree is the same as the divine presence to a human being by grace. In both cases the presence is personal on the side of God. But it is a personal presence that relates to a tree precisely as a tree and that relates to a human being as a grace-filled, self-conscious, dialogical other. Humans are capable of a personal engagement with other creatures which takes delight in them, feeling with them in their struggle and pain, valuing them in their own right for what they are, and respecting them in their specificity and in their interrelationships in an ecological whole. This experience, by way of analogy, enables us to glimpse the differentiated personal presence of the Spirit to each creature, a presence that creates a bond of communion with each, a communion that empowers its being and becoming.

The Spirit is the one who *empowers* and *creates* precisely as the one who *relates* to each creature, bringing each into communion with the Trinity. This empowering personal presence unites each creature in a world of relations with all other creatures in a profoundly relational universe. This communion between each creature and the divine Persons-in-Communion is the relation of ongoing creation. Things exist only because God loves them and because the Spirit of God dwells in them (Wis. 11:24-12:1). The indwelling Spirit is the expression of divine love enabling creatures to exist and to evolve.

In the dynamism of trinitarian life, the Person of the Holy Spirit represents the ecstasy and the excess of divine love. The Spirit is the *ek-static* one—the one who goes out to the other. In the act of creation, the Spirit goes "out" to what is not divine and enables it to exist by participation in the divine being. The Spirit brings what is not divine into relation with the divine persons. As Christian Duquoc has said, the Holy Spirit makes the divine Communion open to what is not divine.[7] The Spirit is God's *ek-stasis* toward creatures. Yves Congar agrees with Duquoc. He understands the Spirit as the Gift of divine Communion directed toward creation. He points out that the Holy Spirit is always understood as a "going out," an "impulse," an "ecstasy." Congar sums this up with the idea that God is Love and Grace, and says that "Love and Grace are hypostasised in the Spirit." This means, he writes, that the "Holy Spirit, who is the term of the communication of the divine life *intra Deum*, is the principle of this communication of God outside himself and beyond himself."[8] The Spirit expresses the dynamism and abundance of the divine Communion. In the free divine choice to create a universe of creatures, it is the Spirit's role to be the dynamic and free overflow of divine Communion that embraces creatures.

This means that what Paul calls the "*koinōnia* of the Holy Spirit" (2 Cor. 13:13) can be understood to describe not only the Spirit's presence in the Christian community but also the Spirit's presence to all of creation. For Paul, the experience of communion in the Spirit is a pledge and foretaste of the reconciliation and communion of all things in Christ. This leads Jürgen Moltmann to suggest that the experience of the Holy Spirit in the church "leads of itself beyond the limits of the church to the rediscovery of the same Spirit in nature, in plants, in animals, and in the ecosystems of the earth." It carries Christians beyond the communion of the church to the greater community of all God's creatures. For Moltmann, then, "the community of creation, in which all created things exist with one another, for one another and in one another, is also the fellowship of the Holy Spirit." He sees it as appropriate to talk about a "community of creation" and to recognize the operation of the life-giving Spirit of God in the trend toward relationship in created things.[9]

In this section, I have been proposing an understanding of the distinctive role of the Holy Spirit as the Creator and Life-Giver, immanent in creatures, who enables them to exist and evolve in an interrelated world, by bringing each creature into a communion with the dynamic Communion of the Three. The Spirit is the ecstatic gift of divine communion with creatures. This is a differentiated communion, because each creature is loved and respected precisely for what it is, and for its own precise participation in the ecological whole. The Creator Spirit is present in every flower, bird, and human being, in every distant quasar and in every atomic particle, closer to them than they are to themselves, enabling them to be and to become.

A *PROPER* ROLE FOR THE SPIRIT OF GOD IN CREATION

There can appear to be a conflict between claiming a distinctive role for the Holy Spirit in creation and the ancient Christian claim that the Trinity's actions toward creation are undivided and one.[10] Athanasius, Basil, Augustine, and many other theologians insist on the close relationship between the unity of the divine persons and the unity of action of the Trinity. The unity of action springs from and points to the unity of the divine nature. As Basil has said, the divine persons act only in full communion with one another. At first glance the undivided nature of the actions of the Trinity can seem opposed to a specific role for the Spirit or for the Word in creation.

I will put the case that in fact there is no such opposition, because the distinct roles occur in the one undivided act. The unity of the act of creation does not exclude but involves the specific and proper roles for the divine persons. As is always the case in trinitarian theology, communion and diversity are not opposed. The distinct and diverse roles appear in the unity of the one divine action. I will propose that the role of the Spirit in creation is *proper* to the Spirit. It is not simply *appropriated* to the Spirit. Words like *proper* and *appropriated* have precise meanings in the history of theology. I will attempt to make their meaning clear in the next few paragraphs. Because this issue demands technical discussion, I will describe my own line of thought with the aid of four summary proposals.

Proposal 1: The Trinity acts in creation in undivided unity, but this undivided unity can involve a proper role of the Spirit in creation. When the Greek theologians of the fourth century stressed the unity of the divine action, they did so in a way that left room for distinguishing specific roles within the one act. A text from Athanasius referred to earlier is a classic example:

There is, then, a Triad, holy and complete, confessed to be God in Father, Son and Holy Spirit, having nothing foreign or external mixed with it, not composed of one that creates and one that originated, but all creative; and it is consistent and in nature indivisible, and *its activity is one*. The Father does all things *through* the Word in the Holy Spirit.[11]

The specificity of the roles of the Three is allowed for in the last sentence. Athanasius goes on to talk in more detail about the roles of the persons. He says that the first person is the "beginning" and the "fountain" of creation, the Word is the one "through" whom things are created, and the Spirit is the one "in" whom things are made.[12] In a similar way, Gregory of Nyssa insists that the Trinity always acts as one, but points to distinct roles in this one act: "every operation which extends from God to the creation, and is named according to our variable conceptions of it, has its origin from the Father, and proceeds through the Son, and is perfected in the Holy Spirit."[13]

In the West, Augustine's emphasis on the radical unity of the Trinity, and with this the unity of the Trinity's action with regard to creation, set the pattern of thought that found expression in the famous axiom that all the Trinity's actions *ad extra* are undivided. This axiom was taken up in church teaching and, in my view, is clearly right in what it affirms. The actions of the Trinity with regard to creation are to be attributed to the Three. They act in the communion of the one nature; but what suffers neglect in the Western tradition are the distinct and proper roles of the divine persons in this one act of creation.

A developed concept of *appropriation* emerged in medieval Western theology. In trinitarian thought, a statement is called an appropriation when something is said of one person that is properly true of the Three. What is said of one is really common to the Three. Thomas Aquinas says that "to appropriate simply means to connect a thing that is common to something particular."[14] The idea is that when we say, for example, that all things are created by the Spirit, we are taking what really belongs to the whole Trinity and applying it to one particular person. According to the theology of appropriation, it is legitimate to do this on the basis of a resemblance between the particular trinitarian person and the work—as long as it is understood that such an assertion is *only an appropriation and not proper to the person*.

I am convinced that this theology of appropriation provides helpful clarification in trinitarian theology, but it has also had a negative effect on the distinction of persons. It has promoted a tendency to think that anything that can be said of any one person in relation to creation is really true of the Three; what is said of one is only *appropriated* to the specific person and is not *proper* to that person. I believe this to be a mistaken use of the idea of appropriation. It is important to distinguish between two levels of application of the theology of appropriation, one of them helpful, the other unhelpful. What I am proposing is that the theology of appropriation has an important and fundamental place at one level of theology, and that it is often misused at another level.

Where appropriation is used to caution against attributing a work such as creation or resurrection exclusively to one person it has an indispensable role to play. In the Christian Scriptures, in liturgy, in theological works, and in popular piety, we find actions attributed and applied to one person that properly belong to all three. The creed attributes creation to the Father, yet Christian tradition and theology attest that the whole Trinity is involved in creation. In this case, then, it is right to say that creation as such is not proper to the Father, but is being appropriated to the Father. (This, by the way, cautions against the well-intentioned idea that the trinitarian word "Father" can be replaced by "Creator.") And we find Jesus called the "resurrection and life" in the Gospel of John (11:25), but other New Testament texts attribute resurrection to the Spirit and to the Father. In this case it is good theology to invoke the tradition of appropriation and to say that resurrection is not proper to the Word, but simply appropriated to the Word. Creation and resurrection belong to the Three. They cannot be attributed to one person without reserve.

But when the theology of appropriation is used at a *second level*, to deny that there is *anything* distinctive about, for example, the Spirit's work in the one work of creation, then I think it is being misused. The fact that creation is to be attributed to the Three does not mean that there is nothing distinctive about the way that each of the Three is involved in the one act. I will argue that what has been described above as the distinctive role of the Spirit, to be the immanent Life-Giver, is proper to the Spirit. It is not simply an appropriation. This argument will involve three further steps. First, I will begin from what contemporary theology has already established about proper roles of the persons in the events of incarnation and Pentecost. Then I will build on the idea that creation is a relationship between each creature and the divine person. Finally, I will suggest that the distinctive relations of the Three come into play in the one act of creation.

Proposal 2: A starting point for a theology of the proper role of the Spirit in creation can be found in recent theologies that argue for proper roles of the divine persons in incarnation and Pentecost. Many contemporary theologians are dissatisfied with an unqualified use of the theology of appropriation, above all when it is used to deny the real and proper roles of the divine persons in the incarnation, Pentecost, and the work of our sanctification. Karl Rahner, for example, has argued convincingly that the incarnation is clearly a case where a divine presence in the world is not merely appropriated to one person, but is proper to the person of the

Word. He does not deny that the whole Trinity is causally involved in the incarnation, but he insists that, in the incarnation of the Word, something occurs that is proper to the Word and can be predicated of this one person alone. Rahner rejects as misleading and false the medieval idea that any person of the Trinity might have become incarnate.[15] In a similar way, theologians such as Heribert Mühlen and David Coffey point out that the outpouring of the Spirit in Pentecost and in the work of sanctification must be understood as proper to the Holy Spirit.[16]

In a different, but not opposed, approach Rahner and Congar both argue that in the work of sanctification and the life of grace, human beings have a real and proper relation to *each* of the divine persons.[17] What is at stake here is a fundamental issue of spirituality. Do we relate to the divine persons or simply to the one divine nature? Rahner and Congar rightly insist that we relate to the persons in a proper and distinctive way. Both theologians understand this relationship between the divine persons and graced humanity in terms of what has been called formal causality. This indicates a causality that involves a real *self-communication* of the triune God to human beings. It points to a divine self-communication that really transforms human beings constitutively, without compromising divine transcendence.[18] Human beings are assimilated to Jesus Christ through the action of the Spirit and become themselves adopted daughters and sons of God. According to Congar and Rahner, this assimilation clearly involves real and proper relations to the divine persons.

There is no contradiction in holding that our sanctification is due to the bestowal of the Spirit on the one hand, and this bestowal of the Spirit brings us into a real relation with the whole Trinity on the other. In fact, I would argue that this is the most obvious interpretation of important biblical texts such as Romans 8:14-17. Furthermore, I would suggest that when contemporary theology rightly claims a proper role for the Word of God in the incarnation and a proper role of the Spirit in Pentecost, this does not exclude, but necessarily includes, a distinctive and proper role for the other persons in these same events. If one adopts a New Testament Spirit Christology, then one must say that not only the Word but also the Spirit has a proper role in the incarnation. It is God's bestowal of the Spirit that constitutes Jesus of Nazareth as messianic Son of God. On the other hand, it seems clear that not only the Spirit but also the Word has a proper role at Pentecost. The outpouring of the Spirit is also a Christ event. It constitutes the church as the Body of Christ, so that the church is *in* Christ and the church *is* Christ. Both great events, the incarnation of the Word and the outpouring of the Spirit, involve not only the Word and the Spirit but also the divine person who is Unoriginate Origin and Source of All.

If the Word and the Spirit both have proper roles in the incarnation and at Pentecost, and if there is one economy that embraces creation and salvation, then we might expect to find that Word and Spirit have proper roles in the one act of creation. After all, theologians like Karl Rahner have long pointed to the inner relationship between God's self-expression in creation and God's self-communication in the Christ event. In fact the Scriptures do suggest distinct and proper roles of the Spirit and the Word in creation. This is the most obvious meaning of a number of biblical texts. Texts such as Genesis 2:7 and Psalm 104:30, for example, point toward the concept of the Spirit as the Breath of Life for all things; texts such as John 1:1-5 and Colossians 1:15-20 suggest a theology of Jesus Christ as the Word through whom all things are created.

Proposal 3: If creation is a relationship between each creature and the Trinity, such a relationship would involve proper relationships with the trinitarian persons. Further support for the idea of a proper role for the divine persons in creation springs from the idea that the trinitarian God creates in a relational way. The simple model of efficient causality is not an adequate way of understanding creation. Karl Rahner is convincing when he argues that God's creative act is not an instance of a causal relationship that can be found elsewhere among creatures.[19] God's creative act cannot be fitted into a system of cause and effect that operates between one empirical reality and another. The relation of Creator and creature is absolutely unique. There is always an infinite difference between the divine "causality" in ongoing creation and the kinds of causality we find at work in the world.

In line with the argument of this book, I am proposing that God's creative act can only be understood as a *relational* causality. This means that God's self-giving and self-expression through grace (described, as I have indicated above, as a kind of formal causality) are the best analogy for understanding God's action in creation. God acts in creation through giving God's self to the creature and through giving to creatures a participation in divine life. If God's being is radically relational, if God's being *is* Communion, then this means that creatures are able to be and to become because of their life-giving relationship with the Persons-in-Communion. In a relational understanding of reality, God, as Persons-in-Communion, can be thought of as creating a relational universe precisely in and through the relation of ongoing creation. In the relational causality of creation, the divine persons would be understood as giving expression to themselves in what is not divine. This divine self-expression constitutes creatures—and allows them to be their own creaturely selves. It gives them existence. It empowers the universe in its evolutionary unfolding.

If the Three give themselves to creatures in the relationship and the act of creation, this seems to suggest that what is proper to the persons is involved with each creature. If God is Persons-in-Communion, and if ongoing creation is a relational act whereby each creature is enabled to be and to become in a community of creatures, then each divine person can be understood as distinctly and properly engaged in the one act of creating.

Proposal 4: What is distinctive about each of the trinitarian persons comes into play in the one work of divine creation. In this last section, I have been suggesting that creation is a being-caught-up-in-relation with the divine Persons-in-Communion. Now I want to propose that this involves each of the divine persons precisely in what distinguishes them from one another—in their relationships as Source of All, Word generated from the Source of All, and Spirit proceeding from the Source of All. In the light of the theological tradition, I think it can be taken for granted that what is proper to the Source of All is to be the Unoriginate Origin of everything that exists. This is the divine person that Bonaventure loved to call the *fontalis plenitudo,* the "overflowing fountain" of life and fecundity for all things. This Source of All can be thought of not only as the Father "from whom are all things" (1 Cor. 8:6) and also as the Mother of all things (Wis. 7:12). Her compassion reaches out to all her creatures: "As a mother comforts her child, so I will comfort you" (Isa. 66:11).

What is distinctive and proper to the Word? Bonaventure saw the Word/Wisdom of God as the *exemplar* and *image* for all creatures. In the eternal generation of the divine Wisdom of God, there springs forth the possibility of the becoming of a universe of creatures. Jesus Christ, the eternal Wisdom of God, is the *icon of God* in whom "all things" were created (Col. 1:15). Bonaventure says: "Every creature is of its very nature a likeness and resemblance to eternal wisdom."[20] Everything that exists gives expression in its own unique way to the generation of divine Wisdom in the eternal life of God. Creatures in all their individuality and distinctiveness give expression to this eternal generativity. Pannenberg has developed some aspects of this tradition in a contemporary approach. He sees the existence of a world of distinct creatures as having its basis "in the free self-distinction of the Son from the Father."[21] The otherness of individual creatures is grounded in the otherness of the eternal Word. The Word of God, who expresses the self-distinction in God, has a mediating role in creation (Heb. 1:2; John 1:3). The self-distinction of the Word is the basis of the self-distinction and the independent existence of all the diverse creatures that make up our universe. The Word is the principle "not merely of the distinction of the creatures but also of their interrelation in the order of creation."[22] This work of the Word in creation comes to its extraordinary fulfilment in the Word made flesh. In both creation and incarnation, Word and Spirit act together: "the Spirit mediates the working of the Logos in creation as also in the incarnation."[23]

The Breath of God is not like the Word, a coming forth in God that would find explicit expression in the human flesh of Jesus of Nazareth. The Spirit is never destined to have a human face. The Spirit proceeds far more mysteriously and, in the economy of salvation, is revealed as the Breath of God that blows where it wills. This mysterious Spirit, who "searches everything, even the depths of God" (1 Cor. 2:10), now "fills" the universe (Wis.

1:7). The Spirit who proceeds from within the eternal depths of God finds expression as the Breath that breathes life into creation, grace, incarnation, and church. This Breath of God can never be pinned down or objectified. The Spirit, who proceeds so mysteriously in the life of the Trinity, appears in creation as the indwelling creative principle, permeating and filling the whole universe in all its diversity. As Pannenberg says, the Spirit is the "principle of the creative presence of the transcendent God" and the "medium of the participation of the creatures in the divine life."[24]

The Spirit expresses the capacity of the Trinity for "going out" (*ek-stasis*) to what is not divine. But the Spirit goes out in order to be able to dwell in creatures, to be present to them in radical immanence. It is thus "in the Spirit" that the divine Persons-in-Communion reach out to embrace what is not God. The Spirit continues in the economy of creation and salvation what the Spirit always is in the divine life. The Spirit is the immanent presence of God, uniting creatures in communion with the trinitarian God, saving them from nonexistence, sustaining, renewing, and directing them toward their fulfillment. While the Spirit is the ecstatic gift of communion only in profound unity with the other divine persons, the work of immanent life-giving and communion-making can be thought of as a reflection in the economy of what distinguishes the Holy Spirit within the trinitarian relations.

Tony Kelly has beautifully drawn the interconnection between the trinitarian life and the roles of the Three in the one work of creation. I conclude this section with his words:

> The originating Love that God is (Father) expresses its fullness in the Word, and rejoices in its infinite excess in the Spirit. In that self-utterance and self-gift, all God is, all that the universe is or will be, is contained. The universe emerging in the long ages of time is ever coming to be out of such Love. . . . That relational vitality which theology calls the "divine processions" of the Word and the Spirit, is creating the universe in its dynamic image. . . . The Word was in the beginning as the primordial self-expression of Love. God is self-differentiated into the Other, and Love becomes self-communication. Now, the universe has been uttered into existence to be a world of endlessly differentiated "words," *logoi,* meanings. . . . But the trinitarian "self-constitution" is achieved in the Spirit. The Love that has differentiated itself, and been expressed in the Other, becomes now a communal activity, "in the unity of the Holy Spirit." Hence, we can understand the relational dynamics of creation as a participation in the ecstasy of the Spirit, leading the differentiated, distinct, and independent realities of creation into self-transcending communion.[25]

THE SPIRIT OF GOD
AS THE "UNSPEAKABLE CLOSENESS OF GOD"

Ecology is concerned with the interrelated systems that support life on our planet. I have been proposing in this book that such living systems can be understood as very much the domain of the life-giving Breath of God. Each creature is a self-expression of divine Wisdom, and each creature is the dwelling place of the Spirit of God. This means that forests, rivers, insects, and birds exist and have value before God. They have value in their own right. They are not simply there for human use. They have their own integrity. They exist as an interdependent network of relationships in which each creature is sustained and held by triune love. They manifest the presence of the Spirit as the ecstasy and fecundity of divine love.

An important foundation for ecological theology is the conviction that the Spirit of God is creatively and lovingly present to all creatures, and present as the *power-in-relation* in our interconnected planetary life.[26] The earth, then, has a sacramental character: it symbolizes the divine that is present in it. Ambrose of Milan sees the Spirit not only as the Life-Giver but also as the one who brings beauty to creation. Beauty is a gift given by the Holy Spirit.[27] Basil of Caesarea develops something of a Christian ecological attitude to creation when he writes: "I want creation to awaken such a profound admiration in you, that in every place, whatever plants you may contemplate, you are overcome by a living remembrance of the Creator."[28]

If Jesus of Nazareth can be understood as the human face of God in our midst, the Holy Spirit can be thought of as God present in countless ways that are far beyond the limits of the human. If, in Jesus, God is revealed in specific human historical shape, in the Holy Spirit, God is given to us in a personal presence that exceeds the human and transcends human limitations. In a lovely phrase used by Moltmann, the Spirit is the "unspeakable closeness of God."[29] We can experience this unspeakable closeness in moments of deep connection with a place, in times of delight in trees, flowers, birds, and animals, and when we stand in silence before the mystery of the universe. We can experience this same unspeakable closeness at the heart of mutual friendship, and as a presence with us in suffering and grief, even in what seems at first like nothing but absence and abandonment. The Holy Spirit is inexpressible personal closeness in these and in many other ways.

The presence of the Spirit cannot be limited by human expectations. The Holy Spirit is radically beyond us—"the wind blows where it chooses, and you hear the sound of it, but you do not know where it comes from or where it is going" (John 3:8). The Spirit transcends our humanity and its self-preoccupation, to embrace all God's creatures. The great symbols of the biblical tradition speak of the Spirit more effectively than anthropomorphic language or abstract theology. The Spirit is living water, untamed wind, blazing fire. The Spirit pervades the whole universe and sees to "the depths of God" (1 Cor. 2:10). To be in communion with this Spirit is to be in communion with the whole of creation.

To be a person of the Spirit is to share the Spirit's love for the creatures that make up our Earth community. It is to love them for their own sake. Sallie McFague says that we should love nature for the same reason we love God and our neighbor, because it is valuable in itself and deserves our love. She sees this love as something to be practiced day by day in a spirituality that involves learning to look on other creatures with a loving eye:

> The love of God and neighbor is based in prayer, as the saints who lasted over the long haul illustrate: praxis must be based in piety. So also a Christian nature praxis rests on the attitude towards nature that emerges from paying attention to it. It rests on respect for otherness and concern for its vulnerability. This sensibility does not develop or endure unless it is cultivated day by day. As we must be open to, present to, God and neighbor, so also we must be to nature. We must be if we are to work, one day at a time over many years, for nature's health and well-being.[30]

NINE

A Relational Universe Evolving within the Relational Life of God

How can we best think about the God–world relationship? Clearly we cannot think of God as literally in the heavens above us. It is just as clearly inadequate to think of the universe and God as two entities over against each other, with God intervening in the universe from time to time. Along with a number of other theologians, I will suggest that a more helpful, but still humanly limited, approach to the God–world relationship is to think of the Spirit of God as "making space" within the divine relational life for a relational world to evolve.[1] This is a form of trinitarian *panentheism*—a word that comes from the Greek and means "all things in God."

In this chapter, I will sketch an understanding of the universe as evolving within the divine Communion that attempts to be faithful to key ideas in both science and theology. Science puts before us a universe that is interrelational, in which individual entities have their own integrity, and which is evolving and emergent. Contemporary theology offers a view of God as a Communion characterized by relational unity and diversity and points to God as the absolute future.

In this chapter, I will propose that when these insights from science and theology are brought into correlation with one another, three fundamental characteristics of reality emerge. First, the entities of the universe are constituted by relationships. Second, individual entities have their own distinct identity. Third, the universe with all its entities has an emergent character and evolves only in time. Each of these characteristics is intimately interconnected with the other two. For the sake of clarity I will consider each in turn. I will conclude this chapter with a brief summary of my own approach to a trinitarian panentheism.

ENTITIES ARE CONSTITUTED BY RELATIONSHIPS

It is all too obvious that we live in an interrelated life community on Earth. Careless or greedy human actions that damage a forest or a sea have unpredictable and devastating effects on countless creatures, including human ones. We are radically interconnected with everything else on the planet. The living systems of our planet, of which we are a part, are characterized by coadaptive, symbiotic, and ecological relationships.

Relationships characterize reality to its very depths. When science looks at anything at all, whether it be a proton, a galaxy, a cell, or the most complex thing we know, the human brain, it find systems of emergent relationships. Every entity seems to be constituted by at least two fundamental sets of relationships. First, there are the interrelationships between the components that make up an entity. Thus, a carbon atom is constituted from subatomic particles (protons, neutrons, and electrons). Second, there is the relationship between the entity and its wider environment. So a carbon atom in my body is constituted as part of a molecule, which forms part of a cell, which belongs to an organ of my body. I am part of a family, a human society, and a community of interrelated living creatures on Earth. The earth community depends upon and is interrelated with the Sun, the Milky Way galaxy, and the whole universe.

Arthur Peacocke tells us that the natural sciences give us a picture of the world as a complex hierarchy, with a series of levels of organization of matter, where each member in the series is a whole constituted of parts that precede it in the series. He provides an example, expressed (incompletely) in the sequence: "atom–molecule–macromolecule–subcellular organelle–cell–multicellular functioning organ–whole living organism–populations of living organisms–ecosystems–the biosphere."[2] At every level things are constituted by lower-level components yet not reducible to them.

The cosmologist William Stoeger describes these emergent patterns, which the natural sciences uncover as "constitutive relationships." He asks: "What makes a thing what it is, endowing it with a definite unity of structure and behavior, persistence, and consistency of action?" His answer is that it can only be an entity's constitutive relationships that make it what it is. He understands constitutive relationships as "those interactions among components and with the larger context which jointly effect the composition of a given system and establish its functional characteristic within the larger whole of which it is a part, and thereby enable it to manifest the particular properties and behavior it does."[3]

Stoeger insists that it is a universal feature of the world revealed by the natural and social sciences that entities are constituted by relationships. At every level from fundamental particles to atoms, molecules, cells, and the brain itself, one level of reality is articulated upon another. At every level, this nested organization is realized through the interrelationships between the components, together with the whole–part relationships that determine the distribution and collective function of components.[4] Constitutive relationships involve all those connections and interactions that incorporate components into a more complex whole and relate that complex whole into another level of unity. These constitutive relationships may be physical, biological, or social in character.

While science suggests a world of constitutive relationships, theology witnesses to a trinitarian God of mutual relations. In chapter 2, I pointed to Basil's theology of God's being as Communion. In this Eastern theology, God exists as a Communion of Persons; in Western theology, Thomas Aquinas insisted that, in God, relation and essence are one and the same.[5] The Persons-in-Relationship are what God is. They constitute the divine nature. As William J. Hill says, "there is no absolute person of the Trinity. There are only the relative Three." There is no reality in God beyond the Three in communion, no additional divine nature, no absolute person.[6] Both Eastern and Western theologies of the Trinity lead to a view of God as radically and essentially relational.

In recent times, trinitarian theologians from diverse backgrounds have argued that if God's being is Communion, then this has implications for the understanding of reality as such. If God's being is radically relational, then this suggests that reality is relational to the core. It suggests a relational ontology—the very *being* of things is relational being. It is this shared insight of theology that I believe can be brought into fruitful dialogue with the world revealed by the natural sciences. John Zizioulas, for example, states: "it is communion that makes things be: nothing exists without it, not even God."[7] He holds that nothing is conceivable as existing only by itself. There can be no true being without communion.[8] Walter Kasper says that understanding the unity of the divine nature as a "unity in love" suggests a "breaking out of an understanding of reality that is characterized by the primacy of subject and nature, and into an understanding of reality in which person and relation have priority."[9] Catherine LaCugna writes that "God's To-Be is To-Be-in-relationship, and God's being-in-relationship-to-us *is* what God is."[10] Her trinitarian theology becomes a sustained argument for what she calls an ontology of relation. So she writes that an ontology that is proper to the God of the economy of salvation "understands being as being-in-relation not being-in-itself."[11] Colin Gunton writes that "of both God and the world it must be said that they have their being in relation."[12] Elizabeth Johnson holds that "the Trinity provides a symbolic picture of totally shared life at the heart of the universe." She says that the Trinity as pure relationality "epitomizes the connectedness of all that exists in the universe."[13]

The theological insight that God is Persons-in-Relation provides a basis for a vision of the fundamental reality of the universe as relational. If the essence of God is relational, if the very foundation of all being is relational, if everything that is springs from Persons-in-Relation, then this points toward an understanding of created reality as "being-in-relation." Science tells us that each creature exists in a nested pattern of constitutive relations. Theology points to the trinitarian relationships of mutual love. A theology done in the light of science suggests a worldview in which a relational universe is thought of as emerging and evolving within the relations of the divine trinitarian Communion. In the worldview I am proposing, continuous creation can be understood as created being-in-relation springing from the divine Communion understood as Persons-in-Relation.

If reality is radically relational, this has applications at many levels, including that of the human person. In much post-Enlightenment thought, the human person has been understood as a self-conscious *individual*. Zizioulas is one of many theologians who, in relation to a theology of God as Communion, argues against all individualistic concepts of the person. He sees the person as essentially oriented toward communion. It is the nature of person to be in relationship with others. Zizioulas insists that the human person is both hypostatic and ecstatic. By *hypostatic* he means that the person is unique, unrepeatable, and free. By *ecstatic* he means that to be a person is determined not by the boundaries of individual existence but by "going out" (*ek-stasis*) beyond the self in relationship to others. To be a person is to be oriented toward communion. Zizioulas insists that the true nature of reality "is not answered by pointing to the 'self-existent,' to a being as it is determined by its own boundaries, *but to a being which in its ekstasis breaks through these boundaries in a movement of communion*." This ecstatic dimension does not diminish individual uniqueness but enables it to exist: "communion does not threaten personal particularity; it is constitutive of it."[14]

Not only human persons, but all the creatures that make up the universe, from atoms to eagles to galaxies, in their highly differentiated ways, are radically interrelational and at the same time possess their own individual integrity. In a trinitarian theology of creation, *all* creatures participate in the life of trinitarian Communion, and their differentiated relationships with each other are already a limited creaturely reflection of this divine Communion. In their different ways every creature, whether an insect, a tree, or a star, exists only in a network of relationships. We live in a radically interrelated universe.

The sciences suggest a world of constitutive relationships. The theology of God as Trinity suggests a view of reality in which relationships are central, where identity comes from being-in-relationship. This kind of theology correlates with what we experience of the world through the natural sciences. Both point toward a view of reality in which relationships have a primary place. Both suggest that things are constituted by relationships.

INDIVIDUAL ENTITIES
HAVE THEIR OWN INTEGRITY

Individual entities have their own identity and degree of self-directed-ness, whether we think of human beings with their experience of being free agents or birds with their glorious freedom in flight. Not every thing has an identity of its own. Some things, such as a pile of papers on my desk, may be simply collections of things that do not form a new whole. Stoeger distinguishes between things that are simply aggregates or collections of components, such as a pile of logs, and those entities that form a new whole and have characteristics that are essentially different from their components. Water has characteristics that are distinctive over and above its components of hydrogen and oxygen. Its functions and attributes cannot be reduced to the functions and attributes of its components.[15]

An individual entity exists only in patterns of constitutive relations but has its own identity, characteristics, and functions. It has a level of autonomous existence. It is both relational and substantive. It is precisely its constitutive relationships that allow it to be particular and substantive. It seems clear that in nature, individuality and distinctiveness are not opposed to relationality but exist only in patterns of relationship.

In a relational theology it is important not to idealize or romanticize relationships as such. Relationships can be of many kinds. A human body has a relationship with the cells that make it up. A predator has a relationship with its prey. An abusive parent has a relationship with an abused child. A lover has a relationship to a beloved. Relationships can be competitive, manipulative, abusive, or hostile. They can also be cooperative, enabling, freeing, and loving. The fact that relationships characterize and constitute reality does not necessarily mean that reality is always characterized by what human beings might think of as healthy and good relationships.

Feminist thinkers have shown how in human affairs patriarchal relationships damage and limit human life. Nancy Victorin-Vangerud in her theology of the Spirit points to the danger of poisonous relationships, which can too easily be sanctioned by what she calls a "poisonous pneumatology." She insists on the central importance of a critical and liberating stance toward the family and the other relationships that constitute our lives.[16] She rightly insists that it matters enormously what *kind* of relationships human beings have with others as infants, children, adolescents, and adults.[17] This line of thought warns against the uncritical embrace of relationships as automatically healthy or good.

What kinds of relationships characterize the world beyond the human? In nature we find amazing and beautiful patterns of mutual dependency, cooperation, and shared life. But we also find competition for survival, predation, and death. Our experience of the relationships that characterize the natural world is deeply ambiguous. I would argue that this ambiguity ought not to be resolved by any kind of simple synthesis. It is a profoundly truthful human experience to celebrate the beauty and wonder of the evolving universe and its creatures. It is just as much a fundamental truth of human experience to face the pain, the violence, and the death. Neither a romantic view of nature that sees only the beautiful nor a bleak view that can see only the pain and loss comes close to facing the full truth of the human experience of being in the world.

If we had only nature as the source for our thinking about relationships, then we would already know that we are part of an interrelational universe, interconnected with all other things. There would already be much to wonder about in this. But we would find that, while many of the patterns of interrelationship in nature are cooperative, others are exploitative, and we would have to admit that the most exploitative species on Earth is our own. Any attempt at understanding human ethical life in terms of natural selection can end only in disaster. A theology of relationships cannot find its source and criteria simply in the relationships that are found in the natural world.

A Christian understanding of relationships will spring in part from nature, but has its fundamental criterion in the compassionate love of God revealed in Jesus Christ and in the outpouring of the Spirit. Its model of relationships is the trinitarian model of mutual and equal love. In spite of the ambiguity we find in nature, a Christian theology dares to suggest that diversity in communion may be the ultimate eschatological nature of all reality, uncreated and created. This theology does not resolve the ambiguity we find in created relations. It leaves us like Job before the mystery. But it also functions as a promise: it proclaims that the ultimate relationships that undergird the expanding universe and the evolution of life on Earth are very specific kinds of relationships. They are relationships of equal and mutual love, of dynamic shared life. In these kinds of relationships, individuals flourish in all their irreducible individuality and otherness.

All of this suggests an understanding of the universe in which each diverse creature has its own distinct integrity. From the perspective of science, this individuality and integrity are given in all the constitutive relationships that make the entity what it is. From the perspective of theology, each individual creature has its own independent value within an interrelated universe springing from its relationship with the indwelling Creator Spirit. The Spirit brings forth from within the divine Communion an interconnected and interdependent universe of creatures. But these created relationships bear the limitations of finitude and death. They come to be only within the limitations of time. They come to be only in a process, a process that is incomplete.

THE UNIVERSE HAS AN EMERGENT CHARACTER
AND EVOLVES IN TIME

The entities of the universe are constituted by relationships and exist with their own integrity only through a process that is both evolutionary and emergent. In chapter 3, I described emergence as occurring when something is constituted from components in such a way that it has new properties, properties that are not reducible to the properties of the components.

Ian Barbour points out that sometimes these new properties can be predicted on the basis of what is known about the properties and organization of component parts. So the wetness of water can be predicted on the basis of dynamical laws concerning molecules, even though it is not a property of the elements of hydrogen and oxygen. But, Barbour continues, there are instances where emergent properties cannot be predicted. Things are far less predictable with the development of an embryo, where higher-level activities alter the structural organization of the components. The functioning of DNA is extremely complex and unpredictable, because its information can be repeatedly reentered to alter existing structures.[18]

Atoms, galaxies, stars, planets, single-celled bacteria, eukaryotes, multicellular organisms, mammals, and human brains are emergent phenomena. They depend on what goes before, but they represent something new. They evolve over long stretches of time. The sciences makes it abundantly clear that time is a fundamental dimension of the way things are in our universe. Admittedly, Einstein has taught us that time is relative. And according to quantum cosmology, time as we presently understand it may not apply to the quantum state from which the Big Bang emerged. But everything in the evolving universe depends on time. Individual creatures exist only in time between their past and an unknown future. The universe evolves over extraordinary lengths of time, and, without the patient unfolding of things in time, nothing at all could ever happen. Individual entities exist in relationship to all the creatures that preceded them, and with the unknown creatures that will follow. This understanding of ourselves and other living creatures, as beings who evolve over enormous lengths of time within an evolving universe, demands a different view of reality from anything that was available to Plato or Aristotle, Aquinas or Bonaventure, Galileo or Newton.

As individual human beings, we exist only for a brief moment. We are fragile, contingent, and, in the perspective of the universe, as transitory as a butterfly. But we are parts of the tapestry, interconnected with all that comes to be in time. Cosmology offers an example of this interconnection in time in what is called "anthropic" reasoning.[19] This refers to the insight that there is a relationship between the presence of human beings in the universe and the kind of universe that they inhabit. A universe with human beings in it is necessarily a universe that has certain characteristics rather than others. One aspect of this involves the age and size of the universe. Both can leave human beings overwhelmed. But cosmologists tell us that the universe has to be roughly as old as it is and as big as it is, if it is to be a place in which human beings could evolve. Because we are made up of atoms of carbon and other elements cooked in stars, we could not exist unless galaxies formed in the early universe, and the first stars began to convert hydrogen into the heavier elements that are needed for living creatures. The universe has to be as old as it is for galaxies to form, stars to ignite, elements like carbon to be synthesized, a solar system incorporating these elements to form around the Sun, and for life to evolve on Earth. And, of course, a universe that has been expanding for fourteen billion years has to be something like the size of our universe. As Martin Rees says, "The size of our universe shouldn't surprise us: its extravagant scale is necessary to allow *enough time* for life to evolve on even one planet around one star in one galaxy."[20]

Cosmologists tell us that a small, apparently insignificant change to one of the constants that characterize the forces and the particles of the universe would make the universe lifeless. The universe has to be fine-tuned in amazing ways if galaxies are to form, stars to light up, and carbon-based life to appear on the planet Earth. To take just two examples: without just the right level of irregularity or clumpiness in the early universe, and without the right balance between the expansive force and gravity, galaxies could never have formed. Without these fine balances, there would be no carbon-producing stars and no carbon-based life. Frogs and clams are as dependent on this fine-tuning as human beings. We are interrelated with every dimension of the expanding evolving universe and can come to exist only at a certain point in its time. We human beings bear the fourteen-billion-year story of the universe within us. Each of us is a product of the universe and part of its history.

A second, obvious example of the way entities like us are radically time-dependent comes from evolutionary biology. I pointed out earlier that life emerged on Earth in bacterial form about 3.8 billion years ago, developed into more complex and then multicellular forms over billions of years, expanded rapidly in the Cambrian period half a billion years ago, and then evolved into all the extraordinary forms we find today, including that of human beings. Pondering the place of death in the emergence of life can further this reflection on the way we are related to time. Evolutionary change in complex organisms is dependant on death. Without death there would be no series of generations, and without the series of generations there would be no evolution. Ursula Goodenough points out that death is part of the evolutionary strategy of complex sexual organisms in a way that is not true for simple bacteria. Bacteria do not have death programmed into their life cycle, although they can be killed or die for lack of food. But the evolutionary strategy of sexual multicellular creatures involves death. Early in the formation of an embryo, some cells switch on genes that commit them as germ-line cells. These are precursors of the egg or sperm cells, with the role of transmitting the genome to the next generation. The other cells are committed to become ordinary somatic cells, with the role of negotiating an evolutionary niche. These ordinary cells are programmed to die. It is only because they are programmed to die that there is the possibility of rapid evolutionary change, which can allow something as intricate as the eye to develop. It is precisely because of sexual recombination and death that we have the variety of complex creatures we find on Earth today. Without death there would be no wings, hands, or brains. Goodenough writes: "Death is the price paid to have trees and clams and birds and grasshoppers, and death is the price paid to have human consciousness."[21]

When we turn to the Christian theology of God, we find that it always has an inescapable orientation toward the future. Divine Communion has an eschatological character. We live from it yet we do not possess it. It comes toward us from the future. Biblical revelation has the character of promise and hope. The biblical sources of Christian theology teach us to value and love the present moment as the gift of grace. They teach us to look back on the past and to hold it in memory as a story of what God had done for us. But in a unique way the Scriptures orient us toward God's future for us. For Israel this has taken the shape of the divine promises, prophetic hope, and messianic expectation. In Jesus it found expression in his preaching and praxis of the coming reign of God. For those who follow the way of Jesus and live in the light of the promise of resurrection and new creation, it means living in constant expectation of God as the eschatological future.

Karl Rahner sees the biblical God as the Absolute Future—the future not only of human beings but also of all creation. In chapter 3, I discussed Rahner's contribution to an evolutionary theology of creation. He insists that the discovery that we are part of an evolving world demands a new understanding of reality, a new metaphysics. God now must be understood not simply as the dynamic cause of the existence of creatures, but as the dynamic ground of their becoming what is radically new. Rahner calls this process "active self-transcendence."[22] Like Rahner, and with Pannenberg, I see the Spirit of God as the Power of the Future, immanent in all of the processes of the evolving universe, enabling it to become what is new.[23] The Spirit of God is at work in evolutionary emergence whenever something radically new occurs, whenever nature reaches ecstatically beyond itself in the unfolding of the universe and in the dynamic story of life.

In his recent contribution to a theology of evolution, John Haught argues that we need a view of reality that makes sense of the fact that evolution brings about *new* forms of being. He too sees God as the power of the future. The entire universe is always being drawn forward by "the power of a divinely renewing future." With Rahner, he sees God as the Absolute Future. Evolution occurs ultimately "because of the 'coming of

God' toward the entire universe from an always elusive future."[24] This coming of God does not enter coercively or violently into cosmic and biological evolution, but energizes it from within in ways that are fully respectful of the world's autonomy.

Like Pannenberg, Ted Peters sees God as God of the future. His emphasis is on the promise of the future given in Christ. A central theme is that of *prolepsis*—meaning that in Jesus we experience an anticipation of God's future. God *is* the future of the world. Jesus Christ is the presence of this future in anticipation. This future involves not only human beings but the physical universe. He writes: "What happens to persons depends upon what happens to the cosmos. . . . If there is no cosmic transformation, then there is no resurrection; and if there is no resurrection, then Christian faith is in vain and believers are of all people the most to be pitied (1 Cor 15:14, 19)."[25] This strong statement, with which I fully agree, opens up a truly major issue in the science-theology discussion. How can this future in God be made intelligible in the light of the extremely bleak long-term predictions that science makes about the fate of our universe? There is an important issue of dissonance here between science and theology, one that demands much more attention in the science-theology discussion. I cannot attempt to address it here, but can simply point out that it has begun to be addressed recently by, among others, Robert John Russell of the Center for Theology and the Natural Sciences at Berkeley.[26]

The Spirit of God is the Power of the Future, immanent in all of the processes of the evolving universe, enabling the universe to become what is new. The Spirit is the immanent Life-Giver present in all things, who is at the same time the bond of communion between all things and the trinitarian God. The Spirit of God is at work in evolutionary emergence whenever something radically new occurs, whenever nature reaches ecstatically beyond itself in the unfolding of the universe and in the dynamic story of life. The Spirit's work does not supplant creaturely causes. It is not an intervention from outside. The Spirit is immanent in the whole process, working cooperatively and adventurously in and through the laws of nature and in and through contingent events. The Creator Spirit is immanent in a time-bound universe, deeply involved with its becoming and with the emergence of what is new. But the Spirit is also the eschatological Spirit, who, in a way that is not yet understood coherently in relation to scientific predictions of the future, draws the universe and its creatures to their future in the divine Communion.

A PARTICULAR FORM OF PANENTHEISM

In this chapter, I have been arguing that it is helpful and coherent to envisage the universe of creatures as emergent, interrelated and substantive, evolving within the dynamic relations of the divine Communion. As I bring this chapter to an end, it may be helpful to make some summary points about the kind of view of all-things-in-God that I have in mind.

1. *A panentheism that is trinitarian.* In this form of panentheism, the universe is understood as created from, and existing within, the shared life of the Trinity. Creation is seen as the free expression of the fecundity of this dynamic divine life. The universe and all its creatures exist and unfold from within the communion of the Three. All things are created through the eternal Wisdom of God, the very same Wisdom who has become incarnate in Jesus of Nazareth. All things are created in the Spirit of God. The Spirit is the interior divine presence empowering the evolution of the universe from within, enabling the emergence of stars, planets, bacteria, birds, and humans.

2. *A panentheism that understands God as wholly other to creatures and, precisely as such, as radically interior to them.* Divine transcendence and divine immanence in creation are understood not as polar opposites but, with the great theologians of the past, as presupposing each other. Some critics of classical theism misrepresent the past when they suggest that the emphasis on transcendence in great theologians of the past like Augustine and Aquinas makes God remote from creation. Nothing could be further from the truth. It is precisely when God is understood as transcendent that God can be thought of as immanent in creatures in a way that is not possible for a finite created being. It is because God is wholly other that God can be *interior intimo meo*—closer to me than I am to myself.[27] In this form of all-things-in-God, then, the infinite ontological distinction between God and creatures is maintained. It is precisely this distinction that enables God to be understood as radically *interior* to creation.

3. *A panentheism that understands the spatial image of all-things-in-God as an appropriate but limited analogy.* Human beings find it impossible to think of the God–world relationship without some form of image or analogy. The image of all-in-God is useful in that it appears to fit better with both science and theology than competing mental pictures, such as those of a God in the heavens or of God as a being outside creation who intervenes in it from time to time. Because Christian theology understands God as involved with the whole space-time universe in creation and redemption, but also as beyond space and time, it seems appropriate to think of the universe as evolving within the life of God. While I believe that the image and language of all-things-in-God are useful, it is important that this is not taken in a literal sense. God is not literally a container. In the position taken here, the language of all-things-in-God is a limited analogy based on God's creative and redemptive relationship with space and time. It seeks to respect God's radical transcendence of all finite notions of space and place.

4. A panentheism that conceives of the Creator as enabling creatures to have their own proper autonomy and integrity. Aquinas sees creation as fundamentally an ongoing relationship between the Creator and the creature—"a certain relation of the creature to the Creator as to the principle of its very being."[28] He insists that this creative relationship does not overpower or eliminate a creature's own proper action, but rather enables the creature to be and to act with its own proper autonomy. There is an infinite difference between God's *creatio continua* (primary causality) and all the interacting connections and causal relationships between creatures (secondary causality).[29] In this view, which I believe is foundational for discussion between science and theology, God is understood as creating a world of interacting creatures that have their own integrity and proper autonomy. God creates through natural processes that enable a life-bearing universe to evolve. In the light of this insight, it is appropriate in a contemporary theology of creation to think of God as committed to the integrity of natural processes.

5. A panentheism that sees creation as a free act of divine self-limitation. Faced with what science tells us about the pain and struggle of the long history of life on Earth, theologians have begun to rethink the issue of divine power. As I have made clear in earlier chapters of this book, along with other theologians, I think of God as freely self-limiting in love in creation. Love involves making space for another, and God can be thought of as supremely loving. In Jesus, God is revealed not in dominating or tyrannical power but in defenseless and vulnerable love. This love is certainly also powerful. It involves the promise of resurrection life and liberation for all. But the God revealed in the Jesus event is one who is present in human history as self-limiting and loving, who accompanies those who suffer, promising freedom and life. This pattern of vulnerable and self-limiting love can be understood to govern not only the story of Jesus but also God's ongoing creation of all creatures. Creation then can be seen as a form of divine self-limiting love that enables creatures and creaturely processes to unfold according to their own potentialities and limits. A God committed to the processes of the evolving universe may not be free to override them, but may well be thought of as being present in the Spirit with each creature, companioning each in compassionate love and leading each to its fulfillment in the divine Communion.

6. A panentheism that understands creation as a relationship that has an impact on God as well as creatures. I mentioned above my strong agreement with Aquinas on his understanding of creation as a relation between each creature and the Creator as the principle of its being. But I believe it is important to hold, against Aquinas, that the relationship with creation must be seen as real on the side of God as well as on the side of creatures. I have argued in chapter 7 that we need to be able to think of God as capable of suffering—in a divine way—with suffering creation. In this view, God can be thought of as supremely and transcendently capable of feeling with finite creatures. The trinitarian God can be understood as *transcendently* capable of loving creatures, making space for them, feeling with them, suffering with them, and delighting in them and bringing them to their eschatological fulfillment.

In this chapter, I have sought to describe a relational and evolving universe that is the expression of a relational God who makes space for and embraces the whole and all its parts. This universe can be understood as an emergent and radically interrelational world, a world in which individual creatures have their own integrity, and a world that is evolving in time at every level. The Creator Spirit can be thought of as the one who makes space in the shared dynamic life of the Three for a universe of entities to be and to become and who empowers the process of an emergent life-bearing universe.

PART 4

Two Particular Issues in Spirit Theology

TEN

The Procession of the Spirit

Any reflection on the inner life of the Trinity can be grounded only in what we know of God from the economy of creation and salvation. In chapter 5, I put the case that what we find in the Christ event is that Word and Spirit always go together. In other chapters, I have proposed that this mutuality of Word and Spirit is to be found not only in the Christ event but also in creation, grace, and the life of the church. Now it is time to take this line of thought further. In this chapter, I will suggest that the reciprocity we find in the economy can be understood as pointing to reciprocal relations between Word and Spirit in the eternal life of God. It is my hope that this discussion will make at least a small ecumenical contribution on an issue that has long been a source of division between East and West, the *filioque*. I hope, by locating reciprocity of Word and Spirit *in the trinitarian life of God,* to contribute to a renewed vision of Word and Spirit as reciprocally involved in Christian life today.

Orthodox theologians have recently focused attention on the reciprocal relations between Word and Spirit. Dumitru Staniloae, for example, while understanding the procession of the Spirit as from the Father alone, sees the Spirit as *accompanying* the Son, *reposing on* the Son, and *shining forth* from the Son.[1] In a recent book, Boris Bobrinskoy sums up the Eastern tradition's concept of the Spirit as always accompanying the Word in a way that I have found helpful. He moves carefully in the direction of a claim to reciprocal relations between Word and Spirit not only in the economy but in the eternal life of God.[2] From the Western tradition, Gary Badcock develops the idea of reciprocal relations in trinitarian life, but does not apply this directly to the relations of origin as I will below.[3] Thomas Weinandy argues for a theology of the immanent Trinity, which has parallels with the position I will take below but also differs from it.[4] My own approach will be to begin from Basil's theology of the procession of the Spirit. Then I will attempt a constructive proposal in which the Word is understood as involved in the procession of the Spirit from the Father, and the Spirit as understood as involved with the generation of the Word from the Father.

BASIL AND THE OTHER CAPPADOCIANS
ON THE PROCESSION OF THE SPIRIT

Basil develops his thought on the procession of the Spirit in the context of the Arian theology of Eunomius and his followers. Eunomius starts from the assumption that God is unbegotten. He then argues that if God's essence is to be unbegotten, and the Word is begotten, then the Word cannot be God. Basil's response is to show that being unbegotten belongs not to the divine essence but to a person, the person of the Father.[5] He sees the person of the Father as eternally the Unbegotten and the person of the Word as eternally the Begotten. It is precisely this relationship of begetting that enables us to distinguish the two persons. But if this is so, what makes the Spirit distinct? In their opposition to the divinity of the Spirit, some Arians had argued that the claim that the Spirit is divine must mean that God has two sons. This issue of the distinctiveness of the Spirit needed to be addressed. How can the coming forth of the Spirit be distinguished from the begetting of the Son?

A first response is given in Basil's favorite biblical image for the Spirit. The Holy Spirit is the Breath of God. Already in his *Against Eunomius* (ca. 364), Basil had appealed to Psalm 33:6: "By the *word of the Lord* the heavens were made, and all their host by the *breath of his mouth*."[6] In his later work on the Spirit, he makes frequent references to this text and speaks of the Holy Spirit as the Breath of the mouth of God. He points out, however, that the expressions *Word* and *Breath* are not to be taken literally. The Word is not to be thought of as air set in motion by the organs of speech. Nor is the Breath of God's mouth to be thought of as a literal breathing out of the lungs. What is meant, he tells us, is that "the Word is the one who was with God from the beginning and who is God, and the Breath of the mouth of God is the Spirit of truth who *proceeds* from the Father."[7] In this passage, Basil links the image of the Breath of God's mouth with the idea of the Spirit's procession that is found in John 15:26: "the Spirit of truth who *proceeds* from the Father."

If Basil's key image for the Spirit is the Breath of God, his key theological concept is that of *procession* (*ekporeusis*). This word will become the technical term in Greek theology for the coming forth of the Spirit. It will be used only of the Holy Spirit. It is not used of the Word. The Spirit *proceeds* and the Word *is generated*. In Latin theology, by contrast, both Word and Spirit are thought of as proceeding, so that Western theologians tend to speak of two processions in the Trinity. These two processions then need to be distinguished from each other, as they are in Augustine's idea that the

Spirit is unique because the Spirit proceeds from both the Father *and the Son (filioque)*.

For Basil, what is distinctive about the Spirit is that the Spirit is the *Breath of the mouth of God* (Ps. 33:6), who *proceeds from the Father* (John 15:26). Toward the end of his *On the Holy Spirit*, Basil focuses again on the distinctiveness of the Spirit. He points out that the Spirit comes from God, but not in the way that creatures do, and not like "the Word who comes forth by way of generation," but as "the Breath of the mouth of God."[8] Again, he insists that we must respect the limits of the image: God does not have a physical mouth. The otherness and mystery of God must be respected. The image must be used in a way that is worthy of God. What the image of the Breath of God points to, Basil tells us, is the Spirit as the "essence of life and divine sanctification."[9] He sees the biblical images of Breath and Word as bringing out the intimate relationship between the persons, while respecting their unspeakable mystery. Gregory of Nyssa and Gregory of Nazianzus both join Basil in using Psalm 33:6 as a foundation for seeing the Spirit as the Breath of God always mutually interrelated with the Word.[10]

In a further attempt to describe what is specific to the Spirit, Basil argues that if we are to give an adequate account of what distinguishes the persons, we need to identify their particular characteristics. These are expressed in their modes of coming to be, or their relationships. What are the particular characteristics that distinguish the modes of existence of the divine persons? Several times Basil speaks about these distinguishing characteristics in biblical terms as *paternity, sonship,* and *sanctifying power*.[11] The last of these was not a success. It was clear to the theologians who followed Basil that sanctification refers to the Spirit's work in the economy of salvation. It cannot be used successfully to point to what is distinctive in God's eternal life. Gregory of Nazianzus would improve on Basil by incorporating the idea of procession (*ekporeusis*) from John 15:26, to which Basil so often referred, as the distinguishing property of the Holy Spirit. Gregory then suggests that the distinguishing properties of the Three can be understood as being *unbegotten*, being *begotten,* and *proceeding*.[12] Gregory of Nyssa attempted a further line of thought, to which I will return in the next section: while the Father is the only Source in the Trinity, the Spirit comes from the Father *through the Son*. Gregory of Nyssa also describes the Spirit, in a phrase taken from John 16:14, as one who proceeds from the Father and *receives from the Son*.[13]

In summary, for the Cappadocians, the Word is the only-begotten and the Spirit is the Breath of God who proceeds from the Father. The word procession (*ekporeusis*) taken from John 15:26 is reserved for the coming forth of the Spirit. Its literal meaning is "to come out from." I believe that its very lack of definition is useful. The coming forth of the Spirit is mysterious and inexpressible. After all, in the economy of salvation the Word is

made flesh, but the Spirit has no human face and transcends all human cat-
egories. The Breath of God is like the wild wind that blows where it wills.
The Spirit is often spoken of in images from nonhuman nature—wind, fire,
and rivers of water. This does not mean that the Spirit is impersonal. In the
theology of the Cappadocians, the Spirit is thought of as entirely personal,
but far more than humanly personal. Gregory of Nazianzus puts us
squarely before the limits of our knowledge in relation to the mystery of
the divine life:

> What then is procession? Do you tell me what is the unbegottenness
> of the Father, and I will explain to you the physiology of the genera-
> tion of the Son and the procession of the Spirit, and we shall both of
> us be frenzy-stricken for prying into the mystery of God. And who are
> we to do these things, we who cannot even see what lies at our feet,
> or number the sands of the sea, or the drops of rain, or the days of
> eternity, much less enter into the depths of God, and supply an
> account of that nature which is so unspeakable and transcending all
> words?[14]

Gregory sets the tone for the rest of the theology of the East. The *procession* of the Spirit is not a clearly defined concept. It merely points to the
ineffable character of the coming forth of the Spirit. It does not exhaust the
mystery. But it does distinguish the Spirit from the Begetting of the Word.
As Bobrinskoy points out, it does this on the basis not of any kind of logical necessity but of revelation and of the experience of the Spirit in the life
and liturgy of the church.[15]

TOWARD A THEOLOGY OF RECIPROCAL RELATIONS
OF WORD AND SPIRIT

In the West, where Word and Spirit were both thought of as proceeding,
one of the fundamental ways by which the procession of the Spirit was distinguished from that of the Word was by means of what is often called the
"psychological" analogy. This is an analogy taken from human interiority,
where the Trinity is understood in relationship to a person who knows (the
Word) and loves (the Spirit). Augustine reflects on a series of triads that can
be found in the activity of the human spirit, beginning with the triad of the
interior self, knowing and *loving* and concluding with the human person's
remembering, knowing and *loving* God.[16] But Augustine finds a second,
sharper way of distinguishing the procession of the Spirit from the generation of the Word. The Spirit can be thought of as distinct in origin, because
while the Son proceeds from the Father, the Spirit proceeds from the Father
and from the Son (filioque).[17] This *filioque* would be unilaterally added to
the Nicene Creed in the West, with disastrous ecumenical consequences. As

Yves Congar has made clear, Augustine never abandons the ancient idea that the Spirit proceeds *principaliter* from the Father.[18] But he thinks of the Spirit's procession as distinctive because, while the Son proceeds from the Father, the Spirit proceeds from *both* Father and Son. He thinks of the Spirit as Gift and as Love in the economy of salvation and, in the divine life, as the mutual love of Father and Son.[19]

Thomas Aquinas builds on Augustine. He understands the Trinity in terms of his profound insight into the structure of a spiritual being: its being, its knowledge, and its love. This provides the fundamental analogy for understanding the two trinitarian processions of the Word and the Spirit. Aquinas also sees the Spirit as Love and Gift and refers to the theme of the Spirit as the mutual love between Father and Son. Along with other Latin theologians, he follows the principle that the persons are distinguished from one another only by their *opposing* and interrelated relationships such as Father–Son. These relationships are constitutive of the persons and are identical with the divine essence (this is Aquinas's theology of *subsistent relations*). Because in the spiration (meaning the "breathing out") of the Spirit, Father and Son are not opposed, Aquinas sees the procession of the Spirit as common to both of them. He thinks of the Father as giving the Son all that he has, apart from being Father, and this includes the capacity to breathe out the Spirit. The procession of the Spirit from the Father *and the Son* clearly distinguishes the procession of the Spirit from that of the Son. The Spirit proceeds from the Father and the Son as from one principle. Nevertheless, for Aquinas, as for Augustine, the Father remains the *principal* source of the Spirit, as the one who gives the Son the capacity to give the Spirit.[20]

I believe there is much that is profound in this Western line of theology and in its further development by more recent theologians, but I am convinced that the West has important things to learn from the East on the Holy Spirit. Congar has written: "I have a very high regard for the eastern way of doing theology and . . . I should like to place myself in a tradition common to both East and West."[21] This is also my aim in these reflections. As a Western theologian, I believe it is appropriate to listen to and learn from the East on the theology of the Holy Spirit without rejecting the Western heritage. And by working from Basil's theology, I am attempting to draw on the common tradition of East and West.

Eastern theology has maintained a living sense of the fullness of the personal mystery of the Spirit. There has been no tendency toward the Christomonism (an exclusive focus on Christ to the exclusion of the Spirit) that has been a danger for the West. The Spirit has not become a less important third, or an impersonal force, or simply a bond of love. While I would argue that there is no intrinsic reason why the *filioque* need lead to Christomonism, I think at a popular level it has tended to result in a reduced role for the Spirit. And at the same popular level, the idea of the Spirit as the mutual love between Father and Son has been misunderstood and reified,

resulting in an inadequate view of the Spirit of God as something impersonal that exists between the other two trinitarian persons.

Eastern theology contains a strong tradition of the *reciprocal relations*
between the Word and Spirit. These reciprocal and mutual relations are
expressed in the history of salvation, in the life and ministry of Jesus, in his
death and resurrection, and in the life of the Christian community. This
economic reciprocity, I believe, can be more explicitly grounded in a trinitarian theology of reciprocal relations. In attempting to develop this, I will
work primarily on the foundations built by Basil, with an eye to the way in
which this tradition has developed in the East. At the same time, I will
attempt to incorporate what I take to be the essential ideas of Augustine's
filioque—that the Word is fully divine, that the Word is to be understood
as fully involved with the procession of the Spirit, and that the Spirit must
be adequately distinguished from the Word. With Basil, I will think of the
Breath of God and the Word of God as always acting together. With him,
I will see the Word as eternally generated and the Spirit as eternally proceeding from the Source of All. And with him, I will understand the Three
as eternally *with* each other in a Communion that is entirely mutual and
equal. I will sketch out my own position with five summary statements.

**1. The Mother/Father is the Source of Word and Spirit, in a commu-
nion of radical equality and mutuality that is a primordial given.** The
Cappadocians speak of the Father not only as the source (*pēgē*) but also as
the personal cause (*aitia*) within the life of the Trinity. This one who is
Source of All communicates the absolute fullness of divinity to the Word
and to the Spirit, so that the Three share divinity in a communion of complete equality and mutuality. In the view of the Cappadocians, the idea of
one person being the Source of the Word and of the Spirit does not point
to the slightest inequality in the Three. It points only to the *personal* distinctiveness and diversity of the Three in communion.[22] It points to an
ongoing relationship of *being from another*.

It is through these relationships of origin that we are able to distinguish
the persons. But the Greek theological tradition does not reduce the persons to the relationships. *The distinctive and diverse persons are primary.*
They are given to us by God's self-revelation. Vladimir Lossky says that the
diversity of the persons is an "absolute reality." The mystery of God,
revealed to us in Jesus Christ and the outpouring of the Spirit, is of a primordial Three. The absolute diversity flourishes in primordial trinitarian
communion. This diversity, Lossky insists, is always ternary. It cannot be
collapsed into a duality or into the opposition in relations of Western theology.[23]

John Zizioulas writes: "The Holy Trinity is *a primordial ontological
concept* and not a notion that is added to the divine substance."[24] The
Source of All is not prior to the Spirit in any way. There is no before or after
either chronologically or conceptually, but only the Three in relationship.

As Lossky says, the Trinity "is not the result of a process, but a *primordial given.*"[25] If the Trinity is radically primordial, this can only mean that the Three depend equally on one another.

Vladimir Lossky sees the generation of the Word and the procession of the Spirit as "in a certain way simultaneous, the one implying the other."[26] The use of the word *simultaneous* points to Word and Spirit coming forth in identical *eternity*. It denies temporal or conceptual priority within the Trinity and points positively to the mutual and reciprocal nature of the divine relations. There can be no Source of All without the Spirit, no Word without the Spirit, no Trinity without the Spirit. There is no God without the Spirit.[27] Although there is only one who is Source of All in the Trinity, the Three are equally and eternally foundational to the Trinity.

2. The Word is fully involved in the procession of the Spirit: the Spirit proceeds from the Source of All **through** *the Word.* In the economy of salvation, the Word of God is profoundly involved with the mission of the Spirit. The Spirit is revealed as not only the Spirit of the Father (Matt. 10:20; John 15:26) but also the Spirit of Christ (Gal. 4:6; Matt. 12:28; John 14:26; 15:26; 20:22). The Scriptures present Jesus as anointed by the Spirit and doing the works of the Spirit (Luke 4:18-19). The risen Christ sends the Spirit from the Father (John 15:26). The Spirit will glorify the risen Christ, because he will take from what is Christ's and declare it to the disciples (John 16:14).

Because the Spirit is given *through* Christ and can be said to *take from* Christ in the economy, many theologians in the Greek tradition have thought that this indicates some kind of role of the Word in the eternal procession of the Spirit from the Father. They have spoken of the Spirit proceeding from the Father *through* the Son, or of the Spirit proceeding from the Father and *taking from* the Son. I will mention only three important examples. First, Gregory of Nyssa teaches that while the Father is the only cause of the Spirit, the Spirit proceeds *through* the Son:

> We do not deny the difference between that which is the cause and that which is caused. By this alone can we conceive of one being distinguished from the other, that is by the belief that one is cause and another is from the cause. In the case of those who are from the cause we recognize another distinction. One is derived immediately from the first, and the other *through that which comes immediately from the first.* So the mediating position of the Son in the divine life guards his attribute of being only-begotten, while not excluding the Spirit's relation by way of nature to the Father.[28]

A second example is Maximus the Confessor (580-662). In 645, Maximus wrote to the Cypriot priest Marinus. He argues the case that the Latin theology of the Spirit is capable of being understood in a way that is not opposed to the Greek theology of procession *through* the Word. He writes: "They [the Romans] have shown that they have not made the Son the cause [*aitian*] of the Spirit—they know in fact that the Father is the only cause of the Son and the Spirit, the one by begetting and the other by *ekporeusis* [procession]—but that they have manifested the procession through him [*to dia autou proieniai*] and have thus shown the unity and identity of the essence."[29]

A third witness to this tradition is John of Damascus (675-749), a major influence on the theology of East and West. He teaches that the Spirit is not only the Spirit of the Father but also the Spirit of the Son, "not because he proceeds from the Son but because he proceeds *through* him from the Father, for there is only one cause, the Father."[30] Like Gregory and Maximus, John of Damascus carefully guards the idea that the Father is the only personal cause in the Trinity, but allows that the Spirit proceeds *through* the eternal Word.

The contemporary Orthodox theologian John Zizioulas refers to the text I have cited from Gregory of Nyssa. He argues that at the heart of Gregory's theology is the idea that the ultimate theological category is the person rather than substance. According to Zizioulas, this is the meaning of the claim that the Father is the only personal cause in the Trinity. But, he argues, this claim does not exclude a mediating role of the Son in the procession of the Spirit, as long as the Son does not acquire the role of being the cause of the Spirit. Based on Congar's work, Zizioulas finds that when the Spirit is understood as proceeding *principaliter* from the Father, a *filioque* theology does not *necessarily* exclude the thesis that the Father is the only personal cause in the Trinity.[31]

I believe that Zizioulas is right, even though it must be admitted that the Latin approach has sometimes failed to make clear the role of the Father as Source and Origin. I also think that when theologians in the Greek tradition maintain that the Spirit proceeds *through* the Son, this can be understood as incorporating what is the most central insight of Latin theology concerning the procession of the Spirit. I propose, then, to hold with many Greek theologians that the Father is the only Source and Origin in the Trinity and that the Spirit proceeds from the Father through the Word.

3. The Spirit is fully involved with the generation of the Word: the Spirit eternally rests upon the Word. In Luke, Jesus is the one who is *anointed with the Holy Spirit* (Luke 4:18; Acts 10:37). In John, Jesus is the one on whom the Spirit *rests* or in whom the Spirit abides (John 32-33). I have outlined Basil's concept of the Spirit as the Breath that *accompanies* the Word in all the events of creation and salvation. The Spirit accompanies Jesus in every aspect of his life and mission.[32] Gregory of Nyssa develops this idea. He brings out the *mutual* interrelation between the Word of God and the Breath of God. He points to everyday experience where we find that our breath always accompanies our words. So, he says, the Breath of God "*accompanies* the Word" and "*manifests* its energies."[33] Word and Spirit come forth in an ineffable "reciprocal concomitance," that is beyond all unilateral causation.[34] John of Damascus also speaks of the Holy Spirit accompanying and manifesting the Word:

> The Spirit *accompanies* the Word and makes his energies *manifest.*
> . . . The Spirit is a power proceeding from the Father and *resting* on the Word, *expressing* and *manifesting* him. Moreover he cannot be separated from God in whom he is, nor from the Word whose *companion* he is.[35]

The long Eastern tradition of reciprocal relations between Word and Spirit includes Irenaeus's image of Word and Spirit as the two hands of God, and continues in the theology of Athanasius, Basil, Gregory of Nyssa, and John of Damascus. Bobrinskoy sees Gregory of Nyssa as central to this tradition:

> St. Gregory of Nyssa, taking over the intuition, not yet made explicit, of the "Hands of God" of St Irenaeus, will mark the entire Orthodox trinitarian vision up to our time by his concept of the simultaneity of the double origin of the Son and the Spirit. The Son will therefore be the "*raison d'être*" of the procession of the Spirit who is simultaneously the Spirit of the Father and the Spirit of the Son. *The Spirit will be linked no less—ineffably—to the paternal generation of the Son, resting on the Son who is spirit-bearing from all eternity.*[36]

There is an often-stated principle of Orthodox theology of the *always trinitarian* relations of the Trinity. This means that the Word cannot but be involved with the procession of the Spirit and the Spirit cannot but be involved with the procession of the Word. Paul Evdokimov has written of the Spirit's role in the generation of the Son: "The Spirit is no stranger to the mystery of the relation Father-Son, because the former is a triadic, not a dyadic, relation."[37] Perhaps the best expression of the way that the Spirit is "no stranger" to the generation of the Word is in the language of John of Damascus, who sees the Spirit as *resting* on the Word, and *manifesting* the Word, and as inseparable *companion* to the Word. This tradition is encapsulated in the Orthodox liturgy of vespers for the feast of Pentecost, where the Spirit is addressed as "the Spirit of comfort, who proceeds from the Father, and rests in the Son."[38]

   4. *The Word and Spirit are eternally coexistent and reciprocally related in their eternal life in God.* This principle is meant to restate the content of what has been said in the previous two in a way that brings out the reciprocal nature of the relations between the Word and Spirit. Spirit and

Word are always reciprocally related in the life of God and in the economy of salvation. The Word comes forth by way of generation, as a child is generated from a parent, and as an image or thought is generated in the mind. The Spirit comes from the Source of All Being by way of procession (*ekporeusis*). This word points to a more mysterious, elusive way of coming forth. It faithfully reflects the mysterious and elusive way that the Spirit is experienced in the economy of creation and salvation.

The Spirit proceeds from the Father, through the Son. The Word is generated from the Father, with the Spirit resting upon the Word. There is no before or after in the coming forth of the Spirit and the Word, no priority of time, rank, or honor. This reciprocal nature of the relation of origins finds expression in every aspect of divine action with regard to creatures. The Spirit is involved with the Word in creation, grace, the call of Abraham and Sarah, the exodus from Egypt and the covenant, the inspiration of the prophets and sages, the incarnation, the ministry of Jesus, his death on the cross, his resurrection, Pentecost, the life of the church, eternal life in God, and the final transformation of all things. Word and Spirit are inseparable in every aspect of the economy of creation and salvation because they are reciprocally related in trinitarian life.

5. Trinitarian life cannot be limited to the structural relations of origin, but involves mutual relations of unspeakable variety, depth, and intimacy. The relations of origin should be understood in the context of the mutual relations of the Three. This involves the important step of distinguishing the relations of origin, which describe the structural interconnection between the Three, from the countless dynamic interactions in the divine trinitarian communion. As Jürgen Moltmann puts it, we need to distinguish between the constitution of the Trinity and the Trinity's inner life.[39] This inner life is what John of Damascus spoke of in terms of *perichoresis*, a word that means a mutual embrace. It points to the mutual indwelling of the divine Three, to their mutual communion. It involves relationships of unthinkable communication of self to the other, of play, of creativity, of delight in the otherness of the other and of supreme intimacy. As Congar has said of this perichoretic relationship, "we should welcome this idea of the in-existence of the hypostases one within the other, the idea, in other words, of exchange and reciprocity. It points to the fact that *there is a Trinitarian life that does not simply consist of processions or relationships of origin.*"[40]

It is important to insist that the relations of origin do not exhaust the trinitarian relations. They are an inadequate human description, based on revelation, of eternal structuring relations. They do not limit divine communication. I make this point because it is not unusual in the theology of the Spirit to come across comments that at least appear to limit divine relationships to the relations of origin. Thus, it is said, for example, that "the

Spirit is pure receptivity." As it stands, this is a statement about the relations of origin. If such a statement is interpreted as an attempt to describe the whole life of the Spirit within the trinitarian relations, then I believe it is dangerously misleading. The Spirit is then thought of as completely passive. In such a view, the Spirit is incapable of active relating. This undermines any idea of the Spirit as fully personal and can lead to a domesticated understanding of the Spirit. The wild Wind of the Spirit is reduced to a passive receptivity.

The Spirit proceeds from the Father through the Son, but this relation of origin does not limit the Spirit's dynamic and diverse perichoretic relations with the other persons. On the contrary, the relation of origin enables the Spirit to participate in the infinite range of responses of the Three to each other. The Spirit is a fully personal participant in the endless dynamism of giving and receiving that makes up the perichoretic communion of the Three. As Dumitru Staniloae says, "There is a reciprocity of infinite richness in its complexity between the Three Persons of the Holy Trinity, and it is this which gives them their fully personal character." And, he says, there is a "special reciprocity" between Word and the Spirit that is reflected in their contact with the world.[41]

6. The Trinitarian Relations do not legitimate patriarchy but support diversity in communion. Feminist theology and liberation theology in general are rightly critical of the way in which the doctrine of the Trinity has been co-opted to serve the cause of patriarchal oppression. In my view such co-option is a perverse misuse of a liberating doctrine, a doctrine that calls us to a life of equal and mutual relations. The critical stance of feminist and liberation theology leads not only to an important critique of exclusively male language in trinitarian theology but also, at times, to concern about the idea that two in the Trinity are *from another.* Do the relations of origin lend support to a dangerously hierarchical approach to reality?

It needs to be said that the relations of origin can be, and have been, used to justify earthly hierarchies. One response to this is to abandon or minimize the relations of origin. Some theologians have moved in this direction out of concern to avoid legitimating hierarchies as well as for other reasons. One example is Leonardo Boff, who claims that "everything in God is triadic, everything is *Patreque, Filioque* and *Spirituque.*"[42] Gavin D'Costa, in a determined effort to undermine patriarchy, abandons the relations of origin altogether and argues that the distinction of persons can be safeguarded at the economic level.[43] Joseph Bracken, in a creative integration of process thought and trinitarian theology, to some extent transcends the relations of origin. He sees the three persons as "three individual processes of interpretation which merge, more deeply than the members of any human community could ever imagine, to form the communal process of interpretation which is their reality as one God."[44] Wolfhart Pannenberg does not abandon the relations of origin but seeks to go beyond them. He sees the variety of richly textured relationships between the persons witnessed to in the Bible as constituting the distinction of persons.[45]

I would not reject or minimize the relations of origin. These relations—of the Word and the Spirit coming from the Source of All—are minimal statements about the eternal life of God that the Christian tradition has made on the basis of biblical revelation. The experience of Christ and the Spirit point beyond themselves to the mystery of the Source of All. This is a deep structure that Christian faith discerns in the economy—God is revealed to us in Word and Spirit who come to us from the Source of All. If God reveals God's self to us, if God is faithful and true, if the economic Trinity is the immanent Trinity, then I believe that the Christian tradition is right to understand the eternal life of God in terms of the relations of origin.

I believe, however, that it is fundamental to insist that the idea that Word and Spirit come from the Source of All does not imply subordination or hierarchy. What is communicated is the absolute fullness of divinity. The Three exist in radical equality and in mutual relations from all eternity. Gregory of Nazianzus points out that, while the Father remains the source of monarchy or unity in the Trinity, this monarchy is shared: "Monarchy is that which we honour. It is, however, a Monarchy that is not limited to one Person." It is a monarchy of the Three, one that is constituted by equality of nature, unity of mind, and the return to unity of those who come from it.[46] This concept of a shared monarchy is a radically new concept that challenges all forms of patriarchy.[47] In this view, reality is determined by mutual relations in shared Communion. And while the Cappadocians always see the Father as Unoriginate Origin of the divinity, they also recognize that the Father cannot be Origin without the Word and the Spirit. Each person exists only in relation to the others. The Cappadocians insist that the Father cannot be Father without the Son. The name "Son" does not imply any kind of deficiency with regard to the Father, but *mutual relations (scheseis)* between the two.[48] Each person can exist only in the eternal interrelationship of the Three. In this sense, they exist on account of each other. They eternally determine each other's existence.

In my view, then, the relation of coming-from-another, when rightly understood, does not lend support to hierarchical and patriarchal views of reality but undermines them. As I argued above, the relations of origin exist in the context of the *perichoresis* of the Three. These perichoretic relations, far from legitimating patriarchal subordination, profoundly subvert it. What they place at the absolute center of reality, both divine and creaturely, are relationships of radically mutual and equal love.

In both anthropology and theology, it is important to challenge the idea that when one person comes from another, this necessarily implies inequality. My mother is the source of life for me, her son. The two of us will always be in a mother–son relationship—even, I hope, in our eternal life in

God. This does *not* mean that my mother is necessarily in any way superior to me. She may well be better at some things than I. But my point is that a relation of origin does not mean superiority and need not and ought not lead to the domination of one over the other. As an adult, I can relate to my mother as a complete equal, and in fully mutual love. Yet I will always be from my mother. Human relationships of origin can sometimes be oppressive, but they certainly need not be so. They are compatible with mutuality and equality.

Human relations of origin are but a pale analogy of the divine trinitarian relations. For one thing, there is no beginning of life for the Word and Spirit. They are coeternal and coequal with the Mother/Father who is Source of All. In spite of the infinite gulf between human and divine relations, human relations of origin can illuminate the divine relations. In particular they can help bring into focus the distinction between structural relations and the relationships of mutual love. A daughter's structural relation with her mother, her relation of origin, means that she will always be from her mother. She will always be a daughter. But this does not limit the endless possibilities of mutual love between mother and daughter. They may be able to communicate with each other, share experiences with each other, be with each other in painful times, be playful with each other and take delight in each other. In spite of human limitations and weakness, they may share a profoundly equal and mutual love. This kind of human relationship at its best can give us a faint glimpse into the mutual relations of the Three.

ELEVEN

Discernment of the Spirit

According to the Gospels, Jesus was "led by the Spirit" in his life and ministry (Luke 4:1). Those who follow the way of Jesus today will seek to be led by the same Spirit. This raises the fundamental question of discernment. How can Christians of today make decisions in their lives that are faithful to the promptings of the Spirit of God? How can we know what is faithful to the Spirit?

From the beginning, Christian believers have always been concerned about distinguishing the experience of the Holy Spirit from other experiences. It has been a constant teaching of the tradition that it is all too easy to fall into self-deception and to be led astray by outside influences. Teachers of Christian spirituality have warned that discernment is often difficult. They have recognized that the human mind and heart are complex and that human consciousness is many-layered.

In more recent times we have come to understand this complexity in new ways. Psychology has taught us that we are capable of acting out of needs and drives that are partly or completely unconscious. The sociology of knowledge and feminism have shown us how easy it is to be unaware that we are operating in ways that reinforce the privilege of our own economic status, class, race, or sex. The drive to maintain a privileged position can shape our consciousness, limit our awareness, impinge on our freedom, and influence our decisions. We have learned that we are not neutral interpreters of reality, but inclined, often unconsciously, towards what serves our own interest and maintains our own privilege. We have learned that a measure of freedom comes only in bringing into the open and acknowledging our interests and biases.

This new awareness reinforces the traditional understanding of the complexity of Christian decision making. How can I tell, for example, whether a desire I feel to abandon what I am doing and take on a new project or a new relationship comes ultimately from the Spirit of God or from a self-serving tendency to secure my sense of myself in relationship to others?

This kind of question points to the importance of what has traditionally been called the "discernment of spirits." In this chapter I will outline some key findings on discernment from Ignatius of Loyola and John of the Cross, and from Karl Rahner's interpretation of the Ignatian tradition.

DISCERNMENT OF THE SPIRIT AS FOLLOWING JESUS

The first thing that needs to be said about the specifically Christian view of discernment is that, as in all other areas of Spirit theology, the Breath of God and the Word of God are reciprocally related. On the one hand, we come to faith in Jesus as the Wisdom of God only in and through the Spirit of God. On the other hand, whenever we experience the Spirit, the Spirit is always the Spirit of Jesus Christ. For the Christian community, Jesus is the explicit shape of God's self-revelation. Jesus-Wisdom is the criterion for all Christian discernment of spirits.

It is not surprising, then, to find that the Scriptures connect discernment with faith in Jesus Christ. Paul speaks explicitly of the "discernment" or "distinguishing" of spirits (*diakriseis*) and sees this capacity as itself a gift of the Spirit of God (1 Cor. 12:10). He tells us that the sure sign of the Spirit's work is confession of faith in Jesus: no one who curses Jesus is led by the Spirit, and anyone who confesses genuine faith in Jesus is led by the Spirit (1 Cor. 12:3). In a similar way, the first letter of John speaks of the need to "test" the spirits (1 John 4:1). Here we are told not to believe every spirit but to test the spirits to see if they are from God. The criterion by which we can know the Spirit of God is this: "Every spirit that confesses that Jesus Christ has come in the flesh comes from God" (1 John 4:2).

What these texts require is not simply an abstract *orthodoxy,* but a following of Jesus that expresses itself in love, a Christian life lived in *orthopraxis.* Paul's test for the authenticity of gifts of the Spirit is that they contribute to the common good of the community (1 Cor. 12:7). They are for the building up of the community (12:1, 26). He points out that there is one gift that stands out above all the others so that it becomes a criterion for all the others, "Faith, hope and love abide, these three; and the greatest of these is love" (1 Cor. 13:13). First John puts it just as directly: "Beloved let us love one another, because love is from God; everyone who loves is born of God and knows God. Whoever does not love does not know God, for God is love" (4:7).

Jon Sobrino, a liberation theologian from El Salvador, has reflected on Christian discernment. He locates this discernment in the following of Jesus in one's own life amid all its complexities and ambiguities.[1] This does not mean a slavish imitation of Jesus, but the attempt to discern the call of God in day-to-day events as Jesus did in his own context. Central to Sobrino's reflection is that, while for Jesus God is the *always greater God,* the God beyond all human institutions, yet this God is met in the specific and limited experience of one's neighbor, above all, in the poor and oppressed neighbor. This leads Sobrino to insist that the place of Christian discernment is in solidarity with those who are oppressed and poor.

In developing this line of thought, Sobrino offers four criteria for discernment as a follower of Jesus. First, the place in which God's will is to be discerned is in the stance of *partiality for the poor*. Second, this stance needs to involve a genuinely *effective* love. Third, this love will need to find expression in the *sociopolitical* dimensions of life. Finally, this love must be prepared to be involved in situations of *conflict*. A love that is partial, effective, and sociopolitical will stand with the oppressed in conflictual situations and over against those who oppress them—in the hope of bringing freedom to both.

Feminist theology joins with Latin American liberation theology in pointing to the interpretative importance of the experience of the oppressed. Rosemary Radford Ruether proposes that the critical principle of feminist theology is the promotion of the full humanity of women. This means that "whatever diminishes or denies the full humanity of women must be presumed not to reflect the divine."[2] For feminist theology, the authentic movement for the full humanity of women is the place of the Spirit of God. The place for discernment, then, can only be in the company of those who seek the full humanity of women—and of all who are excluded or marginalized in today's world. The God of the Bible, the God of Jesus, is a God who is found in the company of women, children, the sick, and the poor.[3]

Choosing this company is already a gift of the Spirit that can bring to light and challenge our prejudices. It can lead us toward freedom. It provides the place for discernment. But there is still the question of *how* to test the spirits and discern the promptings of the Holy Spirit. The most highly developed response to this question in the Christian tradition is found in the *Spiritual Exercises* of Ignatius of Loyola.

THE COGNITIVE DIMENSION OF DISCERNMENT

Ignatius presumes that a person engaged in discernment has taken account of the teaching of the Scriptures and the church and is seeking to make a choice between options that are understood to be morally good. He distinguishes three "times" or ways in which a person can seek to find and follow the will of God. The first time is when God's invitation is clear and unmistakable. The second time is when a person is pulled in different directions and there is need for a discernment of these different movements. The third time is when a person who is peaceful and not moved in different directions uses a more cognitive approach to discernment.

In his life, Ignatius combined all three approaches and moved easily from one to the other. A number of commentators point out that Ignatius makes these distinctions for the sake of clarity and that many life choices may have elements of all three ways. Harvey Egan, for example, writes that in the concrete, "the Three Times are not three distinct ways of finding God's will, but actually aspects of one core experience and election in which all three aspects are present in varying degrees of intensity."[4] In what follows I will begin with some thoughts on cognitive discernment, then consider some key ideas from Ignatius on the discernment of interior movements. Finally I will consider how decisions can be made in the light of consolation that clearly comes from God.

The cognitive approach to discernment is particularly useful at the beginning of the spiritual journey and at other times when we do not experience turbulent feelings. But it is a helpful part of all discernment. It begins with prayer for enlightenment and freedom. Freedom is present when a person recognizes and accepts that, in a choice between two possibilities, God might be leading in either direction. It involves the acceptance of the idea that God might be leading in the least attractive direction. This kind of freedom comes as God's gift given in engagement with the gospel. By taking on the "mind of Christ" (Phil. 2:5), we learn that God's new life can come in ways that cannot be predicted. Pondering Jesus' experience of the cross and the apparent total collapse of his project can create the possibility of going beyond attachment to one direction to accept the real possibility that God's call might be in either direction.

Cognitive discernment involves using our minds to evaluate all the information we have. This includes not only the Scriptures and tradition of the church but also what we have learned from literature, biology, sociology, and psychology. Current events may point to "signs of the times."[5] If, for example, the ecological movement is judged to be a "sign of the times," a movement that in spite of all its human limitations is to be understood as response to the stirring of the Spirit, then this will become relevant in considering some issues.

The process of cognitive discernment is relatively simple. It is an approach that many would see as a matter of common sense. After prayer for freedom and openness to God, the first step in the process is to clarify the options that are before us. Once this is done, it can be helpful to make a list of reasons that support one option over against a list of reasons that support the alternative. The discernment process will involve a time in which these are mulled over and evaluated. It may involve consultation with a friend or spiritual director.

Ignatius tells us that a decision made in this way needs to be confirmed in prayer. The matter is placed before God in prayer and tested to see that it leads to peace and sits well with our being in the place where we are open to God. As we go about our duties, what is truly of God will find confirmation in its effects—above all in our freedom to act with love. What is of

God will lead to a deep peace in God, even in the midst of the complexities of everyday life. Cognitive discernment leads to, and involves to some extent, the discernment of interior movements.

THE DISCERNMENT OF INTERIOR MOVEMENTS

Human beings very often find themselves pulled in different directions. They are influenced by a variety of feelings, thoughts, desires, commitments, and prejudices. It is not unusual to find oneself drawn simultaneously in opposite directions at different levels of one's being. I may, for example, be convinced intellectually that I ought to forgive someone, while finding, at the same time, a level of my being where there is unresolved anger and resentment toward the person.

The early Christian tradition understood the different pulls we experience in terms of the ancient biblical cosmology. In this worldview, good and evil spirits were understood to be at work everywhere, moving the sun and moon and stars and also moving the human heart toward good or evil. In this framework, discernment is understood as distinguishing those movements that have their origin from outside, and then distinguishing which of these come from good spirits and which come from evil spirits. The good spirits are understood as angels of God, bringing God's graces to the person. The Spirit of God might well be moving the mind and heart to good through these angelic spirits.

I pointed out above that in more recent times, psychology and the sociology of knowledge have added to our knowledge of the multilayered nature of human consciousness. We know that our day-to-day decisions and actions are influenced by needs and drives that spring from our preconscious selves. All of this confirms the central importance of discernment as we attempt to assess our feelings, thoughts, desires, moods, and drives. What Ignatius offers are some "rules" that can help to distinguish between various inner movements and promptings. As John Futrell points out, Ignatius's rules for discernment are part of a 1500-year-old tradition. He argues that what is unique about Ignatius is that he offers such a *practical* method of discernment.[6]

Ignatius's approach is embedded in the retreat process of the *Spiritual Exercises*.[7] I will not try to summarize what he says. His approach is wise and subtle and dependent on its context. But I will pick out six of his insights that I believe are useful aids in the everyday discernment to which all Christians are called:

1. The fundamental principle is that the best guide to the discernment of interior movements is the discovery of the direction in which they lead. Ignatius tells us that the best insight into the nature and origin of inner experiences such as thoughts and feelings is through their orientation. We can know the nature of an interior movement only when we see the direction in which it takes us. Futrell puts it succinctly: the goal of discernment is "to discover the *origin* of interior movements by detecting their *orientation.*"[8] The basic question is always: Where does this line of thought lead? Where does this emotional state take me? The ancient biblical maxim provides the foundation for all discernment of interior movements: "You will know them by their fruits" (Matt. 7:16). Does this feeling lead toward God or away from God? Does it lead to a profound sense of peace in God or to a lack of interior peace?

I find myself, for example, desiring to retreat from those around me. How do I know whether this is a God-given, life-affirming instinct or irresponsible escapism? According to Ignatius's principle, I can best answer this question by noticing where my inclination tends to lead me. Does it lead toward interior restoration, to a sense of God's presence, and to a renewed commitment to those I am called to love? Or does it lead to an experience of self-indulgence and emptiness? This principle can also be used to discern in a more communal way. As the Roman Catholic Church ponders its practice of ordaining only celibates as presbyters, key questions in ecclesial discernment will be: Where does the maintaining of the requirement of celibacy lead the church? What effects will it have? Where would the modifying of this requirement lead? What effects would it have? Which direction seems likely to result in a richer eucharistic communion for the People of God throughout the world?

2. In our spiritual lives we can expect to experience both consolation and desolation, and awareness of these can help guide discernment. Ignatius uses the word *consolation* to describe the experience of the interior life when we are inflamed with the love of God. Consolation is an interior movement that leads a person to God. It can involve interior peace, spiritual joy, tears, and an increase in faith, hope, and love (§316). All of these are the gifts of the Holy Spirit. Paul tells us that the fruit of the Spirit is "love, joy, peace, patience, kindness, generosity, faithfulness, gentleness and self-control" (Gal. 5:22-23). *Desolation* involves the opposite: darkness, turmoil, laziness, tepidity, and lack of faith, hope, and love. In desolation, Ignatius tells us, the evil one attempts to guide us, and it is as if we were separated from God (§§317-18).

It is not always easy to distinguish between genuine consolation and desolation. There are times when a choice that is accompanied by an experience of discomfort, which may seem at first like desolation, actually leads to a genuine consolation. The crucial issue is the deepening of relationship with God. Joanne Wolski Conn has offered some examples of how Ignatius's guidelines on consolation and desolation can work in assisting in a feminist approach to Christian spirituality. One example would be that of a woman who has inherited a one-sided and false view of self-sacrifice. She may feel insecure and uncomfortable in her first attempts at learning to care for herself. This discomfort may at first seem to be a kind of desolation; but if it results in the experience of a more mature and loving relationship to God, this would show that the real result of her care for herself is authentic consolation.

Another example would be someone who finds herself experiencing real pain and frustration that give rise to anger. This may seem to be desolation, but if it finds expression in healthy anger, including anger at God, and this results in a more candid and adult relationship to God and others, then the result may not be desolation but consolation.[9] Victorin-Vangerud points out that anger can serve the work of love and right relation. She suggests as further fruits of the Spirit from a maternal feminist perspective: "self-determination, risk, resistance, willfulness, defiance, courage, confrontation, conflict and voice."[10]

What all of this points to is that a choice for good can be accompanied by a superficial lack of peace that comes from choosing to act against cultural assumptions. But this superficial lack of peace may coexist with authentic consolation at a more interior level. Real consolation is a peace that is experienced at the deep levels of our being, the place of the indwelling Spirit of God.

3. Decisions about one's life should not be made in time of desolation. One of the clearest directions Ignatius gives is his insistence that the time of desolation is never the time for making a change (§318). It is not the time to change a previous decision or to make a new decision. He says that in desolation we are easily misled into a path that is not of God. All the good directions of our life seem under attack. Evil seems to be at work in us. We experience turmoil and lack of peace. All of this means we are not in a position to discern the quiet and subtle invitation of the Spirit of God.

Times of desolation include those when we experience emotional conflict with others, confusion, distress, depression at the state of the church or for other reasons, distress at our own failure and inadequacy, dryness in the life of faith, and doubt about God's existence, goodness, or love for us. These and other kinds of experiences can leave us inclined to make a decision that involves abandoning long-held commitments. Ignatius advises, in all such cases, to hold fast to the decisions that have been guiding us. The time of desolation is a time for continuing and deepening our commitment and our prayer. He sees it as a time to remember in humility how much we are in need of God, and to commit ourselves in trust to God, knowing that consolation will come as the gift of God in God's time.

4. Desolation can be a time of grace. Ignatius points to three reasons we may suffer desolation (§322). The first is because of our own tepidity, laziness, or neglect. In this case the right response is to act against the desolation with prayer. The other two instances are times when desolation comes to us as a gift of grace. God may allow a period of desolation as a trial period in which we learn to follow God's call in darkness and dryness. God may be helping us toward an inner purification of spirit. The experience of desolation after consolation can help us recognize that consolation was a pure gift of the Spirit. Ignatius teaches that in these kinds of experiences, God is at work in the dryness and darkness.

This insight of Ignatius has some relation to the experiences that John of the Cross describes in much more detail as the *Dark Night*.[11] It may be, John of the Cross tells us, that a person who experiences only dryness and darkness in the more active forms of prayer is being called by God into a quieter form of contemplative prayer. Such a person should be encouraged to "learn to remain in God's presence with a loving attention and a quiet intellect."[12] Gradually such a person will be led to know the subtle sense of the presence of God in what at first seems to be only darkness. John of the Cross goes on to describe a further, far more painful experience that can occur in the journey of faith. He describes in detail a variety of terrible experiences of emptiness, aridity, and apparent abandonment. He seeks to make clear that the bleakest of experiences can be part of a movement into love. He insists that a person who experiences such painful darkness in his or her life of faith may well be being led by God into a deeper, transforming love, a union with Christ crucified and risen.

John of the Cross was imprisoned in a tiny dark cell in Toledo and was whipped and humiliated for nine months by his own Carmelite brothers. By the time he managed to escape, it seems that his poem *The Dark Night* had taken shape in his mind and heart. He had found love at work in the terrible experience of abandonment and suffering. This dark night he tells us is in fact "the inflow of God."[13] It is the "night more lovely than the dawn" the night "which unites the lover with the beloved."[14] In her reflection on the insights of John of the Cross, Constance Fitzgerald points out that the Dark Night is not primarily *some thing*, an impersonal darkness, but *someone*—a presence leaving an indelible imprint on the human spirit and on one's whole life. The Dark Night is the presence of Jesus as the loving Wisdom of God.[15]

5. Consolation can be the work of evil. According to Ignatius, it is proper to God and God's angels to give true spiritual gladness and consolation. It is the enemy who normally fights against this with subtle and fallacious reasoning, raising up doubts and anxieties (§329). But he insists that the experience of consolation needs to be tested, because some forms of consolation can come from an evil source. When a person is striving to live a good life, the pull of evil may take on the appearance of good. In this case, evil can appear as an angel of light, present in apparently good thoughts, desires, or ambitions (§§331-32). The presence of a deceptive angel of light is revealed when an apparently good beginning ends in being drawn away from God into disturbance, distraction, and evil. What seems good at the beginning ends up as something distorted.

I might find myself, for example, reacting to a situation with what at first appears to be righteous anger, but eventually I discover that I am actually being self-righteous and intolerant. Or I may find myself taking on extra commitments in response to those with whom I work, but find that this apparent generosity leads to a situation that damages family or community relationships. In these cases what appears in the beginning to be good is revealed to be evil masquerading as an angel of light. Ignatius insists that when we find this pattern at work in ourselves, it is an occasion for learning about discernment. It gives us the opportunity to grow in discernment, by noting all the stages we have passed through from the apparently good beginning through to its evil conclusion (§§333-34). This will enable us to be aware of the way we are moved, to be on guard against this pattern, and to be free to recognize it when it occurs.

6. *When a person is being drawn toward God, interior movements that are of God will tend to be at one with this direction, while those that are evil will be disruptive. When a person is being drawn away from God, evil movements will tend to be at one with this direction, while those that are of God will be disruptive.* This rule is fundamental for Ignatius. It appears in different forms at the beginning and the end of his rules for discernment (§§314-15 and 335). He tells us that in those who are going in a good direction, the grace of the Holy Spirit touches the person sweetly and gently, like a drop of water being absorbed into a sponge. In this case, evil appears as incongruent and disruptive. It is violent and noisy, like water falling onto stone. With those who are going in a direction that is away from God, it is precisely the opposite. For them, the promptings of the good spirit will be disruptive and challenging, while those of the bad spirit appear sweet and gentle.

If I find myself carrying a state of hurt feelings after a disagreement, I might eventually come to see that this direction does not lead to authentic life or to God. Then I might use Ignatius's principle to see that the apparently "sweet and gentle" tendency to remain locked in a state of self-pity is actually of the bad spirit. I might come to see that the "disruptive and challenging" voice that suggests a movement toward creative rebuilding of connections is ultimately of the Holy Spirit.

When evil is being done, the promptings that come from the Holy Spirit are not gentle and soothing but opposing and resistant. This principle applies beyond the personal sphere to the communal and political. It appears in Spirit-led prophetic resistance to injustice and evil. When Catherine of Siena came to see that the popes of her time were leading the church in a direction that was not of God, she recognized that remaining passive and being "sweet and gentle," was the way of complicity in evil. She knew that she was called by the Spirit to offer an active and disruptive challenge to church authorities.[16] When Archbishop Romero came to know the extent of the oppression of the poor in El Salvador, he saw that the call to remain quiet and peaceful, to be at peace with everyone and to "keep out of politics," was the voice of collusion in evil. He knew that the disruptive path of identification with the poor and the powerless was the way of fidelity to the Spirit of God.

Ignatius's principle suggests that we should be able to learn from our own experiences of the Spirit. If I am in touch with the part of my being where the grace of God is at work, then I should be able to discern whether my feeling, mood, or decision is congruent with the movement toward God or not. It is obvious that this kind of discernment would be greatly helped if we could identify an experience that we could be reasonably sure is an experience of God's grace. Ignatius points to such an experience, a kind of consolation that clearly comes from God alone. Since it clearly comes from God, it has an important role in Christian decision making.

DISCERNMENT ON THE BASIS OF THE EXPERIENCE OF BEING DRAWN WHOLLY INTO GOD'S LOVE

Ignatius speaks of an experience of being drawn wholly into the love of God. Such an experience comes upon us as sheer grace. There is no thought or event that can account for it. Ignatius calls this a "consolation without previous cause" (§330). It may well occur in a time of quiet prayer or meditation on the gospel. But what we experience far transcends our own efforts, our images, thoughts, and words. It appears simply as a gift. Ignatius tells us that we can learn to distinguish such an experience of God from all of the more superficial experiences of peace that may have their source in ourselves. We can trust that such an experience is God-given.

What Ignatius is pointing to is an encounter with God beyond images and words, even though a human subject can only interpret such an encounter in human images and words. John Futrell says that, for Ignatius, this kind of experience involves two characteristics. First, it is always experienced as sheer grace. Second, it is always an experience of the presence of the Other who cannot be contained in any concept, thought, or image. Such an experience can be understood as an experience of the presence and action of the Spirit. It is a gift by which human beings are enabled to taste and experience the presence of the Holy Spirit.[17]

Ignatius wisely points out that in all interpretation of such experience, human limits come into play as we use our images, concepts, and words to express what we have experienced (§336). Contemporary philosophy and theology would say that the human person brings an interpretative framework to every new experience. This interpretative framework not only is at work after the experience but also precedes all new experience. It is only because of our already existing understandings that we can actually experience anything new. Our interpretative framework, with all its possibilities and biases, enters into the interpretation of experience at every stage. All experience, no matter how profound, is filtered through our finite human preconceptions and limited human language.

Karl Rahner offers a contemporary reading of Ignatius's "consolation without previous cause." He sees it as a preconceptual experience of God, the kind of experience of grace I discussed in chapter 4.[18] It is a moment when we are open to the mystery of the incomprehensible God, an experience of presence and love that is beyond all concepts, and words. While we interpret this encounter only through human images, concepts and words, these point beyond themselves toward the mystery that transcends them. Rahner believes that these experiences of grace can become the touchstone for finding the will of God in the concrete circumstances of day-to-day life.

The process he has in mind for Christian decision making is a kind of prayerful thought experiment.[19] The idea is to bring to conscious attention both our deepest experience of God's grace and the matter to be discerned. It is a matter of testing to see whether a potential decision "sits" well with the place in our being where we are most open to God. Avery Dulles describes the process: "Through a process of 'play acting' we imaginatively place ourselves in the situation we are on the point of choosing, attempting to measure whether it is translucent to pure consolation."[20] Such testing may need to take place over a long time. In this process, the choice we make is not directly revealed by God. We make the decision in the light of our perception of the "fit" or congruence between the matter being discerned and our experience of God. We attempt to notice whether or not the proposed decision sits with our deepest experience of God in such a way as to produce a sense of peace in God.

Rahner suggests that just as philosophers have clarified the systematic logical rules that govern human thinking, so Ignatius has offered a systematic approach to the logic of Christian decision making. While he recognizes that Ignatius builds on the ancient tradition of discernment, he holds that Ignatius offers "the first and so far the only detailed method" for discovering the will of God in the concrete circumstances of everyday life.[21] The experience of grace, the experience of being wholly drawn into the love of God, functions as a kind of first principle in the logic of Christian decision making.[22]

Rahner then suggests that, just as an ordinary person uses logic without having studied it, so ordinary people often make important decisions more or less in the way suggested by Ignatius. So a person might ponder something to be decided over some time, and then make a decision on the basis of what feels right and more or less in harmony with her global sense of herself. This global sense may include her deepest sense of herself before God, the place of God's grace. Her decision may be made not only on the basis of rational analysis but also by a sense of what "suits" her deep down. Many people express the need to "sleep" on a decision. It seems that they need time to find out what is congruent with their sense of self. In the light of this, Rahner suggests that faithful Christians "who have never heard of St. Ignatius's instructions nevertheless instinctively make their decisions by their everyday religious logic in essentially the same way as Ignatius provides for."[23]

Of course, there is always the danger of delusion in this kind of decision making. If I decide something on the basis that I feel "at home" with it, this can easily be a self-centered judgment. It may be no more than an indication that the proposal does not take me out of my comfort zone. The more refined process suggested by Ignatius creates the possibility of finding freedom to make the hard choice. It seeks to ensure that I am testing a decision not against a superficial sense of myself but against a real openness to the otherness of God.

David Fleming encapsulates the heart of discernment when he writes that discernment is "a grace given to a lover." He says that one who loves has a "lover's instinct"—a "sense" or a "feel" for what pleases the one who is loved.[24] So one who loves God will have a lover's instinct for what is of God. Something similar was articulated long ago by Thomas Aquinas in his discussion of wisdom, the gift of the Holy Spirit. Aquinas tells us that in addition to intellectual comprehension, there is another kind of knowing, that of wisdom. Wisdom is precisely a knowing through love, a loving knowledge. He suggests that wisdom (*sapientia*) is a knowledge that can be tasted (*sapida*). By dwelling in the love of God, through the Spirit of God who has been given to us, we are able to taste or sense what is congruent with this love. Wisdom, the gift of the Spirit, enables us to judge rightly about the things that are of God because of an affinity for, or "connaturality" with, the love of God present in our hearts.[25]

By way of conclusion it might be helpful to list some of the key elements in Christian decision making that emerge from this reflection. First, it will involve confrontation with the gospel of Jesus and prayer for the grace of freedom to recognize that God might be leading in either direction of a proposed choice. Second, it may involve the intellectual assessment of the "pros" and "cons" of a proposed decision, perhaps by listing them and pondering them. Third, it may involve the discernment of inner movements, such as thoughts, desires, feelings, and moods, particularly through recognizing whether they lead in the direction of deeper life in God or away from God. Fourth, it may involve calling to mind the central experience of grace in our lives, holding this together with the proposed decision, and seeking to determine whether the union of the two produces a sense of peace in God. Finally, when a decision has been made, it needs to be confirmed in the fruits of a life lived in love and before God in prayer.

CONCLUSION

The Creator Spirit:
Making All Things New

At the end of the journey, it is time to bring together the theology of the Spirit developed in these pages into an overview. Throughout the journey I have attempted to keep in mind the *otherness* of the Spirit—the wind that blows where it wills (John 3:8), the unthinkable and uncontrollable one who knows the depths of God (1 Cor. 2:10-11). But I have thought of this otherness not as a negative but as a positive. It leads to an appreciation of the Creator Spirit in the otherness of the nonhuman, as well as in the mys terious depths of the human. Although I have taken a somewhat different path from Mark Wallace, my exploration in this book leads me to embrace his formulation: "the Spirit is the power of life-giving breath (*ruach*) within the cosmos who continually works to transform and renew all forms of life—both human and non-human."[1] He describes the Spirit as the healing power of God with beautiful words:

> The Spirit comes with healing in her wings to a world that cries out for transformation and renewal. The Spirit comes to a world in need of refreshment as the breath of God and the water of life. The Spirit comes to a world fragmented by violence and suffering with the promise of health and wholeness for all creation.[2]

The Breath of God is healing, transforming, renewing, refreshing, one who promises health and wholeness for all creation. In what follows I will attempt to assemble some key ideas of this book in a overview of the Spirit as the Breath of Life.

1. The Spirit breathes life into the universe and all its creatures. The story of the Spirit begins not with Pentecost but with the origins of the Big Bang. The Spirit of God brooded over our universe from the very begin-

171

ning as the Creator Spirit, the Breath of Life for all things. Creatures exist only because God gives them the "breath of life" (Gen. 2:7; 6:3, 17; 7:15; Job 33:4; 34:14-15; Ezek. 37:9; Ps. 33:6; 104:30; Eccles. 12:7; Jdt. 16:14; Wis. 1:7; 12:1). The Breath of God was at work in our world long before Pentecost, long before Moses led the people of God from slavery, long before Abraham and Sarah were called to leave their home in Ur and journey into the unknown, long before the first hominids appeared in Africa. The Spirit of God was the dynamic, energizing presence that enabled the early universe to exist and evolve from the first part of the first second some 14 billion years ago. As particles of hydrogen and helium separated out from radiation and formed the first atoms, as the clouds of gas compressed to form the first generation of galaxies, as the universe was lit up by the first stars, it was the Spirit of God who breathed life into the whole process. This Breath of God was at work as Earth began to form around the young Sun 4.5 billion years ago, as the first bacterial life emerged on the new planet 3.8 billion years ago, as simple cells became more complex and multicellular creatures emerged, as life forms developed wonderfully in the seas, as life moved onto the land, and as mammals and then hominid species evolved. The Spirit can be thought of as the ecstasy of the divine Communion, the pure abundance and free overflow of the divine life immanent in creation and grace.[3] The Spirit is the bountiful excess of the dynamism of the divine life that animates a world of creatures. The Breath of God, always in the Communion of the Trinity, is the one who goes forth and fills creation as the power of *creatio continua* (Job 33:4; 34:13-15; Wis. 1:7; 12:1). The Creator Spirit can be thought of as the power of becoming, the power that enables the self-transcendence of creation in the emergence of the universe and the evolution of life on Earth. The Spirit of God is creatively at work in the whole process celebrating every emergence, loving life in all its fecundity and diversity, treasuring it in its every instance.

2. The Creator Spirit enfolds human beings in grace. Human beings emerge into a grace-filled universe. Basil of Caesarea insisted that the Spirit of God is not only the Life-Giver but also the Sanctifier. From the beginning the Spirit was present not only as the Creator Spirit but as the Bearer of Grace. Christians understand this as the grace of Christ. What has become clearer in theology, particularly in Roman Catholic theology since the Second Vatican Council, is that this grace cannot be restricted to those human beings who have heard the Gospel, or to those who come after Christ. There is a long story of grace that precedes the historical life of Jesus. From the beginning of human existence, whenever it occurred, the Spirit was already present to human beings not only in the relationship of creation but in grace, as self-offering love that invites a human response. Humans evolve into a gracious world. Alongside this story of grace there is also a tragic story of the willful rejection of grace, a long history of sin that enters into the place of human freedom and inclines to further sin. Humans are born into a world of grace, but one that is also drawn toward lovelessness, ruthlessness, and violence. In the midst of such a world, the Spirit offers freedom and salvation in a way that Christians understand as anticipating, and as directed toward, the Christ event. In Karl Rahner's language, Christ can be interpreted as the final cause of the Spirit and as the *entelechy* or inner orientation of the Spirit at work throughout history. The Spirit of God who graciously accompanies and celebrates every emerging form of life waits patiently for the emergence of creatures who can respond to divine self-offering love in a *personal* way. A grace-filled universe awaits their arrival. The first humans emerged in a process that began with a species of bipedal apes seven million years ago, that continued in species such as *Homo erectus* two million years ago, and that included a number of archaic species like the Neanderthals as well as the modern humans who emerged over the last 150,000 years. Whenever humans emerged who were capable of religious experience and implicit faith, they emerged into a graced world.

3. The Spirit of God brings about the Christ event, sanctifying and transforming the humanity of Jesus that he might be the Wisdom of God. For the Christian community, the foundational revelatory experience of the Spirit occurs in the Christ event. Jesus is conceived of the Spirit (Matt. 1:20; Luke 1:35) and anointed with the Spirit at his baptism (Mark 1:10). In Acts, we are told that "God anointed Jesus of Nazareth with the Holy Spirit and with power," and that this anointed one "went about doing good and healing all who were oppressed by the devil, for God was with him" (Acts 10:36). In John, we are told that Jesus is the one on whom the Spirit descends and *remains* or *rests* (1:32, 33) and that Jesus will give this Spirit *without measure* (3:34). The Holy Spirit sanctifies and transforms the humanity of Jesus from the beginning that he might be the Wisdom of God in our midst. Jesus is the one anointed with the Spirit and, as such, is the bearer of this life-giving and liberating Spirit. He is led by the Spirit in his preaching of the reign of God, in his healing and liberating actions, in his compassion for outcasts and public sinners, in his ministry of the open table and his formation of an inclusive community. Jesus is radically open to the Spirit finally in the abandonment and negativity of the cross. Through the Spirit, the brutal violence of the cross is transformed into an event that brings healing and liberation. The risen Christ, radically identified with the life-giving Spirit, pours out the Spirit in the promised baptism "with the Holy Spirit and with fire" (Luke 3:16). In all of this, as Congar insists, there is a real history of the Spirit in the life, death and resurrection of Jesus. The Spirit accompanies Jesus at every stage. As Basil pointed out long ago, every event in the life and ministry of Jesus is an event of the Spirit. In every aspect of the history of salvation, Word and the Spirit are reciprocally interrelated.

4. The Spirit is poured out on the church. Word and Spirit coinstitute the church. The Western church will be able to respond to the grave crises it faces only by recovering a deeper understanding of the role of the Spirit in the life of the church. What is needed, as opposed to all forms of Christomonism, is a renewed appreciation of the reciprocity between Word and Spirit. Word and Spirit coinstitute the church. The charisms of the Spirit are foundational for the life of the church. The church is always in the process of being built by the Spirit of God. This means that the Spirit always needs to be invoked. The Spirit of God is the source of the local church with its particular gifts and also the source of the communion of the universal church. There is a Spirit-given tension between universal and local that cannot be resolved by coercion and centralism but only through discernment of the Spirit. As Yves Congar insists, the church is open to the Spirit only when it is open to the charisms of all its members. This calls for a renewed appreciation of the theory and practice of listening to the whole church (synodality). It calls for a reciprocity between synodality and ordained ministry. The experience of the communion in the Spirit leads beyond the church to the whole of creation. As Jürgen Moltmann says, the experience of the communion of the Holy Spirit takes the church beyond itself to the communion of all God's creatures.[1] And the church brings creation to the eucharistic table and offers praise on behalf of and in union with all creation.

5. The Spirit is the midwife to the birth of the new as creation groans "in labor pains" (Rom. 8:22). The long history of life on Earth is not only a history of fecundity, beauty, cooperation, and symbiosis but also a history of predation, competition, death, and extinction of species. Death is central to the pattern of biological life. Without death there could be no evolution. It is the price that is paid for birds and butterflies and the human brain. Death is part of the way things are in a finite, limited, bodily world. In this context, Christian theology has no theoretical answers, but can only bear witness to the death and resurrection of Jesus. The death of Jesus reveals a God who enters into the pain of the world, who suffers with suffering creation. At the same time it points to the Spirit transforming death into redemptive love and radical new life. A theology of creation in the light of the cross and resurrection can point to the ideas of divine self-limitation and the promise of new life for all things. It can suggest that the Creator Spirit may be freely self-limiting out of loving commitment to the proper autonomy and independence of creaturely processes. But it also points to the Spirit as *with* creatures in their finitude, death, and incompletion, holding them in redemptive love and drawing each into an unforeseeable eschatological future in the divine life. In the postresurrection experiences of the Spirit, Paul saw the beginning and the guarantee of the transformation of creation. The Spirit is the "down-payment and guarantee" (2 Cor. 1:22;

5:5; Eph. 1:13-15), the "firstfruits" of God's harvest (Rom. 8:23). Creation waits with "eager longing" for its liberation from "bondage to decay" and for "the freedom associated with the glory of the children of God" (Rom. 8:19-23). The Spirit assists and enables the birth of the new: "For we know that the entire creation has been groaning together in the pangs of child-birth up till now" (Rom. 8:22). The Spirit is like the midwife, groaning with groaning creation as the new is being born. The biblical promise points to the unimaginable: the participation of all creatures in the dynamism of the divine life.

6. *The Spirit is the faithful Companion to each creature, accompanying each with love.* The Spirit is the personal presence of God to each creature in all the incompleteness and finitude of things. The triune God is present in the Spirit to each creature here and now, loving it into existence and promising its future. Creation is an act of love. The Spirit companions each, values each, brings each into an interrelated world of creatures, and holds each in the life of the divine Communion. Ruth Page sees God as *companioning* each creature with a love that respects each creature's own identity, possibilities, and proper autonomy. This conviction has immediate ecological consequences. God knows and cares about each creature's experience. God knows and cares about each creature's habitat.[5] This can only mean that the Spirit is grieved (Eph. 4:30) when human beings abuse and destroy habitats. Human beings have their own unique relationship to the indwelling Holy Spirit. And, in the communion of the one Spirit, they are kin to other creatures. They are interconnected in a web of life, in symbiotic relationship, in food chains, in local ecosystems, in a biological community on Earth, in a community that stretches beyond Earth to the solar system and beyond the solar system to the universe. As Rosemary Radford Ruether says, each creature "has its *own* distinct relation to God as source of life." Each has its own value: "Each life form has its own purpose, its own right to exist, its own independent relation to God and to other beings." She insists that when human beings make use of other creatures and exercise their covenantal role as caretakers, they are called to do this only within a larger sensibility of kinship. This is "rooted in the encounter with nature as 'thou,' as fellow beings each with its own integrity."[6]

7. *The Spirit "makes space" within the trinitarian relations for the emergence of a universe in which entities are constituted by relationships.* Even when they acknowledge that God transcends all notions of space and place, human beings still need to imagine the God–world relationship in some way. Some imaginative pictures are clearly inadequate—including the idea of a God who lives in the heavens above us, and the idea of God as an entity alongside the universe who intervenes in it at certain times. A more appropriate image, even though it remains necessarily inadequate, is that of

the divine Trinity as the "place" of the unfolding of the universe. This represents a form of panentheism, the idea that all things are *in* God. In a trinitarian panentheism, the Creator Spirit can be thought of as "making space" within the dynamism of the divine shared life for a world of creatures to emerge. A relational universe can be thought of as evolving within the relational life of God. Contemporary science puts before us an understanding of the entities that make up our world as both emergent and relational. Entities exist and have their own integrity only through their constitutive relationships. In theology, the contemporary retrieval of a trinitarian understanding of God offers a view of God as a Communion characterized by relational unity and diversity. In this theology, it is Communion that makes things be and become. When these insights from science and theology are brought into mutual dialogue, a view of reality emerges in which the entities that make up our universe can be understood as emergent and relational, as having their own integrity, and as evolving within the dynamism of the divine life. The Holy Spirit can be thought of as the ultimate power of relationship, the love that holds all things in the divine Communion.

8. The Creator Spirit is the closeness of God in the otherness of nonhuman creation. If Jesus can be understood as the human face of God in our midst, the Spirit can be thought of as God present in countless ways beyond the limits of the human. The Spirit is not revealed like the Word, who is made flesh in one human being, but as something far more mysterious, the Breath of God, who breathes through the whole of creation and through the lives, minds, and hearts of human beings. The Spirit is not usually described in anthropomorphic terms, but in images taken from the natural world—as breath, wind, water, fire, oil, and anointing. The Spirit's impact on humans is described in the language of grace, above all in terms of the experience of the gratuity of divine love poured out in our hearts (Rom. 5:5). Images such as wind and fire preserve the otherness of the Spirit and challenge the human tendency to domesticate the Spirit. The numinous and mysterious Spirit is experienced in the depths of human relationships and in the beauty and the wilderness of nature. Ambrose of Milan sees the Spirit sweeping over the waters of creation as not only bringing life to creation, but also as bringing it its beauty. Hildegard of Bingen sees the Creator Spirit as the source of *viriditas*, a Latin word that means "greenness" and points to the fecundity at the heart of things. In a similar way, the poet Gerard Manley Hopkins pointed to the Spirit as the source of the "dearest freshness deep down things." The experience of the presence of the Spirit in the otherness of the nonhuman challenges the kind of anthropocentrism that sees God as focused only on the human. It offers a counter to those who would use religious faith to legitimate the ruthless exploitation of other species. It points to the otherness of nonhuman creatures as a place of God.

9. *The Spirit remains wild and uncontrollable, the wind that "blows where it chooses" (John 3:8)*. We can glimpse the wildness of the Spirit in the experiences we have of wilderness in nature and of the mystery of the universe. The experience of wilderness in all its forms can lead to a sense of the incomprehensibility of God. The Spirit is not only the love that stirs in the intimate depths of our own beings but also the love that surrounds and sustains the uncounted insects, animals, and trees that share the exuberant life of a rain forest, the love that is at work in the mysterious and counterintuitive nature of quantum reality and in the nuclear furnaces of twinkling stars. Exposure to astronomy and cosmology takes us far beyond the human comfort zone. We are confronted with nature as profoundly *other*. Nature is radically mysterious, and living with nature means learning to live in mystery. It leads to the knowledge that we cannot domesticate the Creator, that God remains incomprehensible mystery to us. Learning to live with mystery represents what is at the heart of the biblical and theological tradition. It is what we find in Job, when God addresses Job from the whirlwind, asking, "Where were you when I laid the foundation of the earth?" In his encounter with God, Job knows mystery not simply by hearsay, but in the experience of God in the midst of incomprehension (Job 42:5). The acceptance of the presence of the Spirit in what is untameable can be an important step in Christian faith, but also in the emergence of an ecological sensibility that can value the diversity and otherness of the creatures who share life with us.

10. *The Spirit of God and the Word of God can be thought of as reciprocally related not only at every stage of the economy of salvation but also in the eternal life of God.* According to the great Eastern theologians, the Word of God and the Breath of God are always involved together in both creation and redemption. These theologians constantly returned to the words of the Psalmist—"By the Word of the Lord the heavens were made, and all their hosts by God's Breath." As Irenaeus puts it, Word and Spirit can be thought of as the "two hands of God" at work in creation and salvation. In the theology I have outlined, this reciprocal relationship of the Word and the Spirit in the economy of creation and salvation is thought of as pointing back to a reciprocal relationship in the eternal life of God. With theologians such as Gregory of Nyssa and John of Damascus, the Word is thought of as fully involved in the procession of the Spirit: the Spirit proceeds from the Source of All through the Word. And the Spirit is thought of as fully involved in the eternal generation of the Word: the Spirit rests upon the Word, manifests the Word, and is the companion to the Word. These relations of origin, which describe the structural interconnection between the Three, are to be distinguished from the countless dynamic interactions in the divine trinitarian Communion. The mutual indwelling of the divine persons, their *perichoresis*, involves a mutual giving and receiv-

ing in profound mutuality and equality, for which our very best experiences of mutual human friendship provide but a very pale analogy.

11. The Spirit is not less than humanly personal but infinitely more, a personal other, someone who draws us into love. While the Spirit cannot be thought of as a human person, this does not mean that the Spirit is *less* personal than human beings. On the contrary, the Spirit can be thought of as personal in a way that wonderfully transcends the human way of being a person. To say that the Spirit is personal is to say that the Spirit is radically relational. The Spirit is the love of God poured out in our human hearts (Rom. 5:5) and the unspeakable nearness of God immanent in all creatures. This mysterious presence, in which we live and move and have our being, is not a something. It is not finally simply a link or a bond uniting us with God or each other. It is not even simply "mutual love." The Spirit is not only a *presence* but also a mysterious personal *counterpart*, a *personal other*, who relates to us and invites us into love. Jürgen Moltmann reflects on the movement in Christian life from an experience of the Spirit as *presence* to the more personal experience of *counterpart*. He recalls great images of the Spirit: as the fountain of living water (Jer. 2:13; 17:13; John 4:14), as the "flowing light of the Godhead" (Mechthild of Magdeburg) and as the "broad place" that we inhabit (Job 36:16). These images suggest the experience of the Spirit as a presence that is in us and around us—an experience of the Spirit as pure presence. But, Moltmann says, we can discover the Spirit not only as presence but also as *counterpart*. A child first encounters her mother as encompassing presence before discovering her as counterpart and person. Lovers experience each other as both presence and as counterpart. Moltmann suggest that the same can be true of the experience of the Spirit.[7]

The great mystics describe the experience of the Spirit in highly personal images, without going so far as to suggest that the Spirit has a human face. Catherine of Siena depicts the Holy Spirit as a mother who "nurses the soul at the breast of divine charity."[8] Gertrude of Helfta speaks of the Spirit as a "heavenly kiss."[9] This same theme of the kiss is central in the sublime exchange between soprano and countertenor at the heart of one of Bach's cantatas for Pentecost, where the Holy Spirit again and again offers the believer the "the kiss of grace."[10] The image of the kiss suggests an intimate but still mysterious touch of God.

In a contemporary feminist theology of the Spirit, Elizabeth Johnson sees the Spirit as friend and sister. She sees the metaphor of friendship as entailing a reciprocity that makes it possible to cross boundaries of race, sex, class, and even nature. She sees the Spirit as not only making human beings friends of God but also as herself befriending the world.[11] To adapt one of Sallie McFague's metaphors, the Spirit is the Friend of the universe, and we who share in this one Spirit are called to share the Spirit's friend-ships.[12] This one who is our most intimate "soul-friend" also befriends nonhuman creatures, relating to each in all its uniqueness, respecting the integrity of each, delighting in each. This Holy Spirit pervades the whole universe and sees to "the depths of God" (1 Cor. 2:10). To be in commu-nion with this Spirit is to be in communion with all of God's creatures.

Notes

The following abbreviations are used in the notes:

ANF The Ante-Nicene Fathers: Translations of the writings of the fathers down to
A.D. 325, ed. Alexander Roberts and James Donaldson (Grand Rapids:
Eerdmans, [1965]-[1968])

FC Fathers of the Church: Second Series (Washington, D.C.: Catholic University
of America Press)

NJBC *The New Jerome Biblical Commentary,* edited by Raymond E. Brown,
Joseph A. Fitzmyer, and Roland E. Murphy (Englewood Cliffs, N.J.:
Prentice-Hall, 1990)

NPF Nicene and Post-Nicene Fathers: Second Series (Peabody, Mass.: Hendrickson)

PG *Patrologiae cursus completus: Series Graeca,* ed. J.-P. Migne, 161 vols. (Paris:
J.-P. Migne, 1857-66)

SC Sources Chrétiennes (Paris: Éditions du Cerf)

Introduction

1. Anthony Kelly, for example, has developed an appealing, contemporary theology
of the Trinity on the foundations of Aquinas's approach to the psychological analogy.
See his *The Trinity of Love: A Theology of the Christian God* (Wilmington, Del.:
Michael Glazier, 1989). David Coffey has made extensive use of the "mutual love theory" in many writings in which he has developed a creative approach to Spirit Christology and trinitarian theology. See particularly his *Deus Trinitas: The Doctrine of the
Triune God* (Oxford: Oxford University Press, 1999).

2. In addition to the standard encyclopedia articles, see, e.g., C. K. Barrett, *The Holy
Spirit and the Gospel Tradition* (London: SPCK, 1947); James D. G. Dunn, *The Christ
and the Spirit: Collected Essays of James D. G. Dunn,* volume 2, *Pneumatology* (Grand
Rapids: Eerdmans, 1998); F. X. Durrwell, *Holy Spirit of God: An Essay of Biblical The-
ology* (London: Geoffrey Chapman, 1986); Gordon Fee, *God's Empowering Presence:
The Holy Spirit in the Letters of Paul* (Peabody, Mass.: Hendrickson, 1994); Sinclair B.
Ferguson, *The Holy Spirit* (Downers Grove, Ill.: InterVarsity Press, 1996); Alasdair
Heron, *The Holy Spirit* (London: Marshall Morgan & Scott, 1983); Ju Hur, *A Dynamic
Reading of the Holy Spirit in Luke-Acts* (Sheffield, 2002); George T. Mon-
tague, *The Holy Spirit: Growth of a Biblical Tradition* (New York: Paulist Press, 1976);
C. F. D. Moule, *The Holy Spirit* (Oxford: Mowbray, 1978); Ignace de la Potterie and
Stanislaus Lyonnet, *The Christian Lives by the Spirit* (Staten Island, N.Y.: Alba House,
1971); Eduard Schweizer, *The Holy Spirit* (London: SCM, 1980); William H. Shepherd,
Jr., *The Narrative Function of the Holy Spirit as a Character in Luke-Acts* (Atlanta:

Scholars Press, 1994); Michael Welker, *God the Spirit* (Minneapolis, Fortress Press, 1994).

3. I have discussed this in detail in "The Ecological Significance of God Language," *Theological Studies* 60 (1999): 708-22.

1. The Story of the Universe

1. A fourth observation is more recent. Cosmologists have long pointed out that the existence of galaxies shows that matter has emerged in a "clumpy" fashion. This suggests that there would have been a precursor to this variation in the early universe. There should be some slight variations in the background microwave radiation, about one part in 100,000. But the radiation seemed remarkably even. In April 1992 researchers at Berkeley announced that very slight fluctuations had been detected by instruments on the COBE satellite. These fluctuations have been mapped in series of further observations.

2. Stephen Hawking, *A Brief History of Time: From the Big Bang to Black Holes* (New York: Bantam, 1988), 39.

3. In this account I am simply attempting to summarize material that is widely accepted by contemporary scientists. Only in a second theological step will I reflect back on this story as an account of what the Spirit of God is doing. For a different, highly detailed approach to the story of the universe, in which the universe is interpreted as the active subject of the story, see Brian Swimme and Thomas Berry, *The Universe Story: From the Primordial Flaring Forth to the Ecozoic Era: A Celebration of the Unfolding of the Cosmos* (San Francisco: HarperSanFrancisco, 1992). My approach differs too from that of Diarmuid O'Murchu, who seeks to blend science and religion to create a new myth for our time in his *Evolutionary Faith: Rediscovering God in Our Great Story* (Maryknoll, N.Y.: Orbis Books, 2002).

4. The eminent cosmologist P. James E. Peebles offers a brief report on cosmology that distinguishes between what is theoretical speculation and what is established within the discipline in "Making Sense of Modern Cosmology," *Scientific American* 284 (January 2001): 44-45. Books I have found helpful for an overview of developments in cosmology include John D. Barrow, *The Origins of the Universe* (London: Phoenix, 1994); idem, *The Universe That Discovered Itself* (Oxford: Oxford University Press, 2000); Paul Davies, *The Fifth Miracle: The Search for the Origin of Life* (London: Penguin, 1998); Timothy Ferris, *The Whole Shebang: A State of the Universe(s) Report* (London: Phoenix, 1997); John Gribbin, *Stardust: The Cosmic Recycling of Stars, Planets and People* (London: Penguin, 2001); Hawking, *A Brief History of Time*; Martin Rees, *Before the Beginning: Our Universe and Others* (London: Touchstone, 1997); idem, *Our Cosmic Habitat* (London: Phoenix, 2002); Steven Weinberg, *The First Three Minutes* (New York: Basic Books, 1977); Steven Weinberg, *Dreams of a Final Theory* (New York: Pantheon, 1992).

5. Alan Guth developed inflationary cosmology, arguing that the universe went through a period of rapid expansion within the first second of its existence. Andrei Linde's theory of "chaotic inflation" solves some problems in cosmology, while seeing our universe as beginning as a bubble that balloons out from the space-time of a previously existing universe and may exist alongside many such bubble universes. For a brief introduction to Linde's position, see his "Inflationary Cosmology and the Question of Teleology," in *Science and Religion in Search of Cosmic Purpose*, ed. John F. Haught (Washington, D.C.: Georgetown University Press, 2000), 1-17. For fuller treatments, see his *Particle Physics and Inflationary Cosmology* (Chur, Switzerland: Harwood, 1990) and *Inflation and Quantum Cosmology* (Boston: Academic Press, 1990).

6. Rees notes that this new concept is potentially "as drastic an enlargement of our

cosmic perspective as the shift from pre-Copernican ideas to the realization that the Earth is orbiting a typical star on the edge of the Milky Way, itself just one galaxy among many others" (*Before the Beginning*, 3).

7. While revising this chapter for publication, I read a news report of a presentation by cosmologists Alan Guth, Arvin Bode, and Alexander Vilenkin to a conference on "The Future of Theoretical Physics and Cosmology," held at the Centre for Mathematical Sciences in Cambridge, England. Based on the idea that the Hubble parameter never gets below a certain constant value, they argue against the idea of an infinite past filled with inflationary cycles. They see inflation as eternal into the future. Vilenkin is quoted as saying: "Some regions thermalize, while other continue to inflate, and new thermalized regions like our own are being continuously formed." But space-time has a boundary at its origin. It has a beginning. Mike Martin, "Cosmologists Catch Glimpse of the Beginning," *Research News & Opportunities in Science and Religion* 3, no. 5 (January 2003): 1, 27.

8. Specialists differ on the way in which forms of bacteria are related to each other and how they are to be classified. This applies in particular to the archaea or archaebacteria, a primeval form of life that differs from other bacteria in some characteristics. Some of these archaebacteria thrive in extreme conditions such as hot springs, sulfur springs, and brine.

9. Recent insight into the importance of the planetary exchange of matter has also revived speculation about the possibility of life itself having its origin in outer space. See Davies, *Fifth Miracle*, 151-201.

10. Ernst Mayr points to a symbiotic merger and argues that a number of indications support the idea of an origin of eukaryotes about 2.7 billion years ago, even though the first extant fossils of unicellular eukaryotes are only about 1.7 billion years old. See his *What Evolution Is* (London: Weidenfeld & Nicolson, 2001), 48-49. On symbiosis in the origin of eukaryotic cells, see Lynn Margulis, *Symbiotic Planet: A New Look at Evolution* (New York: Basic Books, 1998).

11. See Richard Leakey, *The Origin of Humankind* (London: Phoenix, 1994), xiv; Mayr, *What Evolution Is*, 233-64.

12. Barrow, *Universe That Discovered Itself*, 397.

13. Gribbin, *Stardust*, 178.

14. Martin Rees is building on a story already told by Primo Levi; see Rees, *Before the Beginning*, 17-18.

15. Rees, *Before the Beginning*, 19.

16. George V. Coyne, S.J., and Alessandro Omizzolo, *Wayfarers in the Cosmos: The Human Quest for Meaning* (New York: Crossroad, 2002), 125.

2. Basil on the Holy Spirit

1. This creed was accepted as an official formula by the Council of Chalcedon in 451. Its relationship to the Council of Constantinople has been a matter of debate among historical scholars. See J. N. D. Kelly, *Early Christian Creeds*, 3rd ed. (Harlow, UK: Longman, 1972), 296-331; Kelly follows Ritter in seeing the creed not as a final product of those assembled at Constantinople but as something they had accepted as a negotiating instrument in a failed attempt at compromise with Macedonians who opposed the divinity of the Spirit.

2. On this see Ioannes Karayannopoulos, "St. Basil's Social Activity: Principles and Praxis," in *Basil of Casesarea: Christian, Humanist, Ascetic: A Sixteen-hundredth Anniversary Symposium*, ed. Paul Jonathan Fedwick (Toronto: Pontifical Institute of Medieval Studies, 1981), 1:375-92. On Basil's attitude to slavery, see, in the same volume, Ramón Teja, "San Basilio y las esclavitud: teoría y praxis," 393-403.

3. Philip Rousseau, *Basil of Caesarea* (Berkeley: University of California Press, 1994), 93-132.

4. For a chronology of Basil's life, see Paul J. Fedwick, "A Chronology of the Life and Works of Basil of Caesarea," in *Basil of Caesarea,* ed. Fedwick, 3-19. See also his *The Church and the Charisma of Leadership in Basil of Caesarea* (Toronto: Pontifical Institute of Medieval Studies, 1979).

5. Gregory of Nyssa, *The Life of Saint Macrina,* in *Saint Gregory of Nyssa: Ascetical Works,* trans. Virginia Woods Callahan, FC 58 (1967), 168. Our knowledge of Macrina comes from Gregory's *Life* and his *On the Soul and the Resurrection.* Both can be found in the volume translated by Woods Callahan. Gregory tells of Basil's youngest brother, Peter, and his involvement in a monastic existence at Annisa (pp. 171-72, 189) and of another brother Naucratius, who rejected a career in rhetoric and withdrew to a remote part of the countryside, living a life of prayer and poverty and caring for the aged and the sick, until he was killed in a hunting accident (pp. 168-69).

6. I cannot go into a discussion of the historical debate about the complex range of positions adopted in the fourth century, but will briefly mention Basil's relationship with the more obvious ones. Basil, of course, directly opposed those who followed Eunomius in holding that the Word and the Spirit are *unlike* the Father (the *Anomoeans*). He also opposed those who responded to Eunomius by saying that the Word was *like* the Father (the *Homoeans*), because he found this too close to the Arian position. Then there were the *Homoousians* who followed Athanasius and Nicaea in holding that the Word is of the *same substance* as the Father. And there were the *Homoiousions* who held that the Word was of *like substance* with the Father. They included Basil of Ancyra, Eustathius of Sebaste, and many ordinary Christians, who were far from bring Arians yet found it hard to come to terms with the unbiblical *homoousios.* Basil succeeded in keeping dialogue open between these last two groups. In a letter (Letter 9.3, FC 13L: 42-43) from about 364, he says that while he can accept "like in substance" he has adopted the phrase "of the same substance" (*homoousios*), because it is less open to misunderstanding.

7. Athanasius called them "Tropici" because of their figurative interpretations of Scripture (*tropos* = "figure"). Athanasius's *Letter to Serapion* was written about 360. More than ten years earlier, probably about 348, the conservative church leader Cyril of Jerusalem had strongly defended the divinity of the Spirit in his *Catechetical Lectures.*

8. They were also called Macedonians from the end of the fourth century because it was thought, probably mistakenly, that their position had originated from Macedonius, bishop of Constantinople, who had died around 362.

9. Basil of Caesarea, *On the Holy Spirit* 30, 76-78 in *St. Basil the Great on the Holy Spirit,* trans. David Anderson (Crestwood, N.Y.: St. Vladimir's Seminary Press, 1980), 113-17. Anderson's translation is a revision of that by Blonfield Jackson, in NPF 8. Basil's Greek text can be found in PG 32 and in *Basile de Césarée sur Le Saint-Esprit,* trans. Benoît Pruche, SC 17 (Paris: Éditions du Cerf, 1968). In the notes that follow I will indicate when I am following Sources Chrétiennes (subsequently SC) and when I am making use of Anderson's translation.

10. Anthony Meredith, S.J., *The Cappadocians* (London: Geoffrey Chapman, 1995), 49.

11. John Zizioulas, *Being as Communion* (Crestwood, N.Y.: St. Vladimir's Seminary Press, 1993), 67-122.

12. Rousseau, *Basil,* xv. For his comments on Basil's friendships, see pp. 233-69.

13. Basil, *Homilia in Illud, Destruam Horrea Mea* 7 (PG 31:261-77).

14. Basil, *Homilia Dicta Tempore Famis et Siccitatis* 8 (PG 31:304-28).

15. Gregory of Nazianzus, *Oration* 43.35. This can be found translated by Charles Gordon Brown and James Edward Swallow in *Select Orations of Saint Gregory Nazianzen,* NPF 7:395-422.

16. See Basil's letter to Elias, governor of Cappadocia, Letter 94, in *Saint Basil, Letters Volume 1,* trans. Sister Agnes Clare Way, FC 13:209-11.

17. Gregory of Nazianzus, *Oration* 43.63 (NPF 7:416).

18. Maisie Ward, "Saint Basil and the Cappadocians," in *In Honor of St. Basil the Great 379,* Word and Spirit 1 (Still River, Mass.: St. Bede's Publications, 1979), 18-20.

19. Augustine Holmes, *A Life Pleasing to God: The Spirituality of the Rules of St Basil* (London: Darton, Longman & Todd, 2000), 54.

20. Ibid., 61.

21. Ibid., 89-90.

22. Ibid., 139-43.

23. Basil, *On the Holy Spirit* 26.61 (Anderson, 94).

24. Gregory makes his own position perfectly clear in his *Fifth Theological Oration*: "What then? Is the Spirit God? Most certainly. Well then, is he consubstantial? Yes, if he is God" (NPF 7:321). Gregory's explanation of Basil's "economy" appears in his *On Pentecost* from 379 (*Oration 4*, NPF 7:378-85) and in his panegyric for Basil from 380 (*Oration 43*, NFP 7:395-422). In the panegyric Gregory claims that, while Basil himself undertook the way of economy, he had allowed Gregory freedom to take a stronger stand, so that through their united efforts the Gospel might be firmly established. At one stage, about 372, Gregory had appealed to Basil to clarify his position, informing him of a monk who had been scandalized by what he saw as Basil's lack of clarity on the divinity of the Spirit (Letters 58 and 59, NPF 7:454-56). Basil refused Gregory's request (Letter 71, NPF 8:167). A group of monks had appealed to Athanasius about the same time. Athanasius strongly supported Basil as the glory of the churches, and the fighter for the truth, "who makes himself weak with the weak, in order to win them" (1 Cor. 9:22). Athanasius, *Ad Palladium* and *Ad Joannem et Antiochum* (PG 26:1168).

25. Jean Gribomont, "Intransigence and Irenicism in Saint Basil's '*De Spiritu Sancto*,'" in *In Honor of St. Basil the Great 379,* Word and Spirit 1 (Still River, Mass.: St. Bede's Publications, 1979), 109-36.

26. In Basil's response to those concerned for orthodoxy at Tarsus, he makes it clear that nothing should be added beyond these two conditions (Letter 113, FC 13:239-40). At the end of his letter, he shares his conviction that living the common Christian life, "purified of all evil zeal," will bring about "what would be necessary to see more clearly." He says that this new sight will come as a gift, given by the one who makes all things work together for good for those who love God (Rom. 8:28).

27. Gribomont, "Intransigence and Irenicism," 119. Basil distinguishes between revealed truth held in faith, which he called *dogma*, and proclaimed doctrine, which he called *kerygma*. He gives priority to *dogma*. Dogma is what is received in mystery in the sacramental life and communion of the church. Basil was reticent about making absolute statements about the divinity of the Spirit outside this context. Gribomont says: "more than Athanasius and more than Gregory, Basil values especially this almost ineffable content of the revelation and of the spiritual knowledge of God" (p. 119).

28. See Kelly, *Early Christian Creeds*, 342. Gribomont says that one of the reasons the creed associated with the Council of Constantinople is so strongly stamped with Basil's economy is because of the mediations of Amphilochius and Gregory of Nyssa ("Intransigence and Irenicism," 121). He points out that Gregory of Nazianzus, who supported a more demanding doctrine, not only had to abandon the presidency of the council but also seemed disappointed with its outcome (pp. 120-21).

29. Basil, *On the Holy Spirit* 1.3 (Anderson, 17).

30. Basil, *On the Holy Spirit* 6.13 (Anderson, 28).

31. Basil, *On the Holy Spirit* 23.54 (SC 17: 444).

32. Basil, *On the Holy Spirit* 29.71-75 (SC 17:500-518).

33. Boris Bobrinskoy, *The Mystery of the Trinity: Trinitarian Experience and Vision in the Biblical and Patristic Tradition* (Crestwood, N.Y.: St. Vladimir's Seminary Press, 1999), 244.

34. Ibid., 240.

35. Basil, *On the Holy Spirit* 18.45 (SC 17:406).

36. Basil, *On the Holy Spirit* 13.30 (SC 17:352); 22, heading (SC 17:440).

37. Basil, *On the Holy Spirit* 25.59 (Anderson, 91). Basil points out that the use of the word *with* protects the distinction of persons against Sabellian interpretations that undermine the distinction of persons. At the same time it opposes all Arian interpretations, which treat the Word and the Spirit as inferior and created.

38. J. D. Zizioulas, "The Teaching of the 2nd Ecumenical Council on the Holy Spirit in Historical and Ecumenical Perspective," in *Credo in Spiritum Sanctum = Pisteuō eis to Pneuma to Hagion: Atti del Congresso teologico internazionale di pneumatologia in occasione del 1600° anniversario del I Concilio di Costantinopoli e del 1550° anniversario del Concilio di Efeso: Roma, 22-26 marzo 1982,* ed. J. S. Martins, Teologia e filosofia 6 (Rome/Vatican City: Libreria editrice vaticana, 1983), 1:39.

39. Joseph T. Lienhard argues that the stream of theology that thought of God in terms of one *hypostasis* (which he calls miahypostatic theology) was "more widespread, and more tenacious, than is generally assumed." He points to the evidence that Athanasius remained in communion with Marcellus, as well as with Paulinus in Antioch, and that westerners, particularly the Romans, were sympathetic to this kind of theology. See Lienhard's "*Ousia* and *Hypostasis*: The Cappadocian Settlement and the Theology of One *Hypostasis*," in *The Trinity*, ed. Stephen Davis, Daniel Kendall and Gerald O'Collins (Oxford: Oxford University Press, 1999), 108.

40. The Council of Alexandria of 362, chaired by Athanasius, affirmed the legitimacy of speaking of three *hypostases* in God, as well as of the one *hypostasis*, but Athanasius himself continued to use *hypostasis* and *ousia* as synonyms. See Lienhard, "Cappadocian Settlement," 103-7. Basil's position is made clear in his Letters 210 and 236. In Letter 236, Basil writes: "'Substance' (*ousia*) and 'person' (*hypostasis*) have the same difference as the general has in regard to the particular" (FC 28:171). It is widely recognized that this is not a fully adequate comparison. The trinitarian God is not a generic concept or a class of things. But, of course, for Basil, there is clearly only one God who exists only as the Three, and, as Anthony Meredith says, "in the Basilian scheme, each person of the Trinity can be thought of as a union of the general divine nature and an individual characteristic, sometimes referred to as a *tropos hyparxeos* or way of existing" (*Cappadocians*, 105). The distinction between *ousia* and *hypostasis* is also brought out sharply in Letter 38, which was attributed to Basil, but which Meredith and others now see as the work of Gregory of Nyssa.

41. See Vladimir Lossky, *Orthodox Theology: An Introduction* (Crestwood, N.Y.: St. Vladimir's Seminary Press, 1978), 40-45; and Zizioulas, *Being as Communion,* 27-49.

42. Zizioulas, *Being as Communion,* 17.

43. See, e.g., André de Halleux, "Personnalisme ou Essentalisme trinitaire chez les Pères Cappadociens," *Revue Théologique de Louvain* 17 (1986): 129-55, 265-82.

44. Basil, *Against Eunomius* 3.4; *On the Holy Spirit* 16.38; 18.46; 19.49.

45. Basil, *On the Holy Spirit* 9.23 (SC 17:28).

46. See Cyril Karam, "Saint Basil on the Holy Spirit—Some Aspects of his Theology," in *In Honor of St. Basil the Great 379,* 144-51.

47. Basil, *On the Holy Spirit* 18.47 (Anderson, 74-75).

48. Basil, *On the Holy Spirit* 19.49 (Anderson, 77).

49. Gregory of Nazianzus, *Theological Orations* 5.29 (NPF 7:327).

50. Basil, *On the Holy Spirit* 16.39 (SC 17:384-86).

51. Basil, *On the Holy Spirit* 9.23 (SC 17:324).

52. Basil, *On the Holy Spirit* 9.23 (Anderson, 44).

53. Basil, *On the Holy Spirit* 26.62 (Anderson, 94).

54. Basil, *On the Holy Spirit* 23.54 (SC 17:54); 26.63 (SC 17:472).

55. Basil, *On the Holy Spirit* 26.61 (SC 17:478).

56. Basil, *On the Holy Spirit* 26.64 (Anderson, 97).

57. Basil, *On the Holy Spirit* 26.63 (SC 17:470).

58. Basil, *On the Holy Spirit* 27.68 (Anderson, 102).

3. Breathing Life into a Universe of Creatures

1. Stephen Hawking, *A Brief History of Time: From the Big Bang to Black Holes* (New York: Bantam, 1988), 174 (emphasis added).

2. Arthur Peacocke, *Theology for a Scientific Age: Being and Becoming—Natural, Divine and Human* (Minneapolis: Fortress Press, 1993), 118.

3. David Toolan, *At Home in the Cosmos* (Maryknoll, N.Y.: Orbis Books, 2001), 203.

4. John L. McKenzie, "Aspects of Old Testament Thought," in *NJBC*, 1291.

5. See Joseph A. Fitzmyer, "Pauline Theology," in *NJBC*, 1396.

6. Yves Congar, *I Believe in the Holy Spirit*, 3 vols. (New York: Seabury Press, 1983), 3:xv.

7. Louis Bouyer, *Le Consolateur: Esprit-Saint et Vie de Grace* (Paris: Éditions du Cerf, 1980), 135-42.

8. Boris Bobrinskoy, *The Mystery of the Trinity: Trinitarian Experience and Vision in the Biblical and Patristic Tradition* (Crestwood, N.Y.: St. Vladimir's Seminary Press, 1999), 200.

9. Irenaeus, *Against Heresies* 1.22.1 (ANF 1:347).

10. Ibid.

11. Irenaeus, *Against Heresies* 2.30.9 (ANF 1:406).

12. Irenaeus, *Against Heresies* 5.28.4 (ANF 1:557). For some other examples, see *Against Heresies* 4, Pref. 4 (ANF 1:463); 4.20.1 (ANF 1:487); 5.6.1 (ANF 1:531).

13. Irenaeus, *Against Heresies* 4.38.3 (ANF 1:521-22).

14. Origen, *On First Principles* 1.3.5 (ANF 4:253).

15. Athanasius, *Letter to Serapion* 1.27. See *The Letters of Saint Athanasius Concerning the Holy Spirit,* trans. C. R. B. Shapland (London: Epworth Press, 1951), 133.

16. This important principle of Athanasius's pneumatology is found in the *Letter to Serapion* 3.5 (Shapland, 175).

17. Athanasius, *Letter to Serapion* 3.5 (Shapland, 174).

18. Athanasius, *Letter to Serapion* 1.28 (Shapland, 134-35).

19. Athanasius, *Letter to Serapion* 1.30 (Shapland, 142).

20. Basil, *Against Eunomius* 3.4 (SC 305:156-62).

21. Basil, *On the Holy Spirit* 16.37 (SC 17:374). The example of this "communion" of the Spirit with the Father and the Son in creation that Basil offers is the creation of the angels. He tells us that angels are not holy of their nature but are made holy at creation by the indwelling of the Spirit and that they are maintained in holiness by the same Spirit. Holiness comes "through their communion with the Spirit" (*On the Holy Spirit* 16.38). In the second of his *Longer Rules*, Basil considers the creation of humans and points out that through the Spirit they have the inclination to love God implanted in them at creation, like a seed of the Word that is to be nourished by grace and cultivated with care (see Augustine Holmes, *A Life Pleasing to God: The Spirituality of the Rules of St Basil* [London: Darton, Longman & Todd, 2000], 68-70). Clearly, he sees the foundations of both angelic and human holiness as given by the work of the Spirit in creation, and then continually nourished, sustained and perfected by that same Spirit.

22. Basil, *On the Holy Spirit* 16.38 (SC 17:376-78).

23. Basil, *On the Holy Spirit* 19.49 (SC 17:418).

24. Basil, *Hexaemeron* 2.6 (SC 26:168-70). Basil's contemporary Ephrem the Syrian held a different interpretation. Like some more recent biblical scholars, Ephrem argues

that Genesis is simply referring to a mighty wind. See his *Commentary on Genesis,* in *St. Ephrem the Syrian: Selected Prose Works,* trans. Edward G. Matthews, Jr., and Joseph P. Amar, ed. Kathleen McVey, FC 91 (1994), 79.

25. Basil, *Hexaemeron* 2.1, in *Basile de Césarée, Homélies sur L'Hexaéméron,* trans. S. Giet, SC 26:140.

26. Basil, *Hexaemeron* 7.5 (SC 26:416).

27. Basil, *Hexaemeron* 1.7 (SC 26:116).

28. Basil, *Hexaemeron* 2.2 (SC 26:148).

29. Without naming him, Jerome attacks Ambrose for his lack of originality, claiming that he wrote "bad things in Latin taken from good things in Greek." But Jerome's assessment is unreasonable. Ambrose not only made the theology of the Spirit worked out by Athanasius and the Cappadocians available to the West, which had important effects in the work of Augustine and the whole Western tradition, but also developed and clarified the theology of the Creator Spirit.

30. Ambrose of Milan, *On the Holy Spirit* 2.5.32 (FC 44:107).

31. Ambrose, *On the Holy Spirit* 2.5.33-34 (FC 44:108).

32. Ambrose, *On the Holy Spirit* 2.5.38 (FC 44:108).

33. Ambrose, *On the Holy Spirit* 2.5.41 (FC 44:110).

34. Ambrose, *On the Holy Spirit* 2.7.63-66 (FC 44:117-19).

35. Stephen Jay Gould, *Life's Grandeur: The Spread of Excellence from Plato to Darwin* (London: Vintage, 1996), 4, 197, 216.

36. Ernst Mayr, *What Evolution Is* (London: Weidenfeld & Nicolson, 2001), 82, 216, 218.

37. Gould, *Life's Grandeur,* 230.

38. Philip Clayton, "Neuroscience, the Person, and God: An Emergentist Account," in *Neuroscience and the Person: Scientific Perspectives on Divine Action,* ed. Robert John Russell, Nancey Murphy, Theo C. Meyering, and Michael A. Arbib (Vatican City/Berkeley, Calif.: Vatican Observatory and Center for Theology and the Natural Sciences, 1999), 211.

39. Nancey Murphy and George F. R. Ellis, *On the Moral Nature of the Universe: Theology, Cosmology, and Ethics* (Minneapolis: Fortress Press, 1996), 22.

40. Peacocke, *Theology for a Scientific Age.* For a more recent view, in which he prefers the language of *whole–part influence* to that of *top-down causation,* see "The Sound of Sheer Silence: How Does God Communicate with Humanity?" in *Neuroscience and the Person,* ed. Russell et al., 215-47.

41. Holmes Rolston III, *Genes, Genesis and God: Values and Their Origins in Natural and Human History* (Cambridge: Cambridge University Press, 1999), 297, 351.

42. Stuart A. Kauffman, *The Origin of Order: Self-Organization and Selection in Evolution* (Oxford: Oxford University Press, 1993); idem, *At Home in the Universe: The Search for Laws of Self-Organization and Complexity* (Oxford: Oxford University Press, 1995).

43. Paul Davies, *The Cosmic Blueprint* (London: Unwin, 1987, 1989).

44. Paul Davies, "Teleology without Teleology," in *Evolutionary and Molecular Biology: Scientific Perspectives on Divine Action,* ed. Robert John Russell, William R. Stoeger, S.J., and Francisco J. Ayala (Vatican City/Berkeley, Calif.: Vatican Observatory and Center for Theology and the Natural Sciences, 1998), 160. See also his *Are We Alone?* (London: Penguin, 1995) and *The Fifth Miracle* (New York: Simon & Schuster, 1998).

45. The divine "concursus" or concurrence refers to God's ongoing cooperation, which is always needed to enable creatures to act. In the theological tradition, this concurrence is understood as allowing creatures to act with their own proper autonomy.

46. Karl Rahner, "Evolution," in *Sacramentum Mundi: An Encyclopedia of Theol-*

ogy, ed. Karl Rahner, Cornelius Ernst, and Kevin Smyth (London: Burns & Oates, 1968), 2:289-97.

47. Karl Rahner, "Christology within an Evolutionary View of the World," in *Theological Investigations* (Baltimore: Helicon Press, 1961-79), 1:157-92; see also Karl Rahner, *Foundations of Christian Faith* (New York: Seabury Press, 1978), 178-203.

48. Elizabeth A. Johnson, *Women, Earth, and Creator Spirit* (New York: Paulist Press, 1993), 57-58.

49. Thomas Aquinas, *Summa Theologiae,* 1.45.3.

50. John V. Taylor, *The Go-Between God* (London: SCM, 1972), 64.

4. Enfolding Human Beings in Grace

1. Richard Leakey, *The Origin of Humankind* (London: Phoenix, 1994), xiv-xv.

2. Karl Rahner, "Experience of the Holy Spirit," in *Theological Investigations,* vol. 18 (New York: Crossroad, 1983), 196-97. While Rahner is always thought of as a theologian of grace, he is not always thought of as one of the great theologians of the Spirit. But, of course, for Rahner, grace is first of all always uncreated grace—the Spirit of God. His theology of grace *is* a theology of the Holy Spirit. His theology is encapsulated in the idea of God's self-communication in Word and Spirit (grace). See, e.g., his *Foundations of Christian Faith* (New York: Seabury Press, 1978), 137. What Rahner identified in earlier works as "experience of grace," he tended to call in his later works "experience of God" and "experience of the Holy Spirit"; see, e.g., his "Reflections on the Experience of Grace," in *Theological Investigations,* vol. 3 (New York: Seabury, 1967), 86-90; "The Experience of God Today," in *Theological Investigations,* vol. 11 (New York: Seabury, 1974), 149-65; "Experience of Self and Experience of God," in *Theological Investigations,* vol. 13 (New York: Seabury, 1975), 122-32; "Experience of the Spirit and Existential Commitment," in *Theological Investigations,* vol. 16 (New York: Seabury, 1979), 24-51.

3. Rahner, "Experience of the Holy Spirit," 199.

4. Justin Martyr, *Dialogue with Trypho* 45 (FC 6:215). See Francis Sullivan's *Salvation outside the Church? Tracing the History of the Catholic Response* (New York: Paulist Press, 1992), 14-27.

5. Justin Martyr, *First Apology* 46 (FC 6:83-84).

6. Clement of Alexandria, *Stromata* 7.2 (PG 9:409-10).

7. Origen, *Contra Celsum* 4.7 (PG 11:1035-38).

8. This is what Rahner calls the "supernatural existential." He writes: "Without prejudice to the fact that it speaks of a free and unmerited grace, of a miracle of God's free love for spiritual creatures, the statement that man as subject is the event of God's self-communication is a statement that refers to absolutely all men, and which expresses an existential of every person. Such an existential does not become merited and in this sense "natural" by the fact that it is present in all men as an existential of their concrete existence, and is present prior to their freedom, their self-understanding and their experience. The gratuity of a reality has nothing to do with the question whether it is present in many or only in a few" (*Foundations of Christian Faith,* 127). See also his "Concerning the Relationship between Nature and Grace," in *Theological Investigations,* vol. 1 (New York: Seabury, 1961), 297-317; and "Nature and Grace," in *Theological Investigations,* vol. 4 (New York: Seabury, 1966), 165-88.

9. Rahner, *Foundations of Christian Faith,* 316-18. See also his "Jesus Christ in the Non-Christian Religions," in *Theological Investigations,* vol. 17 (New York: Crossroad, 1981), 46. David Coffey has explored Rahner's idea of the entelechy of the Spirit in his "The Spirit of Christ as Entelechy," *Philosophy and Theology* 13 (2001): 365-98.

10. Rahner, *Foundations of Christian Faith,* 283-85. For Rahner's understanding of symbol, see his "The Theology of Symbol," in *Theological Investigations,* 4:221-52.

11. For a fuller treatment of original sin and its relationship to biological evolution, see my "Original Sin and Saving Grace in Evolutionary Perspective," in *Evolutionary and Molecular Biology: Scientific Perspectives on Divine Action,* ed. Robert John Russell, William R. Stoeger, S.J., and Francisco J. Ayala (Vatican City/Berkeley, Calif.: Vatican Observatory and The Center for Theology and the Natural Sciences, 1998), 377-92; and *The God of Evolution: A Trinitarian Theology* (New York: Paulist Press, 1999), 60-72.

12. Holmes Rolston III, *Genes, Genesis and God: Values and Their Origins in Natural and Human History* (Cambridge: Cambridge University Press, 1999), 300.

13. Translated as *On the Permanent Validity of the Church's Missionary Mandate* (Homebush, NSW: St Paul, 1991), 23.

14. Translated as *Redeemer of Man* (Homebush, NSW: St Paul, 1979), 20-21.

15. *Redeemer of Man,* 36-37.

16. See Sullivan, *Salvation outside the Church?* 190, 193.

17. Translated as *The Holy Spirit in the Life of the Church and the World: Dominum et Vivicantem* (Boston: St Paul, 1986), 91. Here again, John Paul II calls to mind the Second Vatican Council's teaching that the Holy Spirit acts "outside the visible body of the church."

18. Rahner, *Foundations of Christian Faith,* 314.

19. This typology has certainly facilitated discussion over the last twenty years. It was popularized by Alan Race in *Christians and Religious Pluralism: Patterns in the Christian Theology of Religions* (London: SCM, 1983). For other important approaches to these issues, see Paul F. Knitter, *No Other Name? A Critical Survey of Christian Attitudes toward the World Religions* (Maryknoll, N.Y.: Orbis Books, 1985); and Jacques Dupuis, *Toward a Christian Theology of Religious Pluralism* (Maryknoll, N.Y.: Orbis Books, 1997). See also Jacques Dupuis, *Christianity and the Religions: From Confrontation to Dialogue* (Maryknoll, N.Y.: Orbis Books, 2002). On the pluralist approach, see *The Myth of Christian Uniqueness: Toward a Pluralistic Theology of Religions,* ed. John Hick and Paul Knitter (Maryknoll, N.Y.: Orbis Books, 1987).

20. Paul F. Knitter, *Introducing Theologies of Religion* (Maryknoll, N.Y.: Orbis Books, 2002).

21. Gavin D'Costa, *The Meeting of Religions and the Trinity* (Maryknoll, N.Y.: Orbis Books, 2000), 99-142; Dupuis, *Toward a Christian Theology of Religious Pluralism,* 222-23.

22. D'Costa, *Meeting of Religions,* 115.

23. Aloysius Pieris, *Fire and Water: Basic Issues in Asian Buddhism and Christianity* (Maryknoll, N.Y.: Orbis Books, 1996), 150-51.

24. Michael Amaladoss, "Pluralism of Religions and the Proclamation of Jesus Christ in the Context of Asia," *Catholic Theological Society of America Proceedings* 56 (2001): 7-12.

25. Ibid., 11.

5. Bringing About the Christ Event

1. Ambrose, *On the Holy Spirit* 2.5.41 (FC 44:110).

2. D. Lyle Dabney, "The Justification of the Spirit: Soteriological Reflections on the Resurrection," in *Starting with the Spirit,* ed. Stephen Pickard and Gordon Preece (Adelaide: Australian Theological Forum, 2001), 70. Morna Hooker speaks of Mark *framing* the whole story of Jesus in terms of the Spirit (*The Gospel according to Saint Mark,* Black's New Testament Commentaries [Peabody, Mass.: Hendrickson, 1991], 38).

3. Hooker, *Gospel according to Saint Mark,* 38.

4. See Joel Marcus, *Mark 1-8: A New Translation with Introduction and Commentary,* Anchor Bible 27 (New York: Doubleday, 2000), 159-60.

5. John R. Donahue and Daniel Harrington note: "This text contains a 'surplus of meaning,' combining royal and servant motifs along with language from the tradition of the suffering just persons (Wis 2:12-20, especially vv. 13, 18). It also provides an echo of 1:1 where a similar density of titles appears" (*The Gospel of Mark*, Sacra Pagina 2 [Collegeville, Minn.: Liturgical Press, 2002], 65). Morna Hooker points out that in the Old Testament "beloved" often has the sense of "only," and its use after "son" here and in the words of the transfiguration account (Mark 9:7) points to the uniqueness of Jesus as God's beloved son (*Gospel according to Saint Mark*, 47-48).

6. On the messianic promise of the Spirit, see Michael Welker, *God the Spirit* (Minneapolis: Fortress Press, 1994), 108-82.

7. Michael Trainor, *The Quest for Home: The Household in Mark's Community* (Collegeville, Minn.: Liturgical Press, 2001), 82.

8. Eduard Schweizer, *The Good News According to Mark* (Richmond, Va.: John Knox Press, 1970), 39.

9. Marcus, *Mark 1-8*, 284.

10. See, e.g., Ulrich Luz, *Matthew 1-7: A Continental Commentary* (Minneapolis: Fortress Press, 1989), 171-72; Daniel Harrington, *The Gospel of Matthew*, Sacra Pagina 1 (Collegeville, Minn.: Liturgical Press, 1991), 59.

11. James D. G. Dunn, *The Christ and the Spirit*, volume 2, *Pneumatology* (Grand Rapids: Eerdmans, 1998), 93-102.

12. Joseph A. Fitzmyer, S.J., *The Gospel According to Luke I-IX*, Anchor Bible 28 (Garden City, N.Y.: Doubleday, 1981), 227.

13. Ibid., 227-28.

14. At the beginning of Acts, the risen Christ tells the disciples to wait in Jerusalem for the fulfillment of God's promise: "for John baptized with water, but *you will be baptized with the Holy Spirit* not many days from now" (1:5).

15. See Luke Timothy Johnson, *The Gospel of Luke*, Sacra Pagina 3 (Collegeville, Minn.: Liturgical Press, 1991), 18.

16. As Fitzmyer insists, the Holy Spirit of Luke-Acts is clearly the same Spirit who was the life-giving, energizing, and inspiring presence of God throughout Israel's history. This is made explicit when we find Peter talking of the Holy Spirit as speaking through David (Acts 1:16; 4:25) and Paul pointing to the Spirit speaking through Isaiah (Acts 28:25). Two texts are key for Luke: Isaiah 61:1-2 for the anointing of Jesus (Luke 4:16-21) and Joel 2:28-29 for Pentecost (Acts 2:16-21). See Fitzmyer, *Gospel According to Luke I-IX*, 228.

17. See Luke Timothy Johnson, *The Acts of the Apostles*, Sacra Pagina 5 (Collegeville, Minn.: Liturgical Press, 1992), 14.

18. Ibid.

19. Ibid., 15. On the Holy Spirit as a *character*, see William H. Shepherd, Jr., *The Narrative Function of the Holy Spirit as a Character in Luke-Acts*, Society of Biblical Literature Dissertation Series 147 (Atlanta: Scholars Press, 1994).

20. A number of scholars have argued that the figure of the Paraclete may originally have been independent of the Holy Spirit—perhaps as an angelic protector of the righteous. For a summary of discussion on the Paraclete, see Raymond E. Brown, *The Gospel According to John (xiii-xxi)*, Anchor Bible 29A (Garden City, N.Y.: Doubleday, 1970), 1135-44. Brown sees the Paraclete as the Holy Spirit in a special role, as the personal presence of Jesus in the disciples. But, as Francis J. Moloney points out, the Paraclete is always presented as distinct from Jesus, does not become flesh, and is not lifted up in death (*The Gospel of John*, Sacra Pagina 4 [Collegeville, Minn.: Liturgical Press, 1998], 401). In my view the Paraclete is best seen as the presence of the Spirit of Truth, as a helper like Jesus.

21. Moloney, *Gospel of John*, 504-5. Raymond Brown suggests that this is a symbolic reference to the Spirit that points toward the actual giving of the Spirit in 20:22 (*Gospel According to John (xiii-xxi)*, 931).

22. See Denis Edwards, *Jesus the Wisdom of God: An Ecological Theology* (Maryknoll, N.Y.: Orbis Books, 1995); and "The Ecological Significance of God Language," *Theological Studies* 60 (December 1999): 708-22.

23. See the works of Elizabeth A. Johnson, particularly *She Who Is: The Mystery of God in Feminist Theological Discourse* (New York: Crossroad, 1992). A Sophia theology has been developed by a number of other feminist theologians including Elisabeth Schüssler Fiorenza in, among other works, *Jesus: Miriam's Child, Sophia's Prophet* (New York: Continuum, 1994).

24. See Jean Daniélou, *The Theology of Jewish Christianity* (London: Darton Longman & Todd, 1964); and Hans-Joachim Schoeps, *Jewish Christianity: Factional Disputes in the Early Church* (Philadelphia: Fortress Press, 1969).

25. See Stanley M. Burgess, *The Holy Spirit: Ancient Christian Traditions* (Peabody, Mass.: Hendrickson, 1984), 18-19. Burgess has helpfully collected important texts on the Holy Spirit in this volume and in *The Holy Spirit: Medieval Roman Catholic and Reformation Traditions* (Peabody, Mass.: Hendrickson, 1997) and *The Holy Spirit: Eastern Christian Traditions* (Peabody, Mass.: Hendrickson, 1989).

26. See Burgess, *Holy Spirit: Ancient Christian Traditions*, 22-24.

27. James D. G. Dunn, *Jesus and the Spirit: A Study of the Religious and Charismatic Experience of Jesus and the First Christians as Reflected in the New Testament* (Philadelphia: Westminster, 1975), 43, 90-92.

28. Ibid., 322-26.

29. See, e.g., Victor Pfitzner, "'The Spirit of the Lord': The Christological Focus of Pauline Pneumatology," in *Starting with the Spirit*, ed. Pickard and Preece, 113-33; Gordon D. Fee, *God's Empowering Presence: The Holy Spirit in the Letters of St. Paul* (Peabody, Mass.: Hendrikson, 1994), 837-38; Joseph A. Fitzmyer, S.J., "Pauline Theology," in *NJBC*, 1396-97.

30. Geoffrey Lampe, *God as Spirit* (London: SCM, 1977). For further developments, see Paul W. Newman, *A Spirit Christology: Recovering the Biblical Paradigm* (Lanham, Md.: University Press of America, 1987); and Michael E. Lodahl, *Shekhina/Spirit: Divine Presence in Jewish and Christian Religion* (New York: Paulist Press, 1992).

31. James Mackey, *The Christian Experience of God as Trinity* (London: SCM, 1983), 241-51.

32. Piet Schoonenberg, *De Geest, het Woord en de Zoon* (Averbode: Altiora, 1991). See also his "Spirit Christology and Logos Christology," *Bidragen* 38 (1977): 350-73; and his *The Christ: A Study of the God-Man Relationship in the Whole of Creation and in Jesus Christ* (New York: Herder & Herder, 1971). For a helpful description of Schoonenberg's Spirit Christology, see Michael E. O'Keeffe, "The Spirit Christology of Piet Schoonenberg," in *Christology: Memory, Inquiry, Practice*, ed. Anne M. Clifford and Anthony J. Godzieba (Maryknoll, N.Y.: Orbis Books, 2003).

33. Rosemary Radford Ruether, *Sexism and God-Talk: Toward a Feminist Theology* (London: SCM, 1983), 137.

34. Ibid., 138.

35. Jürgen Moltmann, *The Way of Jesus Christ: Christology in Messianic Dimensions* (London: SCM, 1990).

36. Ibid., 74, 94, 174.

37. Roger Haight, *Jesus Symbol of God* (Maryknoll, N.Y.: Orbis Books, 1999), 455. See also idem, "The Case for Spirit Christology," *Theological Studies* 53 (1992): 257-87; and idem, "The Point of Trinitarian Doctrine," *Toronto Journal of Theology* 4 (1988): 191-204.

38. David Coffey, *Grace: The Gift of the Holy Spirit* (Manly, NSW: Catholic Institute of Sydney, 1979), 65.

39. See, among others, David Coffey, "The 'Incarnation' of the Holy Spirit in Christ," *Theological Studies* 45 (1984): 466-80; idem, "A Proper Mission of the Holy Spirit," *Theological Studies* 47 (1986): 227-50; idem, "The Holy Spirit as the Mutual

Love of the Father and the Son," *Theological Studies* 51 (1990): 193-229; and idem, *Deus Trinitas: The Doctrine of the Triune God* (New York: Oxford University Press, 1999).

40. Ralph Del Colle, *Christ and the Spirit: Spirit Christology in Trinitarian Perspective* (New York: Oxford University Press, 1994), 203.

41. Haight, *Jesus Symbol of God,* 447.

42. Walter Kasper, *Jesus the Christ* (New York: Paulist Press, 1976), 255.

43. Scholastic theology tended to see the work of the Holy Spirit in the incarnation as not *proper* but only *appropriated* to the Spirit. I will discuss this in detail in chapter 10.

44. Kasper, *Jesus the Christ,* 251.

45. Ambrose, *On the Holy Spirit* 2.5.41 (FC 44:110); see chapter 3 above.

46. Karl Rahner, *Foundations of Christian Faith,* 316-18; see also his "Jesus Christ in the Non-Christian Religions," in *Theological Investigations,* vol. 17 (New York: Crossroad, 1981), 46.

47. Yves Congar, *The Word and the Spirit* (London: Geoffrey Chapman, 1986), 87.

48. Ibid., 89.

49. Ibid., 92.

50. Yves Congar, *I Believe in the Holy Spirit,* 3 vols. (New York: Seabury Press, 1983), 3:267.

51. John Paul II, *The Holy Spirit in the Life of the Church and the World: Dominum et Vivicantem* (Boston: St Paul, 1986), §41, p. 68.

52. Edward Schillebeeckx, *Christ: The Christian Experience in the Modern World* (London: SCM, 1980), 729-30.

53. In the context of this kind of "transcendental christology" Rahner speaks of humanity as the "grammar" of God's possible self-expression in our world. He sees anthropology in its most radical actualization as theology, and Christology as "the beginning and end of anthropology" (see *Foundations of Christian Faith,* 223-25).

54. Coffey, *Grace,* 91-92.

55. Fitzmyer, "Pauline Theology," 1396.

56. Del Colle, *Christ and the Spirit,* 168-69.

57. Dunn, *Jesus and the Spirit,* 326.

58. While some see the developed doctrine of the Trinity as a falling away from the New Testament into speculative metaphysics, I am among those who see trinitarian faith as a hard-won human achievement of the early church that is also a gift of the Spirit to the church. I believe that this position can be justified on the basis of two theological positions: that God can be trusted in revealing God's self to us and that the Spirit was at work in the emergence of the doctrine. The first principle insists that what God reveals of God's self in the history of salvation is faithful to the way God is. The second is based on the biblical promise of the abiding presence of the Spirit of truth, who guides the church into "all truth" (John 16:13). Of course, a critical hermeneutics that takes account of human limitations and ideological distortions is essential for the interpretation of this and other doctrines. But if one accepts that God can be trusted in God's self-communication and also accepts a role for the Spirit in the life of the church, it seems reasonable to see trinitarian doctrine as a truthful but humanly limited understanding of God, one that necessarily finds expression in symbolic and analogical language. The trinitarian structure of Christian experience can be thought of as pointing, however inadequately, to the way God is. To put the matter negatively, if the church were to be radically mistaken about its fundamental understanding of God, it would seem difficult to assert a presence or action of the Spirit anywhere in the life and history of the Christian community—including its origins.

59. Roger Haight and others point to the danger of this kind of figurative speech becoming understood in a literal and realistic way (see *Jesus Symbol of God,* 475-76). This is an important issue. Many seem to have an uncritical, anthropomorphic and reified view of preexisting divine persons. But I would suggest that the appropriate

response to this danger is not a program of demythologization, the typical response of "modern" theology, but a critically aware embrace of, and delight in, the narrative structure and metaphorical character of myth. A critical theological approach will be based on an awareness of the absolute otherness of God, of God as abiding incomprehensible Mystery. It will be aware of the way analogy, metaphor, and myth work, providing a limited but real yield. I am convinced that preexistence language points to something real. It claims that what it is of God in Jesus, what I am identifying as the Wisdom of God, comes from God and was always with God. In a similar way it claims that the Breath of God who anointed Jesus and is poured out in the church comes from God and was always with God. This kind of language points to relational abundance in the mysterious Communion of the divine. I believe that the figurative and mythic language of the Breath of God and the beautiful narrative of Sophia can provide a limited but wonderfully precious yield for contemporary theology.

6. Poured Out on the Church

1. I am conscious that the Pentecostal/charismatic movement deserves far more attention than I can give it in this book, where my focus is on the larger story of creation, grace, incarnation, and church. Fortunately some recent theologies of the Spirit treat this important part of Christian experience more adequately. See, e.g., Veli-Matti Karkkainen, *Pneumatology: The Holy Spirit in Ecumenical, International, and Historical Perspective* (Grand Rapids: Baker Academic, 2002). On the Pentecostal movement, see Walter J. Hollenweger, *The Pentecostals: The Charismatic Movement in the Churches* (London: SCM, 1972), and his *Pentecostalism: Origins and Developments Worldwide* (Peabody, Mass.: Hendrickson, 1997). See also the *Dictionary of Pentecostal and Charismatic Movements*, ed. Stanley M. Burgess and Gary B. McGee (Grand Rapids: Zondervan, 1988).

2. Kilian McDonnell has long reflected on the theology of the Spirit and on the charismatic movement in the Catholic tradition. See, among other contributions, his *Charismatic Renewal and the Churches* (New York: Seabury Press, 1976) and *Charismatic Renewal and Ecumenism* (New York: Paulist Press, 1978). He is the editor of *The Holy Spirit and Power: The Catholic Charismatic Movement* (Garden City, N.Y.: Doubleday, 1975), and of *Presence, Power, Praise: Documents on the Catholic Charismatic Movement*. 3 vols. (Collegeville, Minn.: Liturgical Press, 1980). With George Montague he is the author of *Christian Initiation and Baptism in the Holy Spirit: Evidence from the First Eight Centuries* (Collegeville, Minn.: Liturgical Press, 1991).

3. José Comblin, *The Holy Spirit and Liberation* (Maryknoll, N.Y.: Orbis Books, 1989), 76.

4. Gustavo Gutiérrez, *We Drink from Our Own Wells: The Spiritual Journey of a People* (Maryknoll, N.Y.: Orbis Books, 1984), 106.

5. Rosemary Radford Ruether sees the critical principle of feminist theology as "the promotion of the full humanity of women" (*Sexism and God-Talk: Toward a Feminist Theology* [London: SCM, 1983], 18).

6. Anne M. Clifford, *Introducing Feminist Theology* (Maryknoll, N.Y.: Orbis Books, 2001), 16.

7. Ibid., 9-28.

8. Sandra M. Schneiders, *With Oil in Their Lamps: Faith, Feminism, and the Future* (New York: Paulist Press, 2000), 8.

9. Mark I. Wallace, "The Wounded Spirit as the Basis for Hope in an Age of Radical Ecology," in *Christianity and Ecology: Seeking the Well-Being of Earth and Humans*, ed. Dieter T. Hessel and Rosemary Radford Ruether (Cambridge, Mass.: Harvard University Press, 2000), 51-72.

10. Rosemary Radford Ruether, "Conclusion: Eco-Justice at the Center of the Church's Mission," in *Christianity and Ecology,* ed. Hessel and Ruether, 603-13.

11. Nikos A. Nissiotis, "The Main Ecclesiological Problem of the Second Vatican Council and the Position of the Non-Roman Churches Facing It," *Journal of Ecumenical Studies* 6 (1965): 31-62. See Yves Congar, *I Believe in the Holy Spirit,* 3 vols. (New York: Seabury Press, 1983), 1:157.

12. Yves Congar, *The Word and the Spirit* (London: Geoffrey Chapman, 1986), 117.

13. Yves Congar, "My Path-Findings in the Theology of the Laity and Ministries," *The Jurist* 32 (1972): 181.

14. See Congar, *Word and the Spirit,* 85-100.

15. See Congar's chapter under this title in *Word and the Spirit,* 21-41.

16. Ibid., 61.

17. Congar, *I Believe in the Holy Spirit,* 1:156.

18. Congar, *Word and the Spirit,* 66-67.

19. Yves Congar, "Pneumatology Today," *American Ecclesiastical Review* 167 (1973): 443.

20. Congar, *Word and the Spirit,* 80-81.

21. Ibid., 130.

22. Congar, *I Believe in the Holy Spirit,* 2:5-14.

23. Ibid., 2:16.

24. Ibid.

25. Ibid., 2:17.

26. Ibid., 2:27.

27. Ibid., 2:44-47.

28. Ibid., 2:52-72.

29. Denis Doyle, "Journet, Congar and the Roots of Communion Ecclesiology," *Theological Studies* 58 (1997): 475.

30. Elizabeth T. Groppe, "The Contribution of Yves Congar's Theology of the Holy Spirit," *Theological Studies* 62 (2001): 451-78.

31. See, e.g., the comments by Avery Dulles introducing The Dogmatic Constitution on the Church in *The Documents of Vatican II,* ed. Walter M. Abbott (London: Geoffrey Chapman, 1966), 9.

32. Walter Kasper, "On the Church," *The Tablet* (June 23, 2001): 930.

33. *On Some Aspects of the Church Understood as Communion* (1992), par 9.

34. See Joseph Ratzinger, "The Local Church and the Universal Church," *America* 185 (November 19, 2001): 7-11.

35. For a full summary of the debate and further analysis of the issues, see Kilian McDonnell, O.S.B., "The Ratzinger/Kasper Debate: The Universal Church and the Local Churches," *Theological Studies* 63 (2002): 227-50; and "Walter Kasper on the Theology and Praxis of the Bishop's Office," *Theological Studies* 63 (2002): 711-29.

36. Kasper, "On the Church," 930.

37. Congar, *I Believe in the Holy Spirit,* 2:26.

38. Ibid., 2:27.

39. In this section I am making use of ideas presented in the agreed statement of the Anglican–Roman Catholic International Commission, *The Gift of Authority: Authority in the Church III* (New York: Church Publishing, 1999), 26 and *passim.*

40. Ibid., 23.

41. Ibid.

42. John Zizioulas, *Being as Communion* (Crestwood, N.Y.: St. Vladimir's Seminary Press, 1993), 226.

43. *Gift of Authority,* 24.

44. Groppe, "Contribution of Yves Congar's Theology of the Holy Spirit," 472.

45. *Gift of Authority,* 24.

46. Congar, *I Believe in the Holy Spirit,* 3:267.

47. Ibid., 2:46.

48. Congar, "Pneumatology Today," 443. I am grateful to Jennie O'Brien, who is working on Congar in the School of Theology at Flinders University and drew my attention to the importance of this article.

7. The Spirit as Midwife and Companion
as Creation Groans in Giving Birth

1. Celia E. Deane-Drummond, *Creation through Wisdom: Theology and the New Biology* (Edinburgh: T&T Clark, 2000), 222-23.

2. Ibid., 223-31.

3. Jay McDaniel, *With Roots and Wings: Christianity in an Age of Ecology and Dialogue* (Maryknoll, N.Y.: Orbis Books, 1995), 53.

4. Elizabeth A. Johnson, *Women, Earth, and Creator Spirit* (New York: Paulist Press, 1993), 59.

5. Patricia Fox, *God as Communion: John Zizioulas, Elizabeth Johnson, and the Retrieval of the Symbol of the Triune God* (Collegeville, Minn.: Liturgical Press, 2001), 244.

6. This theme has been developed by a number of theologians in recent years, including Jürgen Moltmann, Paul Fiddes, and John Polkinghorne. For a recent discussion that includes articles by these scholars, see *The Work of Love: Creation as Kenosis,* ed. John Polkinghorne (Grand Rapids: Eerdmans, 2001).

7. Ted Peters, "God as the Future of Cosmic Creativity," in *Science, Theology, and Ethics* (Burlington, Vt.: Ashgate, 2003), 89-90. Peters is building on Gordon Kaufman's concept of the divine "master act" of creation and Wolfhart Pannenberg's concept of proleptic eschatology in Christ.

8. Carol J. Dempsey, "Hope Amidst Crisis: A Prophetic Vision of Cosmic Redemption" in *All Creation Is Groaning: An Interdisciplinary Vision of Life in a Sacred Universe,* ed. Carol J. Dempsey and Russell A. Butkus (Collegeville, Minn.: Liturgical Press, 1999), 282.

9. James D. G. Dunn, *The Christ and the Spirit,* volume 2, *Pneumatology* (Grand Rapids: Eerdmans, 1998), 14.

10. Ibid.

11. Wolfhart Pannenberg, *Systematic Theology* (Grand Rapids: Eerdmans, 1991–), 2:101, 102. Pannenberg is speaking of the Spirit imaged as a "field," an image that I do not find very helpful.

12. This is Brendan Byrne's translation from his *Romans,* Sacra Pagina 6 (Collegeville, Minn.: Liturgical Press, 1996), 254.

13. Joseph A. Fitzmyer, S.J., *Romans: A New Translation with Introduction and Commentary,* Anchor Bible 33 (New York: Doubleday, 1993), 509.

14. Ibid., 505.

15. Byrne, *Romans,* 255.

16. *Summa Theologiae,* 1.13.7; 1.28.1; 1.45.3 ad 1. In Aristotelian thought, relation is classified as an accident, and no accident can inhere in the divine being. On this, see Anthony Kelly, "God: How Near a Relation?" *Thomist* 34 (1970): 191-229; William Hill, "Does the World Make a Difference to God?" *Thomist* 38 (1974):146-64; John Wright, "Divine Knowledge and Human Freedom: The God Who Dialogues" *Theological Studies* 38 (1977): 450-77; Catherine LaCugna, "The Relational God: Aquinas and Beyond," *Theological Studies* 46 (1985): 647-63.

17. Jürgen Moltmann, *The Crucified God: The Cross of Christ as the Foundation and Criticism of Christian Theology* (London: SCM, 1974), 274.

18. Jürgen Moltmann, *History and the Triune God: Contributions to Trinitarian Theology* (London: SCM, 1991), 29.

19. Thomas G. Weinandy, *Does God Suffer?* (Edinburgh: T&T Clark, 2000).

20. John Paul II, *The Holy Spirit in the Life of the Church and the World: Dominum et Vivicantem* (Boston: St. Paul, 1986), §39, pp. 62-63.

21. Michael Schmaus, *Dogma 2: God and Creation* (London: Sheed & Ward, 1969), 95.

22. Ruth Page, *God and the Web of Creation* (London: SCM, 1996), 62.

23. Ibid., 71.

24. Ibid.

25. Jürgen Moltmann, *The Spirit of Life: A Universal Affirmation* (Minneapolis: Fortress Press, 1992), 10.

26. McDaniel, *With Roots and Wings*, 54.

27. Ursula Goodenough, *The Sacred Depths of Nature* (New York: Oxford University Press, 1998), 8-14. She writes: "The realization that I needn't have answers to the Big Questions, needn't seek answers to the Big Questions, has served as an epiphany. I lie on my back under the stars and the unseen galaxies and I let their enormity wash over me. I assimilate the vastness of the distances, the impermanences, the *fact* of it all" (p. 12).

28. John Zizioulas, "Preserving God's Creation: Three Lectures on Theology and Ecology," *King's Theological Review* 12 (1989): 1-5, 41-45; 13 (1990): 1-5.

29. Aldo Leopold, "Some Fundamentals of Conservation in the Southwest," *Environmental Ethics* 1 (Summer 1979): 140-41.

8. A Distinctive and Proper Role of the Spirit in Creation

1. Wolfhart Pannenberg, *Systematic Theology* (Grand Rapids: Eerdmans, 1991–), 2:76.

2. Athanasius, *Letters to Serapion* 1.24 (Shapland, 127).

3. Matthew Fox, ed., *Hildegard of Bingen's Book of Divine Works with Letters and Songs* (Santa Fe: Bear, 1985), 373.

4. Barbara J. Newman, "Introduction," *Hildegard of Bingen: Scivias*, trans. Mother Columba Hart and Jane Bishop (New York: Paulist Press, 1990), 25.

5. Elizabeth A. Johnson, *She Who Is: The Mystery of God in Feminist Theological Discourse* (New York: Crossroad, 1992), 134.

6. Walter Kasper, *The God of Jesus Christ* (London: SCM, 1983), 227.

7. See Christian Duquoc, *Dieu différent* (Paris: Cerf, 1977), 121-22; see also Yves Congar, *I Believe in the Holy Spirit,* 3 vols. (New York: Seabury Press, 1983), 3:148.

8. Congar, *I Believe in the Holy Spirit*, 3:149, 150.

9. Jürgen Moltmann, *The Spirit of Life: A Universal Affirmation* (Minneapolis: Fortress Press, 1992), 10, 225.

10. This axiom found expression at the Council of Constantinople II (553) and at the Council of Florence (1442), as well as in the work of major theologians of the Eastern and Western traditions.

11. Athanasius, *Letter to Serapion* 1.28 (Shapland, 134-35).

12. Athanasius, *Letter to Serapion* 1.28 (Shapland, 135).

13. Gregory of Nyssa, *On Not Three Gods*, NPF 5:334.

14. Thomas Aquinas, *De Veritate*, q. 7, a. 3. See his *Summa Theologiae*, 1a, q. 37, a. 2 ad 3; q. 38, a.1, ad 4; q. 39, a. 7; q. 45, a. 6.

15. Karl Rahner, *The Trinity* (New York: Herder & Herder, 1970), 23, 28-30.

16. Heribert Mühlen, *Der Heilige Geist als Person: Beitrag zur Frage nach der dem heiligen Geiste eigentümlichen Funktion in der Trinität, bei der Inkarnation und im Gnadenbund,* Münsterische Beiträge zur Theologie 26 (Münster: Aschendorff, 1963); David Coffey, "A Proper Mission of the Holy Spirit," *Theological Studies* 47 (1986): 227-50.

17. Rahner, *Trinity*, 34-38; idem, "Some Implications of the Scholastic Concept of Uncreated Grace," in *Theological Investigations*, 1:319-46; Yves Congar, *I Believe in the Holy Spirit*, 2:85-92.

18. In order to show that God can constitutively transform human existence by self-communication, without thereby compromising divine transcendence, Rahner and Congar speak of a "*quasi*-formal causality."

19. Karl Rahner, *Foundations of Christian Faith* (New York: Seabury Press, 1978), 76-77.

20. "*Omnis enim creatura ex natura est illius aeternae sapientiae quaedam effigies et simultudo*" (*Itinerarium* 2.12). In the *Hexaemeron*, Bonventure writes: "*Unde creatura non est nisi quoddam simulacrum sapientiae Dei, et quoddam sculptile*" (12).

21. Pannenberg, *Systematic Theology*, 2:30.

22. Ibid., 2:32.

23. Ibid., 2:114.

24. Ibid., 2:32.

25. Tony Kelly, *An Expanding Theology: Faith in a World of Connections* (Sydney: E. J. Dwyer, 1993), 158-59.

26. I have taken the concept of *power-in-relation* from Mary Grey, *Redeeming the Dream: Feminism, Redemption and Christian Tradition* (London: SPCK, 1983), 88-94. See also Isabel Carter Heyward, *The Redemption of God: A Theology of Mutual Relation* (Lanham: University Press of America, 1982).

27. Ambrose of Milan, *On the Holy Spirit* 2.32 (FC 44:107).

28. Basil, *Hexaemeron* 5.2 (SC 26:284).

29. Moltmann, *Spirit of Life*, 12.

30. Sallie McFague, *Super, Natural Christians: How We Should Love Nature* (London: SCM, 1997), 177; see also her *Life Abundant: Rethinking Theology and Economy for a Planet in Peril* (Minneapolis: Fortress Press, 2000).

9. A Relational Universe
Evolving within the Relational Life of God

1. Jürgen Moltmann has developed this idea of a divine *kenōsis* in creation that "makes space" for a world of creatures; see his *God in Creation: A New Theology of Creation and the Spirit of God* (San Francisco: Harper & Row, 1985), 86-93; idem, *The Trinity and the Kingdom: The Doctrine of God* (San Francisco: Harper & Row, 1981), 108-11. See also Elizabeth A. Johnson, *She Who Is: The Mystery of God in Feminist Theological Discourse* (New York: Crossroad, 1992), 234.

2. Arthur Peacocke, *Theology for a Scientific Age: Being and Becoming—Natural, Divine and Human* (Minneapolis: Fortress Press, 1993), 38.

3. William R. Stoeger, "The Mind-Brain Problem, the Laws of Nature, and Constitutive Relationships," in *Neuroscience and the Person: Scientific Perspectives on Divine Action*, ed. Robert John Russell, Nancey Murphy, Theo C. Meyering, and Michael A. Arbib (Vatican City/Berkeley, Calif.: Vatican Observatory and Center for Theology and the Natural Sciences, 1999), 136-37.

4. Ibid., 139.

5. Thomas Aquinas, *Summa Theologiae*, 1.28.2.

6. William J. Hill, *The Three-Personed God: The Trinity as a Mystery of Salvation* (Washington: Catholic University of America Press, 1984), 269. Hill insists: "there is not some fourth reality 'behind,' as it were, the Father, Word and Pneuma." He states that when we think of God as a single absolute person, we are abstracting from the reality of the Three. This abstraction can be rendered concrete and real by identifying it with the first person, the *fons divinitatis*.

7. John Zizioulas, *Being as Communion* (Crestwood, N.Y.: St. Vladimir's Seminary Press, 1993), 17.

8. Ibid.; see also John Zizioulas "The Doctrine of the Holy Trinity: The Significance of the Cappadocian Contribution," in *Trinitarian Theology Today,* ed. Christoph Schwobel (Edinburgh: T&T Clark, 1995), 44-60.

9. Walter Kasper, *The God of Jesus Christ* (London: SCM, 1983), 310; see also 290.

10. Catherine Mowry LaCugna, *God for Us: The Trinity and Christian Life* (San Francisco: HarperSanFrancisco, 1991), 250; see also 310.

11. Ibid., 310.

12. Colin E. Gunton, *The One, the Three and the Many: God, Creation and the Culture of Modernity* (Cambridge: Cambridge Univerity Press, 1993), 230. Gunton suggests that perichoresis, substantiality, and relationality can be seen as what he calls "open transcendentals," ways in which creation bears the marks of its making (pp. 129-231). These bear some relation to the three characteristics of the universe that I outline here, but I find no reason to separate perichoresis and relationality. And I find it important to add, as a third characteristic, the emergence and evolution of things in time.

13. Johnson, *She Who Is,* 22.

14. John Zizioulas, "Human Capacity and Human Incapacity: A Theological Exploration of Personhood," *Scottish Journal of Theology* 28 (1975): 408-9. Patricia Fox comments: "If the triune God is understood most fundamentally as 'persons-in-communion,' then the concept of person certainly is humanity's 'most dear and precious good.' Such a vision elucidated by Zizioulas not only opens life-giving understandings of the potential of human personhood and freedom that endures eternally, but it also reveals a dynamic and thrilling view of God. God disclosed as 'persons in communion' reveals a totally shared personal life at the heart of the universe" (*God as Communion: John Zizioulas, Elizabeth Johnson, and the Retrieval of the Symbol of the Triune God* [Collegeville, Minn.: Liturgical Press, 2001], 51).

15. Stoeger calls this "mereological" reducibility ("Mind-Brain Problem," 140-43). In his view, the claim that an entity is mereologically irreducible does not mean that anything extra is needed to explain it over and beyond its constitutive relationships. Stoeger distinguishes "mereological" irreducibility from "causal" irreducibility: causal irreducibility refers to higher-level causes that are not determined solely by causes operating at a more fundamental level. Stoeger suggests that a good case can be made "that the behaviour of a water molecule, though not mereologically irreducible, is causally reducible" (p. 141).

16. Nancy Victorin-Vangerud, *The Raging Hearth: Spirit in the Household of God* (St. Louis: Chalice Press, 2000).

17. See Victorin-Vangerud's analysis of "poisonous pedagogy" and "poisonous pneumatology" in *Raging Hearth,* 109-12, 117-41.

18. Ian G. Barbour, *Nature, Human Nature, and God* (Minneapolis: Fortress Press, 2002), 6.

19. On "anthropic reasoning" see Martin Rees, *Before the Beginning: Our Universe and Others* (London: Touchstone, 1997), 235-69. Brandon Carter introduced the modern discussion of the "anthropic principle" and distinguished between the "weak" and "strong" forms. My interest is in the weak form—which simply brings out the relationship between the fact of the existence of human beings and the constraints this puts on the nature of the universe. Only a universe with certain characteristics could produce creatures like us. The strong form of the principle suggests that the universe is ordered the way it is *in order that* human beings might emerge. For a full treatment of the anthropic principle, see John D. Barrow and F. Tipler, *The Anthropic Cosmological Principle* (Oxford: Oxford University Press, 1986); for a recent treatment see John D. Barrow, *The Constants of Nature: From Alpha to Omega* (London: Jonathon Cape, 2002), 141-74.

20. Rees, *Before the Beginning*, 242.

21. Ursula Goodenough, *The Sacred Depths of Nature* (New York: Oxford University Press, 1998), 151. In a similar way, Lynn Margulis tells us that death is the price we pay for "fancy tissues and complex life histories" (*Symbiotic Planet: A New View of Evolution* [New York: Basic Books, 1998], 91).

22. Karl Rahner, "Evolution," in *Sacramentum Mundi: An Encyclopedia of Theology*, ed. Karl Rahner, Cornelius Ernst, and Kevin Smyth (London: Burns & Oates, 1968), 2:289-97.

23. Wolfhart Pannenberg writes of the Holy Spirit as "working in all events as the power of the future" and as "the power of the future that gives creatures their own present and their duration" (*Systematic Theology* [Grand Rapids: Eerdmans, 1991–], 2:101-2). Christiaan Mostert summarizes Pannenberg's view: "his argument is that the Spirit is the power of the future, working creatively in all events at both micro and macro levels as a field of force, and that the contingency of present events is not compromised by their coming into existence from a 'possibility field of future events'" (*God and the Future: Wolfhart Pannenberg's Eschatological Doctrine of God* [London: T&T Clark, 2002], 179). Lewis Ford often speaks of God as the power of the future; see, e.g., his "Afterword: A Sampling of an Interpretation," in *Explorations in Whitehead's Philosophy*, ed. Lewis S. Ford and George L. Kline (New York: Fordham University Press, 1983), 337.

24. John F. Haught, *God after Darwin: A Theology of Evolution* (Boulder, Colo.: Westview Press, 2000), 81-104.

25. Ted Peters, *God—The World's Future: Systematic Theology for a Postmodern Era* (Minneapolis: Fortress Press, 1992), 315; see also his *God as Trinity: Relationality and Temporality in Divine Life* (Louisville: Westminster/John Knox Press, 1993), where he argues that the eternal perichoretic Trinity embraces and includes time and natural and world history. He sees the immanent Trinity as "consummated eschatologically, meaning that the whole of temporal history is factored into the inner life of God" (p. 181).

26. Robert John Russell, "Bodily Resurrection, Eschatology and Scientific Cosmology: The Mutual Interaction of Christian Theology and Science," in *Resurrection: Theological and Scientific Perspectives*, ed. Ted Peters, Robert John Russell, and Michael Welker (Grand Rapids: Eerdmans, 2002); idem, "Sin, Salvation, and Scientific Cosmology: Is Christian Eschatology Credible Today?" in *Sin and Salvation*, ed. Duncan Reid and Mark Worthing (Adelaide: ATF Press, 2003), 130-54.

27. Augustine, *Confessions* 3.6.11.

28. Thomas Aquinas, *Summa Theologiae*, 1.45.3.

29. For the distinction between primary and secondary causality in Thomas Aquinas, see his *Summa Theologiae*, la, 19, 6; 19, 7; 19, 8; 22, 2; 22, 3; 23, 5; 23, 8; 103, 7; 104, 1; 104, 3; 105, 2.

10. The Procession of the Spirit

1. Dumitru Staniloae, "The Procession of the Holy Spirit from the Father and His Relation to the Son, as the Basis of Our Deification and Adoption," in *Spirit of God, Spirit of Christ: Ecumenical Reflections on the* Filioque *Controversy*, ed. Lukas Vischer (London: SPCK, 1981), 174-86. For Staniloae's notion of "aeonic eternity" and related issues, see Duncan Reid, *Energies of the Spirit: Trinitarian Models in Eastern Orthodox and Western Theology* (Atlanta: Scholars Press, 1997), 100-104.

2. Boris Bobrinskoy, *The Mystery of the Trinity: Trinitarian Experience and Vision in the Biblical and Patristic Tradition* (Crestwood, N.Y.: St. Vladimir's Seminary Press, 1999), 261-316.

3. Gary D. Badcock, *Light of Truth and Fire of Love: A Theology of the Holy Spirit* (Grand Rapids: Eerdmans, 1997). Badcock's argument (pp. 234-56) is that in the life of the Trinity there are not only the relations of origin but, over and above these, the mutual and reciprocal relations of the Three. Later in this chapter I will support this line of thought, but my fundamental proposal is that there is reciprocity between the Word and the Spirit *in the relations of origin*.

4. Thomas G. Weinandy, *The Father's Spirit of Sonship: Reconceiving the Trinity* (Edinburgh: T&T Clark, 1995). Weinandy rightly seeks to pattern the inner trinitarian relations on what is revealed in the economic missions of the Word and Spirit. His argument is that "within the Trinity the Father begets the Son in or by the Holy Spirit, who proceeds then from the Father as the one in whom the Son is begotten" (p. ix). He seeks a theology in which "all three persons, logically and ontologically, spring forth in one simultaneous, nonsequential, eternal act in which each person of the Trinity subsistently defines, and equally is subsistently defined by, the other persons" (pp. 14-15). While I share a good deal with Weinandy, I differ in my interpretation of the Cappadocians, in my choice to stay with Basil's conception of the Father as Source of divinity, and in the biblical and traditional language I propose for the generation of the Word and the procession of the Spirit.

5. Basil, *Against Eunomius* 2.28, in *Basile De Césarée: Contre Eunome 11*, ed. Bernard Sesboüé, Georges Matthieu de Durand, and Louis Doutreleau, SC 305:18.

6. Basil, *Against Eunomius* 3.4 (SC 305:157).

7. Basil, *On the Holy Spirit* 16.38.

8. Basil, *On the Holy Spirit* 18.46 (SC 17: 408).

9. Basil, *On the Holy Spirit* 18.46 (Anderson, 73).

10. See Gregory of Nyssa, *The Great Catechism* 2 (NPF 5:477); Gregory of Nazianzus, *Oration 41: On Pentecost* 14 (NPF 7:384).

11. Letter 214 (NPF 8:254); Letter 236 (NPF 8:278).

12. See, e.g., Gregory of Nazianzus, *Oration* 29.2 (NPF 7:301); see also J. N. D. Kelly, *Early Christian Doctrines* (New York: Harper & Row, 1960), 265-66.

13. Gregory of Nyssa, *Against the Macedonians* 2.10 (PG 45:1304, 1311B).

14. Gregory of Nazianzus, *The Fifth Theological Oration: On the Holy Spirit* 8 (NPF 7:320).

15. See Bobrinskoy, *Mystery of the Trinity*, 276.

16. Augustine, *De Trinitate* 9.3.3 and 14.12.15.

17. Ibid., 4.20.29; 5.11.12; 5.14.15.

18. Yves Congar, *I Believe in the Holy Spirit*, 3 vols. (New York: Seabury Press, 1983) 3:86; see Augustine, *De Trinitate* 15.17.29 and 15.26.47.

19. Augustine, *De Trinitate* 8.10.4; 9.2.2; 15.19.36.

20. Thomas Aquinas, *Summa Theologiae*, 1.36.2; 1.36.4; 1.42.4 ad. 2. See also Congar, *I Believe in the Holy Spirit*, 3:116-27.

21. Congar, *I Believe in the Holy Spirit*, 3:xix.

22. When the Cappadocians use the word *cause* in the Trinity, it describes the different modes of existence of the divine persons within the one divine substance. It is not referring to an external cause, but only to *causality* within one and the same divine nature. Vladimir Lossky insists that this Cappadocian idea of personal cause does not mean inequality, but points to inexpressible communion, the full communication of personal love. He writes that "the cause as fulfillment of personal love cannot produce inferior effects; it wishes them to be equal in dignity and is therefore also the cause of their equality" (*Orthodox Theology: An Introduction* [Crestwood, N.Y.: St Vladimir's Seminary Press, 1989], 47).

23. Ibid., 43-44.

24. John Zizioulas, *Being as Communion* (Crestwood, N.Y.: St. Vladimir's Seminary Press, 1993), 17.

25. Lossky, *Orthodox Theology,* 47 (my emphasis).

26. Ibid., 44.

27. On this, see Bobrinskoy, *Mystery of the Trinity,* 267.

28. Gregory of Nyssa, *On "Not Three Gods"* (PG 45:133).

29. Maximus, *Letter to Marinus* (PG 91:136). I have taken the translation from Congar, *I Believe in the Holy Spirit,* 3:53.

30. John of Damascus, *De fide orthodoxa* 1.12 (PG 94:949B).

31. J. D. Zizioulas, "The Teaching of the 2nd Ecumenical Council on the Holy Spirit in Historical and Ecumenical Perspective," in *Credo in Spiritum Sanctum,* vol. 1, ed. J. S. Martins (Rome/Vatican City: Libreria Editrice Vaticana, 1983), 42-47.

32. Basil, *On the Holy Spirit* 16.39 (Anderson, 65-66); 19.49 (Anderson, 76-78).

33. Gregory of Nyssa, *The Great Catechism* 2 (NPF 5:476-77).

34. Bobrinskoy, *Mystery of the Trinity,* 278.

35. John of Damascus, *De fide orthodoxa* 1.7 (PG 94:805B).

36. Bobrinskoy, *Mystery of the Trinity,* 295-96 (my emphasis).

37. Paul Evdokimov, *L'Esprit-Saint dans la tradition orthodoxe* (Paris: Cerf, 1969), 77.

38. See Bobrinskoy, *Mystery of the Trinity,* 286.

39. Jürgen Moltmann, *The Trinity and the Kingdom: The Doctrine of God* (San Francisco: Harper & Row, 1981), 183.

40. Congar, *I Believe in the Holy Spirit,* 3:75 (my emphasis).

41. Staniloae, "Procession of the Holy Spirit," 186.

42. Leonardo Boff, *Trinity and Society* (Maryknoll, N.Y.: Orbis Books, 1988), 146. *Patreque* means that the Word proceeds from the Spirit *and the Father; filioque* means that the Spirit proceeds from the Father *and the Son; Spirituque* means that the Word proceeds from the Father *and the Spirit.* Catherine LaCugna responded critically to Boff's suggestion in her *God for Us: The Trinity and Christian Life* (San Francisco: HarperSanFrancisco, 1991), 275-78. For Boff's more recent expression of these ideas see his *Holy Trinity: Perfect Community* (Maryknoll, N.Y.: Orbis Books, 2000), 57-60.

43. Gavin D'Costa, *Sexing the Trinity: Gender, Culture and the Divine* (London: SCM, 2000), 94.

44. Joseph A. Bracken, *The Triune Symbol: Persons, Process and Community* (Lanham, Md.: University Press of America, 1985), 24. Bracken, in a process trinitarian theology, distinguishes between the persons, in that the Father proposes initial aims from the primordial nature, the Son responds with unqualified assent from the consequent nature, and the Spirit is a catalyst for both from the superjective nature. The divine superjective nature is the principle of activity by which God sustains the community of divine persons and the creation. See Joseph A. Bracken, *Society and Spirit: A Trinitarian Cosmology* (Selinsgrove, Pa.: Susquehanna University Press, 1991), 133-34; see also his "Panentheism from a Process Perspective," in *Trinity in Process: A Relational Theology of God,* ed. Joseph A. Bracken and Marjorie Hewitt Suchoki (New York: Continuum, 1997), 101-2. For a reflection on Bracken's work from a feminist perspective, see Lisa Stupar, "Implications of Bracken's Process Model of the Trinity for a Contemporary Feminist Theology," *Horizons* 27 (2000): 257-75.

45. Pannenberg, *Systematic Theology* (Grand Rapids: Eerdmans, 1991–), 1:320.

46. Gregory of Nazianzus, *Third Theological Oration* 29.2 (NPF 7:301).

47. See LaCugna, *God for Us,* 388-400.

48. Gregory of Nazianzus, *Fifth Theological Oration* 31.9 (NPF 7:320-21).

11. Discernment of the Spirit

1. Jon Sobrino, "Following Jesus as Discernment," in *Discernment of the Spirit and of Spirits,* Concilium 119, ed. Casiano Floristan and Christian Duquoc (New York:

Seabury Press, 1979), 14-24. See also his *Jesus in Latin America* (Maryknoll, N.Y.: Orbis Books, 1987), 131-39.

2. Rosemary Radford Ruether, *Sexism and God-Talk: Toward a Feminist Theology* (London: SCM, 1983), 18-19.

3. On this, see Elisabeth Schüssler Fiorenza, *In Memory of Her: A Feminist Theological Reconstruction of Christian Origins* (London: SCM, 1983), 135-36.

4. Harvey D. Egan, *The Spiritual Exercises and the Ignatian Mystical Horizon* (St. Louis: Institute of Jesuit Sources, 1976), 152.

5. See Ernest Larkin, "What to Know about Discernment," *Review for Religious* 60 (2001): 165-66. I have followed Larkin in calling this aspect of the process "cognitive discernment."

6. John Carroll Futrell, "Commentaries on Ignatius' Rules," in Marian Cowan and John Carroll Futrell, *The Spiritual Exercises of St. Ignatius of Loyola: A Handbook for Directors* (St. Louis: Ministry Training Services, 1981), 139.

7. Ignatius provides two sets of rules for the discernment of spirits, the first set appropriate for the first week of the *Spiritual Exercises* (§§313-27), and the second set appropriate for the second week (§§328-36). I am using both the literal translation of Elder Mullan and David Fleming's contemporary version, from David L. Fleming, *The Spiritual Exercises of St. Ignatius: A Literal Translation and A Contemporary Reading* (St. Louis: Institute of Jesuit Sources, 1978). In the text that follows, I will refer to paragraphs of the *Spiritual Exercises* by numbers in parentheses.

8. Futrell, "Commentaries on Ignatius' Rules," 161; see also 142.

9. Joanne Wolski Conn, "Revisioning the Ignatian Rules for Discernment," in *Women's Spirituality: Resources for Christian Development*, ed. Joanne Wolski Conn (New York: Paulist Press, 1986), 315.

10. Nancy M. Victorin-Vangerud, *The Raging Hearth: Spirit in the Household of God* (St. Louis: Chalice Press, 2000), 202.

11. See Futrell, "Commentaries on Ignatius' Rules," 148.

12. John of the Cross, *The Ascent of Mount Carmel* 2.15.5, in *The Collected Works of St. John of the Cross*, trans. Kieran Kavanaugh and Otilio Rodriguez (Washington, D.C.: Institute of Carmelite Studies, 1979), 149. See also *The Dark Night* 1.10.4 (*Collected Works*, 317) and *The Living Flame of Love* 3.33 (*Collected Works*, 622).

13. *Dark Night* 2.5.1 (*Collected Works*, 335).

14. *Collected Works*, 711.

15. Constance Fitzgerald, "Desolation as Dark Night: The Transformative Influence of Wisdom in John of Cross," *The Way Supplement* 82 (1995): 100-101.

16. Mary Catherine Hilkert points out that Catherine's own approach to discernment centered on God as "first truth," on her understanding that it was the role of teachers in the church to be "persons who are in love with truth and enlightened by it—not persons who are insensitive to and ignorant of it," and on her conviction that it was every Christian's responsibility to "pursue truth and clothe herself in it" (*Speaking with Authority: Catherine of Siena and the Voices of Women Today* [New York: Paulist Press, 2001], 89).

17. Futrell, "Commentaries on Ignatius' Rules," 158.

18. Karl Rahner, "The Logic of Concrete Individual Knowledge in Ignatius Loyola," in *The Dynamic Element in the Church* (London: Burns & Oates, 1964), 132-35. For an important commentary on Rahner's insights, see Harvey Egan's *Spiritual Exercises and the Ignatian Mystical Horizon*.

19. Rahner, "Logic of Concrete Individual Knowledge," 155-56.

20. Avery Dulles, "The Ignatian Experience as Reflected in the Spiritual Theology of Karl Rahner," in *Jesuit Spirit in a Time of Change*, ed. Raymond Schroff (Westminster, Md.: Newman Press, 1968), 36.

21. Rahner, "Logic of Concrete Individual Knowledge," 115.

22. Rahner, "Logic of Concrete Individual Knowledge," 130. See Egan, *Spiritual Exercises and the Ignatian Mystical Horizon*, 43-46.

23. Rahner, "Logic of Concrete Individual Knowledge," 166-67.

24. David Fleming, "Thy will be done, on earth as it is in heaven," *Review for Religious* 58 (1999): 565.

25. Thomas Aquinas, *Summa Theologiae*, 1.43.5 ad 2; 2-2.45.2.

12. The Creator Spirit—Making All Things New

1. Mark I. Wallace, *Fragments of the Spirit: Nature, Violence, and the Renewal of Creation* (New York: Continuum, 1996), 1.

2. Ibid., 226.

3. Yves Congar, *I Believe in the Holy Spirit*, 3 vols. (New York: Seabury Press, 1983), 3:148-49; Christian Duquoc, *Dieu différent* (Paris: Cerf, 1977), 121-22; Walter Kasper, *The God of Jesus Christ* (London: SCM, 1983), 226.

4. See Jürgen Moltmann, *The Spirit of Life: A Universal Affirmation* (Minneapolis: Fortress Press, 1992), 10. In another place he says. "In the fellowship of the Holy Spirit, the divine Triunity is so wide open that the whole creation can find room in it" (*The Source of Life: The Holy Spirit and the Theology of Life* [London: SCM Press, 1997], 91).

5. Ruth Page, *God and the Web of Creation* (London: SCM, 1996), 71.

6. Rosemary Radford Ruether, *Gaia and God: An Ecofeminist Theology of Earth Healing* (San Francisco: HarperSanFrancisco, 1992), 227-28 (my emphasis).

7. Moltmann, *Spirit of Life*, 285-89.

8. *Catherine of Siena: The Dialogue*, trans. Suzanne Noffke (New York: Paulist Press, 1980), 141, 74.

9. *The Exercises of Saint Gertrude*, ed. a Benedictine nun of Regina Laudis (Westminster, Md.: Newman, 1956), 5.3.

10. *Erschallet ihr Lieder* (BWV 172).

11. Elizabeth Johnson, *She Who Is: The Mystery of God in Feminist Theological Discourse* (New York: Crossroad, 1992), 145.

12. Sallie McFague says, "God's sustaining work involves an invitation to us to become friends of the Friend of the world" (*Models of God: Theology for an Ecological, Nuclear Age* [Philadelphia: Fortress Press, 1987], 172).

Indexes

SCRIPTURE REFERENCES

NAMES AND SUBJECTS